CONTENTS

Contents

British Vocational Qualifications

11TH EDITION

A Directory of Vocational Qualifications
Available in the United Kingdom

KOGAN
PAGE

London and Philadelphia

Publisher's note

Every possible effort has been made to ensure that the information contained in this book is accurate at the time of going to press, and the publishers and authors cannot accept responsibility for any errors or omissions, however caused. No responsibility for loss or damage occasioned to any person acting, or refraining from action, as a result of the material in this publication can be accepted by the editor, the publisher or any of the authors.

Eleventh edition published in Great Britain and the United States in 2009 by Kogan Page Limited

120 Pentonville Road
London N1 9JN
United Kingdom
www.koganpage.com

525 South 4th Street, #241
Philadelphia PA 19147
USA

© Kogan Page Limited, 2009

The right of Kogan Page Limited to be identified as the author of this work has been asserted by them in accordance with the Copyright, Designs and Patents Act 1988.

ISBN 978 0 7494 5341 1

British Library Cataloguing-in-Publication Data

A CIP record for this book is available from the British Library.

Typeset by AMA DataSet Limited, Preston
Printed and bound in Great Britain by Thanet Press Ltd, Margate

British Vocational Qualifications

Contents

HOW TO USE THIS BOOK

British Vocational Qualifications is divided into five parts:

Part One provides a brief overview of the provision of vocational education for the 19-plus age group within the United Kingdom at the time of publication. It provides current information on regulatory authorities and the main awarding bodies and an overview of the National Qualifications Framework. The main types of vocational qualifications are included within this publication and are described in full.

Part Two is the directory of vocational qualifications. Qualifications are listed under subject headings covering a wide range of professional and careers areas. For each heading the qualifications are set out in the following order: National Vocational Qualifications (NVQs), Scottish Vocational Qualifications (SVQs), Vocationally Related Qualifications (VRQs), and Vocational Qualifications (VQs). Under each heading qualifications are listed alphabetically by title and then by ascending level. Sections do not contain all types of award, they contain only the qualification types available for that particular professional or career area. Each entry gives details of the type of qualifications, course title, level and awarding body.

Part Three consists of a list of acronyms of the awarding bodies together with their full titles and addresses of awarding bodies and sources of further information. Sources of further information include contact details of industry lead bodies and professional institutions and organisations.

Part Four is a directory of Further Education colleges offering vocational qualifications, listed alphabetically by area.

Part Five is an index of all qualifications listed, together with the number of the page on which the entry appears. Qualification titles (with level) are listed in alphabetical order.

A vocational qualification at Tower Hamlets College can give you a kick-start to achieving your aim.

Tower Hamlets
6th Form
College

For course advice contact us on

📞 020 7510 7777
✉ advice@tower.ac.uk
🌐 www.tower.ac.uk

If you have ambitions for a particular career, a vocational qualification at Tower Hamlets College can give you a kick-start to achieving your aim.

At Tower Hamlets 6th Form College, we offer an exciting range of vocational courses, in subjects from science to sport, beauty therapy to business skills, and computing to catering.

The qualifications offer a mix of theory and practice, often including work experience. Progression can lead to gaining professional qualifications.

And if you take a vocational qualification at Level 3, you can gain UCAS points for entry to higher education. For example, a BTEC National Diploma with overall three merit grades is equivalent to two A levels with A grades, therefore you always have the opportunity to change your mind about your future.

THC is right next door to Canary Wharf and the City of London and this has helped us build fantastic connections with many of the world's most successful companies. Many of our students have benefited from work placement schemes with leading firms and some have secured permanent employment with them. So, choosing a Vocational qualification with THC does not end on the completion of your course, we have a commitment into helping you into work.

Contact our advice line for further information
0207 510 7777
advice@tower.ac.uk
www.tower.ac.uk

Part 1

Introduction

Vocational education in the UK is continuing the change and reorganization that got underway in recent years. These developments are in response to various Government strategies including the March 2006 reform strategy, *Further Education: Raising Skills, Improving Life Chances* which sets out to create a new economic mission for further education (FE) with providers of learning and skills supplying a more specialist service. There is also an enhanced role for employers and learners in shaping development and new entitlements to learning and support for those who need it most.

During the academic year 2005–06 the continued expansion of colleges and other training providers enabled a sustained growth in the number of vocational qualifications being taken up by young people and adult learners. There has also been a radical review of qualifications for the 14- to 19-year-old age group under *The Working Group on 14–19 Reform*, led by Mike Tomlinson. The group published its final report in October 2004 and some of its proposals can be seen in the 2005 14–19 Education and Skills White Paper, which introduced the 14–19 diploma. The latest information on this reform is available at: www.dcsf.gov.uk/14-19/.

In parallel with these changes there has been the development of a national qualifications framework (NQF) (see p 7 for table), designed to produce a coherent framework in which vocational qualifications can be viewed alongside comparative academic qualifications.

There are also a number of new bodies that influence qualifications provision at sector and regional level and work together to develop and oversee the education and training provision across the sector/subject classifications set by the regulatory authorities. These bodies include:

- **Learning and Skills Councils (LSCs)**. Responsible for all funding and in support of the qualifications in the NQF.
- **Alliance of Sector Skills Councils (ASSC)**. Comprising all 25 licensed UK Sector Skills Councils (SSCs).
- **Regional Development Agencies (RDAs)**. Create regional workforce plans and Learning Gateways (through consortia of learning providers).
- **Sector Skills Councils (SSCs)**. Industry-specific bodies that ensure education and training provision respond to employer requirements.

The involvement of these bodies reflects the opening up of a variety of settings in which vocational qualifications can be studied. Further education colleges, distance learning, workplaces and higher education institutions are now able to offer vocational qualifications in a new and dynamic way and the increased involvement by industry through the SSCs will inevitably see a continued growth in workplace and home-based provision of vocational education.

This edition of *British Vocational Qualifications* provides an updated listing of vocational qualifications offered in the United Kingdom for the 19-plus age group. While the national framework starts at introductory level and goes up to level 8, this publication offers a listing of qualifications from levels 1 to 5 in keeping with the qualifications most likely to be offered by further education colleges. However, contact details for awarding bodies are also included to ensure that readers are able to identify providers of qualifications that might be offered outside the traditional further education setting. Vocational courses offered by Higher Education institutions can be found in *British Qualifications* (39th edition), also published by Kogan Page.

REGULATORY AUTHORITIES AND AWARDING BODIES

Central to the organization of vocational education is the relationship between the regulatory authorities and the awarding bodies. The checks and balances built into this relationship ensure quality assurance, standardization of awarding bodies and the qualifications they offer and, with the involvement of the Sector Skills Councils, an adequate response to employer and student requirements for qualifications that respond to market needs.

Regulatory authorities

Responsibility for regulating external qualifications lies with three regulatory authorities in England, Wales and Northern Ireland. The Office of the Qualifications and Examinations Regulator (Ofqual), together with Ofqual Northern Ireland (which at the time of writing regulates NVQs and it is planned that in the near future it will be regulating vocational qualifications in Northern Ireland), the Lifelong Learning and Skills (DCELLS), Qualifications and Curriculum Group and the Council for the Curriculum, Examinations and Assessment in Northern Ireland (CCEA) are responsible for establishing a coherent and comprehensive national framework for qualifications in England, Wales and Northern Ireland. The Scottish Qualifications Authority (SQA) regulates qualifications in Scotland. A description of qualifications regulated by the SQA is provided further on in this section.

National Vocational Qualifications (NVQs), other vocational qualifications and key skills qualifications are accredited by the regulatory authorities and are components of the framework. Candidates for these are assessed by awarding bodies, which award qualifications where candidates meet the required standards. The regulatory authorities, in partnership with the awarding bodies, are in charge of quality assurance of the system. They collaborate with the Scottish Qualifications Authority (SQA) to ensure that NVQs and their Scottish equivalent, Scottish Vocational Qualifications (SVQs), are based on national occupational standards and remain aligned with each other. The full list of accredited qualifications in England, Wales and Northern Ireland can be found on the new National Database of Accredited Qualifications (www.accreditedqualifications.org.uk).

The Office of the Qualifications and Examinations Regulator (Ofqual)
Spring Place
Coventry Business Park
Herald Avenue
Coventry
CV5 6UB
Tel: 0300 303 3344
Fax: 0300 303 3348
E-mail: info@ofqual.gov.uk
Website: www.ofqual.gov.uk

Ofqual Northern Ireland
2nd Floor
Glendinning House
6 Murray Street
Belfast
BT16 6DN
Tel: 028 9033 0706
Fax: 028 9023 1621
E-mail: info@ofqual.gov.uk

Department for Children, Education, Lifelong Learning and Skills (DCELLS), Qualifications and Curriculum Group
Castle Buildings
Womanby Street
Cardiff CF10 1SX
Tel: 029 20375400
E-mail: dcells.enquiries@wales.gsi.gov.uk
Website: www.wales.gov.uk

Council for the Curriculum, Examinations and Assessment (CCEA)
29 Clarendon Road
Clarendon Dock
Belfast BT1 3BG
Tel: 028 9026 1200
Fax: 028 9026 1234
E-mail: info@ccea.org.uk
Website: www.ccea.org.uk

Scottish Qualifications Authority (SQA)
The Optima Building
58 Robertson Street
Glasgow G2 8DQ
Tel: 0845 279 1000
Fax: 0845 213 5000
or
Ironmills Road
Dalkeith
Midlothian EH22 1LE
Tel: 0845 279 1000
Fax: 0845 213 5000
E-mail: customer@sqa.org.uk
Website: www.sqa.org.uk

Awarding bodies

Awarding bodies are responsible for the design and assessment of vocational education and training qualifications. The awarding bodies work with the regulatory authorities to develop qualifications and to ensure that standards are met. They manage the assessment, verification and awarding of qualifications and oversee quality assurance. They award certificates for assessed units and for full vocational qualifications, including NVQs.

There are 117 awarding bodies (see p 273 for a full list). Many of these are sector-based and provide specific qualifications for their particular industry. However, there are also a number of key awarding bodies that provide a wide range of vocational qualifications across sectors and subjects. These include:

- Edexcel (offers BTEC qualifications);
- City & Guilds (includes Pitman qualifications);
- Cambridge International Examinations (CIE qualifications are mainly available outside of the UK and not within the national framework);
- OCR;
- AQA;
- EDI.

QUALIFICATIONS

The introduction of the revised National Qualifications Framework (NQF) levels have increased alignment with the Framework for Higher Education Qualifications (FHEQ) levels and improved progression routes between the NQF and Higher Education. The NQF levels span from Entry Level to Level 8 setting out the levels at which qualifications are recognized. A sector and subject classification has also been introduced to sit alongside the Framework.

The National Qualifications Framework (NQF) for England, Wales and Northern Ireland sets out the levels at which qualifications are recognized

The National Qualifications Framework (NQF) helps learners to make informed decisions about the qualifications they need and allows them to select at a glance the full picture of the structure of qualifications in England, Wales and Northern Ireland. They can also compare the levels of different qualifications and identify clear progression routes for their chosen career. The current NQF which took effect from September 2004, has nine levels: entry level to level 8, with levels 4–8 being higher level qualifications. This allows broad comparisons to be made with the FHEQ – certificates of higher education at level 4 through to doctorates at level 8.

What does the current NQF look like?

The following table illustrates the current NQF levels and provides examples of qualifications that can be achieved at each level. It shows how the original and revised NQF levels compare with each other. It also shows how the revised levels broadly compare with the FHEQ.

Comparison of original and current NQF levels with broad indications of FHEQ levels with examples

National Qualifications Framework		Framework for Higher Education Qualification levels (FHEQ)
Original levels	**Current levels**	
5 Level 5 NVQ in Construction Project Management* Level 5 Diploma in Translation	**8** Specialist awards	D (doctoral) doctorates
	7 Level 7 Diploma in Translation	M (masters) masters degrees, postgraduate certificates and diplomas
4 Level 4 NVQ in Advice and Guidance* Level 4 Diploma in Management Level 4 BTEC Higher National Diploma in 3D Design Level 4 Certificate in Early Years Practice	**6** Level 6 Diploma in Management	H (honours) bachelors degrees, graduate certificate and diplomas
	5 Level 5 BTEC Higher National Diploma in 3D Design	I (intermediate) diplomas of higher education and further education, foundation degrees, higher national diplomas
	4 Level 4 Certificate in Early Years Practice	C (certificate) certificates of higher education
3 *(There is no change to Level 3 in the revised NQF)* Level 3 Certificates in Small Animal Care Level 3 NVQ in Aeronautical Engineering A levels		
2 *(There is no change to Level 2 in the revised NQF)* Level 2 Diploma for Beauty Specialists Level 2 NVQ in Agricultural Crop Production GCSEs Grades A*–C		
1 *(There is no change to Level 1 in the revised NQF)* Level 1 Certificate in Motor Vehicle Studies Level 1 NVQ in Bakery GCSEs Grade D–G		
Entry *(There is no change to Entry level in the revised NQF)* Entry Level Certificate in Adult Literacy		

*Revised levels are not currently being implemented for NVQs at level 4 and level 5. For up-to-date information, please visit www.accreditedqualifications.org.uk

Source: Qualifications and Curriculum Authority

Basic Skills

In September 2001 national qualifications in adult literacy and numeracy became available for the first time. The accreditation of these qualifications assures users that they are based on the national standards and ensures consistency in terms of level, demand, content and outcomes. The qualifications are available at entry level and at Levels 1 and 2. The tests for these certificates match the key skills Level 1 and 2 tests used for communication and application of number. The adult literacy qualifications are approved for use pre-16. Students on post-16 full-time programmes are more likely to work towards key skills qualifications.

All adult literacy and adult numeracy qualifications must be based on the national standards. At entry level, fifty per cent of each award must be made up of tasks or assessments which are independently or externally set or validated, externally marked or moderated, and are conducted under supervised and specified conditions. At levels 1 and 2 the assessment of these qualifications is via the shared adult literacy/adult numeracy/key skill test.

Entry Level

Entry level is the first level in the National Qualifications Framework. All Entry level qualifications (known as Entry level certificates) are pitched below an NVQ or Vocationally Related Qualification at Level 1 and below grade G of a GCSE. So that small steps of achievement can be recognized, Entry level is sub-divided into three further sub-levels: Entry 1, Entry 2 and Entry 3, with Entry 3 being the highest. Each sub-level provides progression to the next sub-level while Entry 3 qualifications are specifically designed to help learners progress to related Level 1 qualifications. Qualifications can cover one or more of the Entry sub-levels. They may address any area of learning from, for example, life skills to literacy, religious studies to retail.

Key Skills

Key skills qualifications are available at Levels 1 to 4 in each of the key skills of application of number, communication, ICT, working with others, improving own learning and performance and problem solving. They are offered by a wide range of awarding bodies. In England the first three of these key skills are assessed by an internally assessed portfolio of evidence and an externally set and marked test. Both parts have to be passed; there is no prescribed weighting for each. For the last three, the assessment is portfolio based.

Apprenticeships

Apprenticeships have been designed and developed in partnership with employers and Sector Skills Councils to provide an effective, high-quality, work-based route to the skills employers are looking for.

Thousands of employers in the United Kingdom now recruit apprentices. These employers welcome this opportunity to develop the skills, flexibility, loyalty and confidence that their organizations need – in effect, to grow their own workforce.

Work based learning, in the form of apprenticeships, gives young people the opportunity to gain recognized, career-building qualifications while working in a real job. All apprentice frameworks must comprise:

- a competence based element;
- a knowledge based element;

- transferable or Key Skills;
- employment rights and responsibilities.

The apprenticeship is not a qualification in its own right. Instead, it is described by the Learning and Skills Council as 'the achievement of a collection of qualification components, each requiring differing assessment methods and requiring registration and associated costs'. The training itself is a mix of practical, on-the-job instruction, with elements of off-the-job learning (for example, day release to college).

Introduction

There are 250,000 apprentices enrolled nationwide in more than 180 different apprenticeships. It is possible to take an Apprenticeship or an Advanced Apprenticeship, at levels 2 and 3 respectively. Most apprenticeships are completed in one to three years.

The different occupational areas covered by apprenticeships are as follows. Each of these areas contains several specific occupations shown, and details of each can be found on the website www.apprenticeships.org.uk and individual website addresses in the occupations directory.

Administration and Professional
Accounting; Advice and Guidance; Business Administration; Information Technology and Electronic Services; Information and Library Services; Learning and Development/Direct Training and Support; Management; Payroll; Personnel (Support)

Agriculture
Agriculture, Crops and Livestock; Agriculture and Garden Machinery; Animal Care; Amenity Horticulture; Environmental Conservation; Equine industry; Farriery; Floristry; Production Horticulture; Sea-fishing

Construction
Building Services Engineers; Construction (Craft); Electrical and Electronic Servicing; Engineering; Mechanical Engineering Services; Plumbing

Customer Service, Retailing and Wholesaling
Contact Centres; Customer Service; Floristry; Procurement; Retailing; Sales and Telesales; Wholesale, Distribution, Warehousing and Storage

Engineering
Cleaning and Support Services; Electrical and Electronic Servicing; Electricity Industry; Electrotechnical; Engineering; Gas Industry; Heating, Ventilating, Air Conditioning and Refrigeration; Land-based Service Engineering; Manufacturing; Motor Industry; Communication Technologies (Telecoms); Water Industry (Process Operations)

Finance, Insurance and Real Estate
Insurance; International Trade Services; Newspapers; Personnel; Providing Financial Services; Property Services

Health and Beauty
Beauty Therapy; Hairdressing; Health and Social Care

Health, Care and Public Services
Community Justice; Cultural Heritage; Early Years Care and Education; Emergency Fire Services Operations; Health and Social Care; Housing; Information and Library Services; Occupational Health and Safety; Operating Department Practice; Pharmacy Technicians; Physiological Measurement Technology; Security Sector

Hospitality
Events; Hospitality

Manufacturing

Ceramics; Chemical, Pharmaceutical, Petrochemical Manufacturing and Refining Industries; Clothing Industry; Fibreboard Packaging; Food and Drink Manufacturing; Furniture Manufacture; Glass Industry; Jewellery, Silversmithing and Allied Trades; Laboratory Technician (Generic); Man-made Fibres; Manufacturing; Oil and Gas Extraction; Optical Manufacturing Technician; Paper and Board Manufacture; Polymer Processing; Sign-making; Steel and Metals Industry; Surface Coatings Industry; Textiles

Media and Printing

Arts and Entertainment; Broadcast, Film, Video and Multimedia; Photo Imaging; Print and Print Packaging

Recreation and Travel

Active Leisure and Learning; Amenity Horticulture; Cultural Heritage; Travel Services

Transportation

Aviation; Driving Goods Vehicles; Marine Industry; Motor Industry (Vehicle Body Repair and Paint Operations); Rail Transport Engineering; Rail Operations; Traffic Office

Details of apprenticeships, where appropriate, are given at the head of individual occupations in Part 2.

Apprenticeships and NVQs

During the course of employment, workplace training will enable the apprentice to obtain an NVQ. The learning provider or local college will provide training for Key Skills and also a relevant technical certificate. Completion of an apprenticeship will qualify for an NVQ at level 2, an Advanced Apprenticeship at level 3.

National Vocational Qualifications (NVQs)

NVQs are available for study throughout England, Wales and Northern Ireland. Based on national occupational standards set and developed by industry lead bodies, employers and employees in each field, they are practical and relevant to work. They are designed to cover various aspects of a job or area of work, assessing the skills actually used in the workplace. The standards set define the skills or competences needed by people working in particular occupations.

These qualifications can be completed unit by unit, enabling an individual to build up to a qualification as conveniently as possible. A mix of mandatory and optional units can enable a candidate to tailor the qualification to their particular role.

The NVQ framework sits within the overall National Qualifications Framework. It covers the first five levels, from routine work at Level 1 through to senior management at Level 5. There are no barriers to access, such as age limits or entry requirements. NVQs are open to anyone who can demonstrate they reach the required standard.

Vocational Qualifications (VQs)

A wide range of vocational qualifications (VQs) is accredited into the National Qualifications Framework (NQF). These qualifications cover almost every industry sector, and every level of the NQF. VQs are offered by a large number of awarding bodies. They range from broad-based VQs to specialist qualifications designed for a particular sector. In many cases, suites of qualifications are available, offering progression through the levels of the NQF.

Scottish Vocational Qualifications (SVQs)

Scottish Vocational Qualifications (SVQs) are work-based qualifications which record the 'skills, knowledge and understanding' of an individual in relation to their work. They are based on national occupational standards developed by National Training Organizations. These identify the level of competence expected of people in their work. Competence means the ability to perform tasks, and this is assessed on the job. This may be as an employee, through a Modern Apprenticeship, or as a school or college student through a work placement. Some schools are currently piloting Scottish Progression Awards which offer students vocational subjects at SVQ Level 1 as an alternative to traditional academic subjects. These can act as an opening to Modern Apprenticeships. You would need to contact SQA for an update on this.

The main types of qualification offered are standard Grade and National Qualifications (Access, Intermediate 1, Intermediate 2, Higher and Advanced Higher) usually taken in schools but also offered in some colleges; National Certificate and Higher National modules which can be taken individually or in groups which can lead to qualifications such as a Higher National Certificate or a Higher National Diploma; Scottish Vocational Qualifications which are designed to meet the standards set by the relevant industry sector; and customized Awards and Professional Development Awards.

Qualifications and Credit Framework

The Qualifications and Credit Framework is a new way of recognizing skills and qualifications. This is done by awarding credit for qualifications and units which enable people to go at their own pace to gain qualifications. When it is fully implemented, the QCF will work by ensuring that every unit and qualification in the framework has a credit value, with one credit representing 10 hours of work, and a level between Entry level and level 8. The three sizes of qualification in the QCF are:

- Awards (1 to 12 credits)
- Certificates (13 to 36 credits)
- Diplomas (37 credits or more)

This makes it possible to have an award at level 1 or at level 8 because the type of qualification (award, certificate, diploma) represents the size, not the level of difficulty.

For further information on the Qualifications and Credit Framework and a timetable for implementation, visit the Ofqual website www.ofqual.gov.uk.

Employers' benefits and obligations

The employer benefits from the development of a fully trained skilled workforce at a time of national skills shortages, with the increased expectation of retention of such staff, but are obliged to provide facilities for workplace training and for attendance at day-time courses, as well as financial obligations. For example, the employer contribution to NVQ level 2 rates in Engineering is £3,240 (or 50%), for NVQ level 3 it is £5,874. Specific rates apply to all other occupations.

Employee benefits

Vocational qualifications can be obtained as a result of satisfactory completion of work-based learning, combined with courses conducted at colleges listed in Part 4. Some secondary schools also offer facilities for such courses.

Apart from the great benefit of earning whilst learning, the acquisition of vocational qualifications can have the effect of opening up routes to higher professional or academic qualifications, for those who have not obtained exemptions or entry qualifications through academic studies.

BTEC qualifications (National Certificates and Diplomas) can provide entrance credentials for some university degrees. NVQs and SVQs can provide entrance credentials for entry to various professional bodies; level 3 NVQs/SVQs are acceptable for entry into graduate grades of some professional bodies, leading to higher qualifications.

National Skills Academies – a new LSC initiative

The National Skills Academy is a network of employer-led centres of excellence which deliver the skills required by each sector of the economy. They are focused on vocational education and skills training, delivering to young people and adults. There are currently eleven active sectors:

- Construction
- Creative and cultural
- Fashion retail
- Financial services
- Food and drink manufacturing
- Hospitality
- Manufacturing
- Nuclear
- Process industries
- Retail
- Sport and active leisure

At the time of writing there are two sectors in the business planning stage:

- Fashion, textiles and jewellery
- Materials, production and supply

Find out more at the National Skills Academy website, www. nationalskillsacademy.gov.uk.

Part 2

Directory of Vocational Qualifications and Apprenticeships

Accountancy and Mathematics

APPRENTICESHIPS

Apprenticeship (Foundation
Apprenticeship in Wales); NVQ 2
Advanced Apprenticeship (Modern
Apprenticeship in Wales); NVQ3
www.aosg.org

VOCATIONAL QUALIFICATIONS

Advanced Extension Award

Mathematics – Level 3
Awarding body:
EDEXCEL

Advanced Level Free-Standing Mathematics Qualification

Additional Mathematics – Level 3
Awarding body:
OCR

Modelling with calculus – Level 3
Awarding body:
AQA
OCR

Using and applying decision mathematics – Level 3
Awarding body:
AQA

Using and applying statistics – Level 3
Awarding body:
OCR

Working with algebraic and graphical techniques – Level 3
Awarding body:
AQA
OCR

Entry Level Certificate

Living Mathematics – Entry Level
Awarding body:
CCEA

Mathematics – Entry Level
Awarding body:
WJEC

Mathematics A – Entry 2
Awarding body:
AQA

Mathematics A – Entry 3
Awarding body:
AQA

Mathematics A – Entry Level
Awarding body:
WJEC

Mathematics B – Entry Level
Awarding body:
OCR

Foundation Level Free-Standing Mathematics Qualification

Making sense of data – Level 1
Awarding body:
AQA
OCR

Managing money – Level 1
Awarding body:
AQA
OCR

Working in 2 and 3 dimensions – Level 1
Awarding body:
AQA
OCR

Free-Standing Mathematics Qualification

Using and applying statistics – Level 3
Awarding body:
AQA

Intermediate Level Free-Standing Mathematics Qualification

Calculating finances – Level 2
Awarding body:
AQA
OCR

Foundations of Advanced Mathematics – Level 2
Awarding body:
OCR

Handling and interpreting data – Level 2
Awarding body:
AQA
OCR

Making connections in mathematics – Level 2
Awarding body:
AQA
OCR

Solving problems in shape and space – Level 2
Awarding body:
AQA
OCR

Using algebra, functions and graphs – Level 2
Awarding body:
AQA
OCR

National Vocational Qualification

Accounting – Level 2
Awarding body:
AAT
C&G
EDEXCEL

Accounting – Level 3
Awarding body:
AAT
C&G
EDEXCEL

Administration – Level 1
Awarding body:
AAT

Administration – Level 2
Awarding body:
AAT

Administration – Level 3
Awarding body:
PMI

Administration – Level 4
Awarding body:
C&G

Local Taxation – Level 3
Awarding body:
IRRV

Scottish Vocational Qualification

Accounting – Level 2
Awarding body:
SQA & AAT

Accounting – Level 4
Awarding body:
SQA & AAT

Local Taxation – Level 3
Awarding body:
IRRV

Payroll Administration – Level 2
Awarding body:
AAT

Payroll Administration – Level 3
Awarding body:
AAT

Vocationally Related Qualification (Award)

Personal Finance – Level 2
Awarding body:
　BCS

Vocationally Related Qualification (BTEC National Award)

Personal and Business Finance – Level 3
Awarding body:
　EDEXCEL

Vocationally Related Qualification (Certificate)

Personal Finance – Level 2
Awarding body:
　BCS

Vocationally Related Qualification (Diploma)

Personal Finance – Level 2
Awarding body:
　BCS

Advertising

VOCATIONAL QUALIFICATIONS

BTEC Professional Certificate

Advertisement Production for the Electronic and the Printed Page – Level 4
Awarding body:
　EDEXCEL

Vocationally Related Qualification (Certificate)

Advertising and Promotion – Level 3
Awarding body:
　ABC

Advertising Design and Art Direction – Level 3
Awarding body:
　ABC

Vocationally Related Qualification (Double Award)

Advertising – Level 3
Awarding body:
　ABC

Aeronautical and Avionic Engineering

APPRENTICESHIPS

Apprenticeships leading to NVQ2 or NVQ3 or BTEC or C&G qualifications
www.aerosociety.com

VOCATIONAL QUALIFICATIONS

BTEC National Certificate

Aerospace Engineering – Level 3
Awarding body:
EDEXCEL

BTEC Higher National Certificate

Aerospace Engineering – Level 5
Awarding body:
EDEXCEL

BTEC National Certificate

Aerospace Engineering (Avionic) – Level 3
Awarding body:
EDEXCEL

BTEC National Certificate

Aerospace Engineering (Mechanical) – Level 3
Awarding body:
EDEXCEL

BTEC National Diploma

Aerospace Engineering – Level 3
Awarding body:
EDEXCEL

Aerospace Engineering (Avionic) – Level 3
Awarding body:
EDEXCEL

Aerospace Engineering (Mechanical) – Level 3
Awarding body:
EDEXCEL

National Vocational Qualification

Aeronautical Engineering – Level 2
Awarding body:
EAL
ETCAL

Aeronautical Engineering – Level 3
Awarding body:
C&G
EAL

Aircraft Engineering Maintenance – Level 3
Awarding body:
EAL

Scottish Vocational Qualification

Aeronautical Engineering – Level 2
Awarding body:
EAL

Aeronautical Engineering – Level 3
Awarding body:
EAL

Vocationally Related Qualification

Aeronautical Engineering – Level 2
Awarding body:
C&G

Vocationally Related Qualification (Certificate)

Aeronautical Engineering – Level 2
Awarding body:
   C&G

Agriculture

APPRENTICESHIPS

There are numerous apprenticeship opportunities across a range of subjects in agrriculture. These can lead to NVQs or SVQs at levels 2 or 3 or Vocationally Related Qualifications.
www.lantra.co.uk

VOCATIONAL QUALIFICATIONS

BTEC Higher National Certificate

Agriculture – Level 5
Awarding body:
EDEXCEL

BTEC National Award

Agricultural Production (Grazing Livestock) – Level 3
Awarding body:
EDEXCEL

Agricultural Production (Organic Production) – Level 3
Awarding body:
EDEXCEL

Agricultural Production (Poultry Production) – Level 3
Awarding body:
EDEXCEL

Agriculture (Farm Diversification) – Level 3
Awarding body:
EDEXCEL

Agriculture (Land Based Business) – Level 3
Awarding body:
EDEXCEL

BTEC National Certificate

Agriculture (Agribusiness) – Level 3
Awarding body:
EDEXCEL

Agriculture (Crops) – Level 3
Awarding body:
EDEXCEL

Agriculture (Livestock) – Level 3
Awarding body:
EDEXCEL

BTEC National Diploma

Agriculture (Agribusiness) – Level 3
Awarding body:
EDEXCEL

Agriculture (Crop Husbandry) – Level 3
Awarding body:
EDEXCEL

Agriculture (Livestock) – Level 3
Awarding body:
EDEXCEL

National Vocational Qualification

Agricultural Crop Production – Level 2
Awarding body:
NPTC

Agricultural Crop Production – Level 3
Awarding body:
NPTC

Agriculture – Level 1
Awarding body:
NPTC

Livestock Markets (Droving Livestock) – Level 2
Awarding body:
NPTC

Livestock Production – Level 2
Awarding body:
NPTC

Livestock Production – Level 3
Awarding body:
NPTC

Mixed Farming – Level 3
Awarding body:
NPTC

Scottish Vocational Qualification

Agricultural Crop Production – Level 2
Awarding body:
SQA

Agricultural Crop Production – Level 3
Awarding body:
SQA

Agriculture – Level 1
Awarding body:
SQA

Agriculture – Level 3
Awarding body:
C&G/NPTC

Livestock Markets: Droving Livestock – Level 2
Awarding body:
NPTC

Livestock Production – Level 2
Awarding body:
SQA

Livestock Production – Level 3
Awarding body:
SQA

Mixed Farming – Level 2
Awarding body:
SQA

Mixed Farming – Level 3
Awarding body:
SQA

Vocationally Related Qualification (Advanced National Certificate)

Agriculture – Level 3
Awarding body:
NPTC

Vocationally Related Qualification (BTEC National Award)

Agricultural Production – Level 3
Awarding body:
EDEXCEL

Agriculture – Level 3
Awarding body:
EDEXCEL

Vocationally Related Qualification (BTEC National Certificate)

Agriculture – Level 3
Awarding body:
EDEXCEL

Vocationally Related Qualification (BTEC National Diploma)

Agriculture – Level 3
Awarding body:
EDEXCEL
LANTRA

Vocationally Related Qualification (Certificate of Competence)

Brushcutting Operations – Level 2
Awarding body:
NPTC

**Brushwood Chipper Operations –
Level 2**
Awarding body:
NPTC

**Chainsaw and Related Operations –
Level 2**
Awarding body:
NPTC

Granular Fertiliser Application – Level 2
Awarding body:
NPTC

Livestock Husbandry – Level 2
Awarding body:
NPTC

Sheep Shearing – Level 2
Awarding body:
NPTC

**Tractor Driving and Related Operations
– Level 2**
Awarding body:
NPTC

Vocationally Related Qualification (Certificate)

**Automatic Turf Irrigation Systems –
Level 3**
Awarding body:
NPTC

Vocationally Related Qualification (National Award)

**Agricultural Production (Pig Production)
– Level 3**
Awarding body:
EDEXCEL

Air Transport

APPRENTICESHIPS

Aviation level 2; Aviation Industries or
Aviation level 3 Coordinating Aviation
Operations
Also BTEC qualifications
www.goskills.org/client/industry

VOCATIONAL QUALIFICATIONS

National Vocational Qualification

Control Room Operations – Level 3
Awarding body:
  C&G

Controlling Aircraft Operations – Level 3
Awarding body:
  EAL

Controlling Airport Operations – Level 3
Awarding body:
  EAL

Handling Air Passengers – Level 2
Awarding body:
  EAL

Handling Air Passengers – Level 3
Awarding body:
  EAL

Vocationally Related Qualification (Intermediate Certificate)

Air Cabin Crewing – Level 2
Awarding body:
  EAL

Amenity Horticulture

APPRENTICESHIPS

Apprenticeships and Advanced
Apprenticeships available
www.lantra.co.uk

VOCATIONAL QUALIFICATIONS

BTEC Higher National Certificate

Horticulture – Level 5
Awarding body:
　EDEXCEL

BTEC Higher National Diploma

Horticulture – Level 5
Awarding body:
　EDEXCEL

Certificate

Horticulture – Level 2
Awarding body:
　RHS

National Vocational Qualification

Amenity Horticulture – Level 2
Awarding body:
　NPTC

Amenity Horticulture – Level 3
Awarding body:
　NPTC

Horticulture – Level 1
Awarding body:
　NPTC

Scottish Vocational Qualification

Amenity Horticulture – Level 2
Awarding body:
　SQA

Amenity Horticulture – Level 3
Awarding body:
　SQA

Amenity Horticulture – Level 4
Awarding body:
　SQA

Horticulture – Level 1
Awarding body:
　SQA

Vocationally Related Qualification (BTEC National Certificate)

Horticulture – Level 3
Awarding body:
　EDEXCEL

Vocationally Related Qualification (Certificate)

Amenity Horticulture – Level 3
Awarding body:
　NPTC

Neighbourhood Gardener – Level 2
Awarding body:
　NPTC

Animal Care

APPRENTICESHIPS

Apprenticeships and Advanced
Apprenticeships available

VOCATIONAL QUALIFICATIONS

BTEC National Award

Animal Management (Animal Rehabilitation) – Level 3
Awarding body:
EDEXCEL

BTEC Higher National Certificate

Animal Management – Level 5
Awarding body:
EDEXCEL

Equine Management – Level 5
Awarding body:
EDEXCEL

BTEC Higher National Diploma

Equine Management – Level 5
Awarding body:
EDEXCEL

BTEC National Award

Animal Management (Exotics) – Level 3
Awarding body:
EDEXCEL

Animal Management (Kennel and Cattery Management) – Level 3
Awarding body:
EDEXCEL

Animal Management (Pet Store Management) – Level 3
Awarding body:
EDEXCEL

BTEC National Certificate

Animal Management – Level 3
Awarding body:
EDEXCEL

Animal Management (Care) – Level 3
Awarding body:
EDEXCEL

Animal Management (Science) – Level 3
Awarding body:
EDEXCEL

BTEC National Diploma

Animal Management – Level 3
Awarding body:
EDEXCEL

Animal Management (Care) – Level 3
Awarding body:
EDEXCEL

Animal Management (Science) – Level 3
Awarding body:
EDEXCEL

National Vocational Qualification

Animal Care – Level 1
Awarding body:
NPTC

Animal Care – Level 3
Awarding body:
NPTC

Animal Technology – Level 2
Awarding body:
C&G

Animal Technology – Level 3
Awarding body:
C&G

Farriery – Level 3
Awarding body:
BHEST

Gamekeeping and Wildlife Management – Level 2
Awarding body:
NPTC

Gamekeeping and Wildlife Management – Level 3
Awarding body:
NPTC

Horse Care – Level 1
Awarding body:
BHEST
BHS
NPTC

Horse Care – Level 2
Awarding body:
BHS

Horse Care and Management – Level 3
Awarding body:
BHS
NPTC

Racehorse Care – Level 2
Awarding body:
BHEST

Racehorse Care and Management – Level 3
Awarding body:
BHEST

Veterinary Nursing – Level 2
Awarding body:
RCVS

Veterinary Nursing – Level 3
Awarding body:
RCVS

Scottish Vocational Qualification

Animal Care – Level 1
Awarding body:
SQA

Animal Care – Level 2
Awarding body:
SQA

Animal Care – Level 3
Awarding body:
SQA

Animal Nursing Assistants – Level 2
Awarding body:
BHS

Animal Technology – Level 2
Awarding body:
BHS

Animal Technology – Level 3
Awarding body:
BHS

Basic Stockmanship and Welfare – Level 1
Awarding body:
BHS

Equine Artificial Insemination – Level 3
Awarding body:
BHS

Gamekeeping and Wildlife Management – Level 3
Awarding body:
SQA

Horse Care – Level 1
Awarding body:
BHS

Horse Care – Level 2
Awarding body:
BHS

Horse Care and Management – Level 3
Awarding body:
BHS

Vocational Certificate of Education (Certificate)

Small Animal Veterinary Nursing Theory – Level 2
Awarding body:
RCVS

Small Animal Veterinary Nursing Theory – Level 3
Awarding body:
RCVS

Vocationally Related Qualification

Animal Nursing Assistants – Level 2
Awarding body:
ABC

Horse Knowledge and Care – Level 3
Awarding body:
BHS

Horse Knowledge, Care and Riding – Level 1
Awarding body:
BHS

Horse Knowledge, Care and Riding – Level 2
Awarding body:
BHS

Horse Knowledge, Care and Riding – Level 3
Awarding body:
BHS

Vocationally Related Qualification (Advanced Certificate)

Horse Care – Level 3
Awarding body:
BHEST

Vocationally Related Qualification (Advanced National Certificate)

Animal Care – Level 3
Awarding body:
NPTC

Horse Management – Level 3
Awarding body:
NPTC

Vocationally Related Qualification (BTEC First Certificate)

Animal Care – Level 2
Awarding body:
EDEXCEL

Vocationally Related Qualification (BTEC First Diploma)

Animal Care – Level 2
Awarding body:
EDEXCEL

Horse Care – Level 2
Awarding body:
EDEXCEL

Vocationally Related Qualification (BTEC National Award)

Horse Management – Level 3
Awarding body:
EDEXCEL

Vocationally Related Qualification (BTEC National Certificate)

Horse Management – Level 3
Awarding body:
EDEXCEL

Vocationally Related Qualification (BTEC National Diploma)

Horse Management – Level 3
Awarding body:
  EDEXCEL

Vocationally Related Qualification (Certificate of Competence)

Basic Stockmanship and Welfare – Level 2
Awarding body:
  NPTC

Equine Artificial Insemination – Level 3
Awarding body:
  NPTC

Milking and Dairy Hygiene – Level 3
Awarding body:
  NPTC

Pig Husbandry Skills – Level 2
Awarding body:
  NPTC

Planning and Supervising the Safe Use of Veterinary Medicines – Level 3
Awarding body:
  NPTC

Sheep Shearing – Level 3
Awarding body:
  NPTC

Transport of Animals by Road (Short Journeys) – Level 2
Awarding body:
  NPTC

Vocationally Related Qualification (Certificate)

Equine Veterinary Nursing Theory – Level 2
Awarding body:
  RCVS

Equine Veterinary Nursing Theory – Level 3
Awarding body:
  RCVS

Gamekeeping and Wildlife Management – Level 3
Awarding body:
  NPTC

Health and Safety for those Working in the Equine Industry – Level 2
Awarding body:
  NPTC

Horse Management – Level 3
Awarding body:
  NPTC

Small Animal Care – Level 2
Awarding body:
  ABC

Small Animal Care – Level 3
Awarding body:
  ABC

Vocationally Related Qualification (Diploma)

Farriery – Level 3
Awarding body:
  WCF

Vocationally Related Qualification (Intermediate Certificate)

Horse Care – Level 3
Awarding body:
  BHEST

Vocationally Related Qualification (National Certificate)

Animal Care – Level 2
Awarding body:
  NPTC

Gamekeeping – Level 2
Awarding body:
  NPTC

Horse Care – Level 2
Awarding body:
  NPTC

Veterinary Care Assistants – Level 2
Awarding body:
  C&G

Architectural Studies

APPRENTICESHIPS

Apprenticeships available in
Construction
www.bconstructive.co.uk

VOCATIONAL QUALIFICATIONS

Scottish Vocational Qualification

Architectural Technology – Level 4
Awarding body:
SQA/CIOB/ICE/BIAT

Vocationally Related Qualification (Award)

Digital Modelling for Architectural Environments – Level 3
Awarding body:
ABC

Art and Design

APPRENTICESHIPS

Apprenticeships in Arts and
Entertainment - Media and Printing
www.ccskills.org.uk

VOCATIONAL QUALIFICATIONS

Advanced Award

Creative Skills – Level 3
Awarding body:
  NOCN

Advanced Vocational Certificate of Education

Art and Design – Level 3
Awarding body:
  AQA
  EDEXCEL
  OCR

Advanced Vocational Certificate of Education (Double Award)

Art and Design – Level 3
Awarding body:
  AQA
  EDEXCEL
  OCR

Award

Art and Design – Level 1
Awarding body:
  NOCN

Art and Design – Level 2
Awarding body:
  NOCN

Art and Design – Level 3
Awarding body:
  NOCN

BTEC Higher National Certificate

3D Design – Level 5
Awarding body:
  EDEXCEL

Fine Arts – Level 5
Awarding body:
  EDEXCEL

Graphic Design – Level 5
Awarding body:
  EDEXCEL

BTEC Higher National Diploma

3D Design – Level 5
Awarding body:
  EDEXCEL

Fine Arts – Level 5
Awarding body:
  EDEXCEL

Graphic Design – Level 5
Awarding body:
  EDEXCEL

BTEC Professional Diploma

Set Design Management – Level 5
Awarding body:
  EDEXCEL

Certificate

Art – Level 1
Awarding body:
  OCNW

Art and Design – Level 1
Awarding body:
NOCN

Art and Design – Level 2
Awarding body:
NOCN

Art and Design – Level 3
Awarding body:
NOCN

Art, Design and Creative Studies – Level 1
Awarding body:
ABC

Art, Design and Creative Studies – Level 2
Awarding body:
ABC

Craft and Design – Level 1
Awarding body:
OCNW

Craft and Design – Level 2
Awarding body:
OCNW

Design and Craft – Level 2
Awarding body:
C&G

Design and Craft – Level 3
Awarding body:
C&G

Graphic Design – Level 2
Awarding body:
NCFE

Diploma

Art and Design – Level 1
Awarding body:
NOCN

Art and Design – Level 2
Awarding body:
NOCN

Art and Design – Level 3
Awarding body:
NOCN

Design and Craft – Level 3
Awarding body:
C&G

Foundation Studies (Art and Design) – Level 3
Awarding body:
EDEXCEL

Foundation Award

Creative Skills Development – Level 1
Awarding body:
NOCN

Foundation General National Vocational Qualification

Art and Design – Level 1
Awarding body:
AQA
EDEXCEL
OCR

Higher Professional Diploma

Creative Arts – Level 4
Awarding body:
C&G

Intermediate Award

Creative Skills – Level 2
Awarding body:
NOCN

Intermediate General National Vocational Qualification

Art and Design – Level 2
Awarding body:
AQA
OCR

Intermediate Vocational Qualification

Art and Design – Level 2
Awarding body:
    EDEXCEL

National Certificate

Design – Level 3
Awarding body:
    OCR

National Diploma

Design – Level 3
Awarding body:
    OCR

National Extended Diploma

Design – Level 3
Awarding body:
    OCR

National Vocational Qualification

Craft Pottery – Level 2
Awarding body:
    C&G

Craft Pottery – Level 3
Awarding body:
    C&G

Design – Level 3
Awarding body:
    EDEXCEL

Design and Drafting – Level 3
Awarding body:
    ECITB

Design Support – Level 2
Awarding body:
    EDEXCEL

Other General Qualification (Extended Certificate)

Creative Craft – Level 2
Awarding body:
    NCFE

Scottish Vocational Qualification

Creative Skills – Level 2
Awarding body:
    ECITB

Creative Skills – Level 3
Awarding body:
    EDEXCEL

Design and Drafting – Level 3
Awarding body:
    ECITB

Vocationally Related Qualification

Computer Aided Design – Level 3
Awarding body:
    C&G

Design and Technology – Entry Level
Awarding body:
    WJEC

Vocationally Related Qualification (Award)

3D Graphic Design – Level 3
Awarding body:
    ABC

3D Materials Exploration – Level 3
Awarding body:
    ABC

Colour Management – Level 3
Awarding body:
    ABC

Colour Theory and Practice – Level 3
Awarding body:
    ABC

Communication Drawing – Level 3
Awarding body:
  ABC

Craft Bookbinding – Level 3
Awarding body:
  ABC

Experimental Web Design – Level 3
Awarding body:
  ABC

Life Drawing – Level 3
Awarding body:
  ABC

Merchandising Display and Presentation – Level 3
Awarding body:
  ABC

Time-Based Web Design – Level 3
Awarding body:
  ABC

Vocationally Related Qualification (BTEC Award)

3D Design – Level 1
Awarding body:
  EDEXCEL

3D Design – Level 2
Awarding body:
  EDEXCEL

3D Design – Level 3
Awarding body:
  EDEXCEL

Design Crafts – Level 3
Awarding body:
  EDEXCEL

Graphics – Level 1
Awarding body:
  EDEXCEL

Graphics – Level 2
Awarding body:
  EDEXCEL

Graphics – Level 3
Awarding body:
  EDEXCEL

Visual Arts – Level 1
Awarding body:
  EDEXCEL

Visual Arts – Level 2
Awarding body:
  EDEXCEL

Visual Arts – Level 3
Awarding body:
  EDEXCEL

Vocationally Related Qualification (BTEC Certificate)

3D Design – Level 1
Awarding body:
  EDEXCEL

3D Design – Level 2
Awarding body:
  EDEXCEL

3D Design – Level 3
Awarding body:
  EDEXCEL

Design Crafts – Level 3
Awarding body:
  EDEXCEL

Graphics – Level 1
Awarding body:
  EDEXCEL

Graphics – Level 2
Awarding body:
  EDEXCEL

Graphics – Level 3
Awarding body:
  EDEXCEL

Visual Arts – Level 1
Awarding body:
  EDEXCEL

Visual Arts – Level 2
Awarding body:
  EDEXCEL

Visual Arts – Level 3
Awarding body:
  EDEXCEL

Vocationally Related Qualification (BTEC Diploma)

3D Design – Level 1
Awarding body:
EDEXCEL

3D Design – Level 2
Awarding body:
EDEXCEL

3D Design – Level 3
Awarding body:
EDEXCEL

Design Crafts – Level 3
Awarding body:
EDEXCEL

Graphics – Level 1
Awarding body:
EDEXCEL

Graphics – Level 2
Awarding body:
EDEXCEL

Graphics – Level 3
Awarding body:
EDEXCEL

Visual Arts – Level 1
Awarding body:
EDEXCEL

Vocationally Related Qualification (BTEC First Certificate)

Art and Design – Level 2
Awarding body:
EDEXCEL

Vocationally Related Qualification (BTEC First Diploma)

Art and Design – Level 2
Awarding body:
EDEXCEL

Design – Level 2
Awarding body:
EDEXCEL

Vocationally Related Qualification (BTEC National Award)

Art and Design – Level 3
Awarding body:
EDEXCEL

Vocationally Related Qualification (BTEC National Certificate)

3D Design – Level 3
Awarding body:
EDEXCEL

Art and Design – Level 3
Awarding body:
EDEXCEL

Design – Level 3
Awarding body:
EDEXCEL

Design Crafts – Level 3
Awarding body:
EDEXCEL

Fine Art – Level 3
Awarding body:
EDEXCEL

Graphic Design – Level 3
Awarding body:
EDEXCEL

Vocationally Related Qualification (BTEC National Diploma)

3D Design – Level 3
Awarding body:
EDEXCEL

Art and Design – Level 3
Awarding body:
EDEXCEL

Design – Level 3
Awarding body:
  EDEXCEL

Design Crafts – Level 3
Awarding body:
  EDEXCEL

Fine Art – Level 3
Awarding body:
  EDEXCEL

Graphic Design – Level 3
Awarding body:
  EDEXCEL

Multimedia – Level 3
Awarding body:
  EDEXCEL

Vocationally Related Qualification (Certificate)

2D Computer Aided Design – Level 2
Awarding body:
  C&G

Animation – Level 2
Awarding body:
  NCFE

Applied Graphic Skills – Level 3
Awarding body:
  ABC

Art and Design – Level 2
Awarding body:
  NCFE

Art and Design – Level 3
Awarding body:
  NCFE

Design and Technology – Entry Level
Awarding body:
  AQA
  CCEA
  OCR

Design Production Skills – Level 3
Awarding body:
  ABC

Digital Graphics – Level 3
Awarding body:
  ABC

Experimental Illustration – Level 3
Awarding body:
  ABC

Illustration – Level 3
Awarding body:
  ABC

Information Design – Level 3
Awarding body:
  ABC

Magazine and Publishing Design – Level 3
Awarding body:
  ABC

Typographic Design – Level 3
Awarding body:
  ABC

Web Design – Level 3
Awarding body:
  ABC

Vocationally Related Qualification (Diploma)

3D Modelling and Animation – Level 3
Awarding body:
  ABC

Animation – Level 3
Awarding body:
  ABC

Display Design – Level 3
Awarding body:
  ABC

Vocationally Related Qualification (Double Award)

2D Design Software – Level 3
Awarding body:
  ABC

Animation Skills – Level 3
Awarding body:
  ABC

Publications Design – Level 3
Awarding body:
  ABC

Vocationally Related Qualification (National Award)

Applied Art, Design and Media – Level 1
Awarding body:
  OCR

Art and Design – Level 2
Awarding body:
  OCR

Vocationally Related Qualification (National Certificate)

Art and Design – Level 2
Awarding body:
  OCR

Bakery and Confectionery

APPRENTICESHIPS

Apprenticeships and Advanced
Apprenticeships in Bakery
www.improveltd.co.uk

VOCATIONAL QUALIFICATIONS

National Vocational Qualification

Bakery – Level 1
Awarding body:
  C&G
  HAB

Bakery – Level 2
Awarding body:
  C&G
  HAB

Scottish Vocational Qualification

Bakery – Level 1
Awarding body:
  SAMB & SQA

Bakery (Distribution) – Level 2
Awarding body:
  SAMB & SQA

Bakery (Distribution) – Level 3
Awarding body:
  SAMB & SQA

Bakery (Dough Production) – Level 2
Awarding body:
  SAMB & SQA

Bakery (Flour Confectionery Production) – Level 2
Awarding body:
  SAMB & SQA

Bakery (Functional Management) – Level 3
Awarding body:
  SAMB & SQA

Bakery (Product Development) – Level 3
Awarding body:
  SAMB & SQA

Bakery (Production) – Level 3
Awarding body:
  SAMB & SQA

Bakery (Retail and Service) – Level 2
Awarding body:
  SAMB & SQA

Bakery (Retail) – Level 3
Awarding body:
  SAMB & SQA

Bakery (Service) – Level 3
Awarding body:
  SAMB & SQA

Bakery (Specialist Craft) – Level 3
Awarding body:
  SAMB & SQA

Beauty

APPRENTICESHIPS

Apprenticeships in Beauty Therapy and Hairdressing
www.habia.org.uk

VOCATIONAL QUALIFICATIONS

BTEC Higher National Certificate

Beauty Therapy Sciences – Level 5
Awarding body:
EDEXCEL

BTEC Higher National Diploma

Beauty Therapy Sciences – Level 5
Awarding body:
EDEXCEL

National Vocational Qualification

Beauty Therapy – Level 1
Awarding body:
C&G
EDEXCEL
VTCT

Beauty Therapy – Level 2
Awarding body:
C&G
EDEXCEL
VTCT

Beauty Therapy – Level 3
Awarding body:
C&G
EDEXCEL
VTCT

Nail Services – Level 2
Awarding body:
C&G
EDEXCEL
VTCT

Nail Services – Level 3
Awarding body:
C&G
EDEXCEL
VTCT

Spa Therapy – Level 3
Awarding body:
C&G
EDEXCEL

Scottish Vocational Qualification

Beauty Specialists – Level 2
Awarding body:
C&G

Beauty Therapy – Level 1
Awarding body:
SQA
VTCT

Beauty Therapy – Level 2
Awarding body:
SQA
VTCT

Beauty Therapy – Level 3
Awarding body:
SQA
VTCT

Beauty Therapy (Make-Up) – Level 2
Awarding body:
SQA
VTCT

Beauty Therapy (Make-Up) – Level 3
Awarding body:
SQA

Beauty Therapy (Massage) – Level 3
Awarding body:
SQA
VTCT

Nail Services – Level 2
Awarding body:
SQA
VTCT

Nail Services – Level 3
Awarding body:
SQA
VTCT

Spa Therapy – Level 3
Awarding body:
SQA
VTCT

Vocationally Related Qualification (Advanced Diploma)

Beauty Therapy – Level 3
Awarding body:
VTCT

Vocationally Related Qualification (Award)

Make-up Techniques: Fashion Styling – Level 3
Awarding body:
ABC

Make-up Techniques: TV and Film – Level 3
Awarding body:
ABC

Vocationally Related Qualification (BTEC National Award)

Beauty Therapy Sciences: Beautician – Level 3
Awarding body:
EDEXCEL

Vocationally Related Qualification (BTEC National Certificate)

Beauty Therapy Sciences – Level 3
Awarding body:
EDEXCEL

Vocationally Related Qualification (BTEC National Diploma)

Beauty Therapy Sciences – Level 3
Awarding body:
EDEXCEL

Vocationally Related Qualification (Certificate)

Beauty Consultancy – Level 2
Awarding body:
C&G

Cosmetic Make-Up and Beauty Consultancy – Level 2
Awarding body:
VTCT

Depilation – Level 2
Awarding body:
VTCT

Ear Piercing – Level 2
Awarding body:
VTCT

Electrical Epilation Treatments – Level 3
Awarding body:
C&G

Eyelash and Eyebrow Treatments – Level 2
Awarding body:
C&G

Face and Skin Conditioning using Electrotherapy – Level 3
Awarding body:
C&G

Facial Treatments – Level 2
Awarding body:
  C&G

Manicure – Level 2
Awarding body:
  C&G

Nail Treatments – Level 2
Awarding body:
  VTCT

Pedicure – Level 2
Awarding body:
  C&G

Salon Services – Level 1
Awarding body:
  C&G

Skin Care and Make-up Treatments – Level 2
Awarding body:
  C&G

Specialist Beauty Therapy – Level 3
Awarding body:
  C&G

Vocationally Related Qualification (Diploma)

Beauty Specialist Techniques – Level 2
Awarding body:
  VTCT

Beauty Specialists – Level 2
Awarding body:
  ITEC

Beauty Therapy – Level 3
Awarding body:
  C&G

Body Treatments – Level 3
Awarding body:
  ITEC

Epilation – Level 3
Awarding body:
  ITEC
  VTCT

Facial Electrical Treatments – Level 3
Awarding body:
  ITEC

Nail Technology – Level 3
Awarding body:
  ITEC

Spa Treatments – Level 3
Awarding body:
  ITEC

Tanning Treatments – Level 3
Awarding body:
  ITEC

Boats and Boatbuilding

APPRENTICESHIPS

Apprenticeships available in
Boatbuilding and Maintenance
www.senta.org.uk

VOCATIONAL QUALIFICATIONS

National Vocational Qualification

**Boat Building and Maintenance –
Level 3**
Awarding body:
EAL

**Boat Production and Support Services –
Level 2**
Awarding body:
EAL

Vocationally Related Qualification (Certificate)

**Boat Production, Maintenance and
Support – Level 3**
Awarding body:
C&G

Brickwork and Masonry

APPRENTICESHIPS

Apprenticeships available in Brickwork and Masonry
www.bconstructive.co.uk

VOCATIONAL QUALIFICATIONS

Vocationally Related Qualification (Certificate)

Dry Stone Walling – Level 1
Awarding body:
LA

Dry Stone Walling – Level 2
Awarding body:
LANTRA

Building

APPRENTICESHIPS

Apprenticeships available in complete range of Building occupations
www.bconstructive.co.uk

VOCATIONAL QUALIFICATIONS

Advanced Vocational Certificate of Education

Construction and the Built Environment – Level 3
Awarding body:
AQA
EDEXCEL
OCR

Advanced Vocational Certificate of Education (Double Award)

Construction and the Built Environment – Level 3
Awarding body:
AQA
EDEXCEL
OCR

Higher Professional Diploma

Building Services Engineering – Level 4
Awarding body:
C&G

National Vocational Qualification

Accessing Operations and Rigging (Construction) – Level 1
Awarding body:
CIOB

Accessing Operations and Rigging (Construction) – Level 2
Awarding body:
C&G/CITB

Accessing Operations and Rigging (Construction) – Level 3
Awarding body:
C&G/CITB

Associated Industrial Services Occupations – Level 2
Awarding body:
C&G/CITB

Constructing Capital Plant Steel Structures (Erecting) – Level 3
Awarding body:
ECITB

Construction – Foundation
Awarding body:
C&G/CITB

Construction and Civil Engineering Services – Level 1
Awarding body:
C&G/CITB

Construction Contracting Operations – Level 3
Awarding body:
ABBE

Construction Contracting Operations – Level 4
Awarding body:
ABBE

Demolition – Level 3
Awarding body:
C&G/CITB

Plastering – Level 1
Awarding body:
C&G/CITB

Plastering – Level 2
Awarding body:
C&G/CITB

Plastering – Level 3
Awarding body:
    C&G/CITB

Production of Glass Supporting Fabrications – Level 2
Awarding body:
    GQA

Production of Glass Supporting Fabrications – Level 3
Awarding body:
    GQA

Refractory Installations – Level 2
Awarding body:
    C&G/CITB

Roadbuilding (Construction) – Level 2
Awarding body:
    C&G/CITB

Specialist Concrete Occupations – Level 1
Awarding body:
    C&G/CITB

Specialist Concrete Occupations – Level 2
Awarding body:
    C&G/CITB

Specialist Installations – Level 3
Awarding body:
    C&G/CITB

Trowel Occupations (Construction) – Level 2
Awarding body:
    EDEXCEL

Tunnelling Operations – Level 1
Awarding body:
    C&G/CITB

Tunnelling Operations – Level 2
Awarding body:
    C&G/CITB

Scottish Vocational Qualification

Building Control – Level 4
Awarding body:
    SQA & ABBE

Constructing Capital Plant Steel Structures (Erecting) – Level 3
Awarding body:
    ECITB

Construction and Civil Engineering Services – Level 1
Awarding body:
    SQA & CITB

Construction and Civil Engineering Services: Construction Operations – Level 2
Awarding body:
    SQA & CITB

Construction Contracting (Buying) – Level 4
Awarding body:
    SQA & CIOB & ICE

Construction Contracting (Estimating) – Level 3
Awarding body:
    SQA & CIOB & ICE

Construction Contracting (Estimating) – Level 4
Awarding body:
    SQA & CIOB & ICE

Construction Contracting (Planning) – Level 3
Awarding body:
    SQA & CIOB & ICE

Construction Contracting (Planning) – Level 4
Awarding body:
    SQA & CIOB & ICE

Construction Contracting (Surveying) – Level 3
Awarding body:
    SQA & CIOB & ICE

Construction Contracting (Surveying) – Level 4
Awarding body:
    SQA & CIOB & ICE

Construction Contracts Management – Level 5
Awarding body:
    SQA & CIOB & ICE

Construction: Accessing Operations and Rigging – Level 2
Awarding body:
   CIOB
   ECITB
   SQA & CITB

Construction: Accessing Operations and Rigging – Level 3
Awarding body:
   CIOB
   ECITB
   SQA & CITB

Construction: Applied Waterproof Membranes (Built Up Bituminous Roofing) – Level 2
Awarding body:
   SQA & CITB

Construction: Applied Waterproof Membranes (Liquid Waterproofing Systems) – Level 2
Awarding body:
   SQA & CITB

Construction: Applied Waterproof Membranes (Single Ply Roofing) – Level 2
Awarding body:
   SQA & CITB

Construction: Bricklaying – Level 2
Awarding body:
   SQA &SBATC

Construction: Bricklaying – Level 3
Awarding body:
   SQA & SBATC

Construction: Carpentry and Joinery – Level 2
Awarding body:
   SQA & SBATC

Construction: Carpentry and Joinery – Level 3
Awarding body:
   SQA & SBATC

Construction: Floorcovering Occupations (Impervious) – Level 2
Awarding body:
   SQA & CITB

Construction: Floorcovering Occupations (Impervious) – Level 3
Awarding body:
   SQA & CITB

Construction: Floorcovering Occupations (Textile) – Level 1
Awarding body:
   SQA & CITB

Construction: Floorcovering Occupations (Textile) – Level 2
Awarding body:
   SQA & CITB

Construction: Floorcovering Occupations (Textile) – Level 3
Awarding body:
   SQA & CITB

Construction: Floorcovering Occupations (Timber) – Level 1
Awarding body:
   SQA & CITB

Construction: Floorcovering Occupations (Timber) – Level 2
Awarding body:
   SQA & CITB

Construction: Floorcovering Occupations (Timber) – Level 3
Awarding body:
   SQA & CITB

Construction: Formworking – Level 2
Awarding body:
   SQA & CITB

Construction: Heritage Skills – Level 2
Awarding body:
   SQA & CITB

Construction: Interior Fixer and Sheeter – Level 2
Awarding body:
   SQA & CITB

Construction: Interior Systems (Access Flooring) – Level 2
Awarding body:
   SQA & CITB

Construction: Interior Systems (Ceiling Fixing) – Level 2
Awarding body:
    SQA & CITB

Construction: Interior Systems (Dry Lining - Finishers) – Level 2
Awarding body:
    SQA & CITB

Construction: Interior Systems (Dry Lining - Fixers) – Level 2
Awarding body:
    SQA & CITB

Construction: Interior Systems (Relocatable Partitioning) – Level 2
Awarding body:
    SQA & CITB

Construction: Painting and Decorating – Level 1
Awarding body:
    SQA & CITB

Construction: Painting and Decorating – Level 2
Awarding body:
    SQA & CITB
    SQA & SBATC

Construction: Painting and Decorating – Level 3
Awarding body:
    SQA

Construction: Plant Maintenance – Level 1
Awarding body:
    SQA & CITB

Construction: Plant Maintenance – Level 2
Awarding body:
    SQA & CITB

Construction: Plant Maintenance – Level 3
Awarding body:
    SQA & CITB

Construction: Plastering – Level 1
Awarding body:
    SQA

Construction: Plastering – Level 2
Awarding body:
    SQA & SBATC

Construction: Plastering – Level 3
Awarding body:
    SQA & SBATC

Construction: Roof Sheeting and Cladding – Level 2
Awarding body:
    SQA & CITB

Construction: Roof Sheeting and Cladding – Level 3
Awarding body:
    SQA & CITB

Construction: Roof Slating, Tiling and Cement Work – Level 2
Awarding body:
    SQA & SBATC

Construction: Roof Slating, Tiling and Cement Work – Level 3
Awarding body:
    SQA & SBATC

Construction: Shopfitting – Level 2
Awarding body:
    SQA & CITB

Construction: Shopfitting – Level 3
Awarding body:
    SQA & CITB

Construction: Site Management (Conservation) – Level 4
Awarding body:
    SQA/CIOB/ICE/COTAC

Construction: Site Management (Consulting Engineering) – Level 4
Awarding body:
    SQA & CIOB & ICE

Construction: Site Management (Contracting) – Level 4
Awarding body:
    SQA & CIOB & ICE

Construction: Site Supervision (Building and Civil Engineering) – Level 3
Awarding body:
    SQA & CIOB & ICE

Construction: Site Supervision (Highways Maintenance) – Level 3
Awarding body:
    SQA & CIOB & ICE

Construction: Steelfixing – Level 2
Awarding body:
    SQA & CITB

Construction: Stonemasonry – Level 2
Awarding body:
    SQA & SBATC

Construction: Timber Frame Erection – Level 2
Awarding body:
    SQA & CITB

Construction: Trowel Operations – Level 1
Awarding body:
    SQA

Construction: Water Jetting – Level 2
Awarding body:
    SQA & CITB

Construction: Wood Machining – Level 2
Awarding body:
    SQA & SBATC

Construction: Wood Machining – Level 3
Awarding body:
    SQA & SBATC

Demolition – Level 2
Awarding body:
    EDEXCEL

Demolition – Level 3
Awarding body:
    EDEXCEL

Demolition (Construction) – Level 2
Awarding body:
    EDEXCEL

Demolition (Construction) – Level 3
Awarding body:
    EDEXCEL

Drilling and Sawing – Level 2
Awarding body:
    SQA & CITB

Erection of Precast Concrete (Construction) – Level 2
Awarding body:
    EDEXCEL

Fabricating of Steel Structures (Plating) – Level 3
Awarding body:
    ECITB

General Building Operations – Level 2
Awarding body:
    SQA & SBATC

General Highways Operations – Level 2
Awarding body:
    EMP

Roadbuilding – Level 2
Awarding body:
    SQA & CITB

Site Technical Support – Level 3
Awarding body:
    SQA & CIOB & ICE

Spatial Data Management – Level 4
Awarding body:
    SQA & ABBE

Vocationally Related Qualification

Advanced Construction Award – Level 3
Awarding body:
    ABBE

Foundation Construction Award – Level 1
Awarding body:
    C&G/CITB

Intermediate Construction Award – Level 2
Awarding body:
    C&G/CITB

Vocationally Related Qualification (BTEC First Certificate)

Construction – Level 2
Awarding body:
EDEXCEL

Vocationally Related Qualification (BTEC First Diploma)

Construction – Level 2
Awarding body:
EDEXCEL

Construction – Level 3
Awarding body:
EDEXCEL

Vocationally Related Qualification (BTEC National Award)

Construction – Level 3
Awarding body:
EDEXCEL

Vocationally Related Qualification (BTEC National Certificate)

Construction – Level 3
Awarding body:
EDEXCEL

Vocationally Related Qualification (BTEC National Certificate)

Building Services Engineering – Level 3
Awarding body:
EDEXCEL

Vocationally Related Qualification (BTEC National Diploma)

Building Services Engineering – Level 3
Awarding body:
EDEXCEL

Construction – Level 3
Awarding body:
EDEXCEL

Vocationally Related Qualification (Certificate)

Construction Technology and the Built Environment (Pilot) – Level 2
Awarding body:
C&G

Site Supervisory Studies – Level 3
Awarding body:
CIOB

Vocationally Related Qualification (Diploma)

Remedial Camouflage – Level 3
Awarding body:
VTCT

Vocationally Related Qualification (Foundation Certificate)

Building Craft Occupations – Level 1
Awarding body:
C&G/CITB

Vocationally Related Qualification (Introductory Certificate)

Construction – Level 1
Awarding body:
EDEXCEL

Vocationally Related Qualification (Introductory Diploma)

Construction – Level 1

Awarding body:
EDEXCEL

Business Studies and Services

VOCATIONAL QUALIFICATIONS

BTEC Award

Business Administration – Level 2
Awarding body:
  EDEXCEL

BTEC Diploma

Business Administration – Level 2
Awarding body:
  EDEXCEL

BTEC Professional Diploma

Business and Management for the Arts: Music Production – Level 5
Awarding body:
  EDEXCEL

Entry Level Certificate

Business Administration – Entry 2
Awarding body:
  OCNW

Business Administration – Entry 3
Awarding body:
  OCNW

Higher Level (BTEC Professional Diploma)

Small Business Financial Management – Level 3
Awarding body:
  SQA

National Vocational Qualification

Business – Level 2
Awarding body:
  AQA
  C&G
  CMI
  EAL
  EDEXCEL
  EDI
  ILM
  OCR
  VTCT

Business – Level 3
Awarding body:
  AQA
  C&G
  CMI
  EAL
  EDEXCEL
  EDI
  ILM
  OCR
  VTCT

Business and Administrartion – Level 3
Awarding body:
  C&G

Business and Administration – Level 1
Awarding body:
  C&G
  EDI
  OCR

Business and Administration – Level 2
Awarding body:
  EAL
  EDI
  IMI
  OCR

Business and Administration – Level 3
Awarding body:
EDEXCEL
EDI
IMI
OCR

Business Improvement Techniques – Level 2
Awarding body:
C&G
EAL
EDEXCEL
ETCAL
PAA/VQSET

Business Improvement Techniques – Level 3
Awarding body:
C&G
EAL
EDEXCEL
ETCAL
PAA/VQSET

Business Information – Level 3
Awarding body:
OCR

Business Start Up – Level 3
Awarding body:
CMI
EDEXCEL
EDI
ILM
OCR
VTCT

Business Studies and Services – Level 2
Awarding body:
C&G

Combined Working Practices – Level 2
Awarding body:
PAA/VQSET

Combined Working Practices – Level 3
Awarding body:
PAA/VQSET

Qualifications and Credit Framework (Award)

Self Employment and Enterprise – Level 2
Awarding body:
NOCN

Self Employment and Enterprise – Level 3
Awarding body:
NOCN

Qualifications and Credit Framework (Certificate)

Self Employment and Enterprise – Level 3
Awarding body:
NOCN

Scottish Vocational Qualification

Business – Level 3
Awarding body:
CMI
ILM
SQA

Business Administration – Level 1
Awarding body:
EAL

Business Administration – Level 2
Awarding body:
EAL

Business Administration – Level 3
Awarding body:
EAL

Business Advice – Level 4
Awarding body:
EDEXCEL
SQA

Business and Administration – Level 1
Awarding body:
C&G
EDI
SQA

Business and Administration – Level 2
Awarding body:
   C&G
   EDI
   SQA

Business and Administration – Level 3
Awarding body:
   C&G
   EDI
   SQA

Business and Administration – Level 4
Awarding body:
   C&G
   EDI
   SQA

Business and Management for the Arts: Music Production – Level 4
Awarding body:
   EDEXCEL

Business Development – Level 4
Awarding body:
   SQA

Business Improvement Techniques (Process Improvement Pathway) – Level 2
Awarding body:
   SQA

Business Improvement Techniques (Process Improvement Pathway) – Level 3
Awarding body:
   SQA

Business Improvement Techniques (Process Improvement Pathway) – Level 4
Awarding body:
   SQA

Business Improvement Techniques (Process) – Level 2
Awarding body:
   EAL

Business Improvement Techniques (Process) – Level 3
Awarding body:
   EAL

Business Improvement Techniques (Process) – Level 4
Awarding body:
   EAL

Business Improvement Techniques (Quality Improvement Pathway) – Level 2
Awarding body:
   SQA

Business Improvement Techniques (Quality Improvement Pathway) – Level 3
Awarding body:
   SQA

Business Improvement Techniques (Quality Improvement Pathway) – Level 4
Awarding body:
   SQA

Business Improvement Techniques (Quality) – Level 2
Awarding body:
   EAL

Business Improvement Techniques (Quality) – Level 3
Awarding body:
   EAL

Business Improvement Techniques (Quality) – Level 4
Awarding body:
   EAL

Business Information – Level 3
Awarding body:
   SQA

Business Start Up – Level 3
Awarding body:
   CMI
   SQA

Combined Working Practices – Level 2
Awarding body:
   PAA/VQSET
   SQA

Combined Working Practices – Level 3
Awarding body:
PAA/VQSET
SQA

Vocational Certificate of Education

Starting Your Business – Level 3
Awarding body:
SQA

Vocational Certificate of Education (Double Award)

Starting Your Business – Level 3
Awarding body:
SQA

Vocational Certificate of Education Advanced Subsidiary

Trade Union Representatives – Level 3
Awarding body:
SQA

Vocationally Related Qualification (Advanced Award)

Business Improvement Techniques – Level 2
Awarding body:
EDEXCEL

Business Improvement Techniques – Level 3
Awarding body:
EDEXCEL

Business Improvement Techniques – Level 4
Awarding body:
EDEXCEL

Vocationally Related Qualification (Advanced Certificate)

Business Improvement Techniques (Process) – Level 2
Awarding body:
EDEXCEL

Business Improvement Techniques (Process) – Level 3
Awarding body:
EDEXCEL

Business Improvement Techniques (Process) – Level 4
Awarding body:
EDEXCEL

Vocationally Related Qualification (Award)

Creative Arts Business Start-up – Level 3
Awarding body:
ABC

Starting a Business Venture – Level 3
Awarding body:
OCR

Vocationally Related Qualification (BTEC First Diploma)

Business Improvement Techniques (Quality) – Level 2
Awarding body:
EDEXCEL

Business Improvement Techniques (Quality) – Level 3
Awarding body:
EDEXCEL

Business Improvement Techniques (Quality) – Level 4
Awarding body:
EDEXCEL

Vocationally Related Qualification (BTEC National Award)

Business Information – Level 3
Awarding body:
EDI

Business Language Competence – Level 1
Awarding body:
EDI
OCR

Business Language Competence – Level 2
Awarding body:
EDI
OCR

Business Language Competence – Level 3
Awarding body:
EDI
OCR

Vocationally Related Qualification (BTEC National Certificate)

Business Practice – Level 2
Awarding body:
EDI
OCR

Business Practice – Level 3
Awarding body:
EDI
OCR

Business Start Up – Level 3
Awarding body:
ETCAL

Vocationally Related Qualification (BTEC National Diploma)

Business Start Up – Level 3
Awarding body:
IAB

Vocationally Related Qualification (Certificate)

Business and Administration – Level 2
Awarding body:
EDI

Business and Administration – Level 3
Awarding body:
EDI

Business Improvement Techniques – Level 2
Awarding body:
ILM

Business Improvement Techniques – Level 3
Awarding body:
ILM

Business Improvement Techniques – Level 4
Awarding body:
ILM

Business Travel – Level 2
Awarding body:
ILM

Combined Working Practices – Level 3
Awarding body:
NCFE

E-business – Level 3
Awarding body:
NOCN

E-business (Applied) – Level 3
Awarding body:
OCR

Enterprise (Young Enterprise) – Level 1
Awarding body:
OCR

Enterprise (Young Enterprise) – Level 2
Awarding body:
OCR

Exploring Enterprise (Pilot) – Level 2
Awarding body:
OCR

Starting a Business Venture – Level 3
Awarding body:
OCR

Vocationally Related Qualification (Diploma)

Business Administration – Level 3
Awarding body:
IMIAL

International Trade and Services – Level 2
Awarding body:
OCR

International Trade and Services – Level 3
Awarding body:
OCR

International Trade and Services – Level 4
Awarding body:
OCR

Vocationally Related Qualification (Introductory Certificate)

International Trade and Services – Level 2
Awarding body:
OCR

International Trade and Services – Level 3
Awarding body:
OCR

International Trade and Services – Level 4
Awarding body:
OCR

Vocationally Related Qualification (National Certificate)

Key Account Management – Level 4
Awarding body:
OCR

Vocationally Related Qualification (National Diploma)

Preparation for Business – Level 3
Awarding body:
OCR

Vocationally Related Qualification (National Extended Diploma)

Running a Small Business – Intermediate
Awarding body:
OCR

Care

APPRENTICESHIPS

Apprenticeships available in Early Years Care and Education and in Health and Social Care
www.skillsforhealth.org.uk

VOCATIONAL QUALIFICATIONS

Entry Level Certificate

Preparing for Work in the Care Sector – Level 3
Awarding body:
C&G

National Vocational Qualification

Custodial Care – Level 2
Awarding body:
C&G
EDEXCEL
OCR

Custodial Care – Level 3
Awarding body:
C&G
EDEXCEL
OCR

Custodial Healthcare – Level 3
Awarding body:
C&G
EDEXCEL

Scottish Vocational Qualification

Care – Level 3
Awarding body:
C&G
EDEXCEL

Custodial Care – Level 2
Awarding body:
SQA & Scottish Prison Service

Custodial Care – Level 3
Awarding body:
SQA & Scottish Prison Service

Vocationally Related Qualification (Award)

Supervising Exercise with Disabled People – Level 2
Awarding body:
CYQ

Vocationally Related Qualification (BTEC First Diploma)

Caring – Level 2
Awarding body:
EDEXCEL

Vocationally Related Qualification (BTEC National Certificate)

Care – Level 3
Awarding body:
EDEXCEL

Vocationally Related Qualification (BTEC National Diploma)

Care – Level 3
Awarding body:
EDEXCEL

Vocationally Related Qualification (Certificate)

Contributing to the Care Setting – Level 2
Awarding body:
  C&G

Dementia Care – Level 2
Awarding body:
  EDI

Enhancing Movement Activities with Older People (Care) – Level 3
Awarding body:
  C&G

Non-Care Staff in the Care Environment – Level 2
Awarding body:
  EDI

Non-Care Workers in Care Settings – Level 2
Awarding body:
  NCFE

Vocationally Related Qualification (National Certificate)

Care – Level 3
Awarding body:
  C&G

Vocationally Related Qualification (National Diploma)

Care – Level 3
Awarding body:
  EDEXCEL

Catering and Hospitality

APPRENTICESHIPS

Apprenticeships available in Food Preparation and Cooking, Restaurant Supervision, Housekeeping Skills and Bar Service
www.people1st.co.uk

VOCATIONAL QUALIFICATIONS

Advanced Vocational Certificate of Education

Hospitality and Catering – Level 3
Awarding body:
AQA
EDEXCEL
OCR

Advanced Vocational Certificate of Education (Double Award)

Hospitality and Catering – Level 3
Awarding body:
AQA
EDEXCEL
OCR

Award

Effective Augmentative and Alternative Communication – Entry Level
Awarding body:
C&G

BTEC Higher National Certificate

Hospitality Management – Level 5
Awarding body:
EDEXCEL

BTEC Higher National Diploma

Hospitality Management – Level 5
Awarding body:
EDEXCEL

BTEC Professional Award

Aspects of Financial Management for Hospitality – Level 4
Awarding body:
EDEXCEL

Human Resource Practices in Hospitality – Level 4
Awarding body:
EDEXCEL

Managing Business Performance in Hospitality – Level 4
Awarding body:
EDEXCEL

Marketing for Hospitality – Level 4
Awarding body:
EDEXCEL

Staff Training and Development for Hospitality – Level 4
Awarding body:
EDEXCEL

Certificate

Catering – Entry Level
Awarding body:
OCR

Food Studies – Entry 1
Awarding body:
C&G

Food Studies – Entry 2
Awarding body:
C&G

Food Studies – Entry Level
Awarding body:
 CCEA
 WJEC

Home Economics – Entry Level
Awarding body:
 CCEA

Hospitality and Catering – Entry Level
Awarding body:
 C&G

Foundation General National Vocational Qualification

Hospitality and Catering – Level 1
Awarding body:
 AQA
 EDEXCEL
 OCR

Higher Professional Diploma

Hospitality and Catering – Level 4
Awarding body:
 C&G

Intermediate General National Vocational Qualification

Hospitality and Catering – Level 2
Awarding body:
 AQA
 EDEXCEL
 OCR

National Vocational Qualification

Bar Service – Level 2
Awarding body:
 C&G
 HAB

Drink Service Advanced Craft – Level 3
Awarding body:
 GOAL
 HAB

Drinks Dispense Systems – Level 3
Awarding body:
 C&G
 HAB

Events – Level 2
Awarding body:
 C&G

Events – Level 3
Awarding body:
 C&G

Events - Temporary Structures – Level 3
Awarding body:
 C&G

Food and Drink Service – Level 2
Awarding body:
 EDI

Food Processing and Cooking – Level 2
Awarding body:
 EDI

Front Office – Level 1
Awarding body:
 EDI

Front Office – Level 2
Awarding body:
 C&G
 HAB

Guest Service – Level 1
Awarding body:
 C&G
 HAB

Hospitality – Level 1
Awarding body:
 C&G
 EDI
 HAB

Hospitality Quick Service – Level 2
Awarding body:
 C&G
 HAB

Hospitality Service – Level 2
Awarding body:
 C&G
 GOAL
 HAB

Hospitality Supervision – Level 3
Awarding body:
   C&G
   EDEXCEL
   EDI
   GOAL
   HAB

Housekeeping – Level 1
Awarding body:
   C&G
   HAB

Housekeeping – Level 2
Awarding body:
   C&G
   EDI
   GOAL
   HAB

Kitchen Portering – Level 1
Awarding body:
   C&G
   HAB

Multi-Skilled Hospitality Services – Level 2
Awarding body:
   C&G
   EDI
   HAB

Preparing and Serving Food – Level 1
Awarding body:
   C&G

Professional Cookery – Level 2
Awarding body:
   EDI

Professional Cookery – Level 3
Awarding body:
   EDI

Scottish Vocational Qualification

Customer Service – Level 2
Awarding body:
   C&G
   SQA

Front Office – Level 2
Awarding body:
   C&G
   SQA & HAB

Hospitality Conflict Handling – Level 1
Awarding body:
   HAB

Hospitality Customer Relations – Level 3
Awarding body:
   C&G
   EDI
   HAB

Hospitality Quick Service – Level 2
Awarding body:
   C&G
   SQA & HAB

Hospitality Selling – Level 1
Awarding body:
   C&G
   SQA & HAB

Hospitality Supervision – Level 3
Awarding body:
   SQA/HAB/BII

Hospitality: Food and Drink Service – Level 1
Awarding body:
   C&G

Hospitality: Food Preparation and Cooking – Level 1
Awarding body:
   C&G
   SQA & HAB

Hospitality: Front Office – Level 1
Awarding body:
   C&G
   SQA & HAB

Hospitality: Housekeeping – Level 1
Awarding body:
   C&G

Hospitality: Multi-skilled – Level 1
Awarding body:
   SQA & HAB

Hospitality: Quick Service – Level 1
Awarding body:
   C&G

Housekeeping – Level 2
Awarding body:
  C&G
  SQA & HAB

Multi-Skilled Hospitality Service – Level 2
Awarding body:
  C&G
  SQA & HAB

Vocational Certificate of Education (Certificate)

Licensees (On-Licence) – Level 2
Awarding body:
  GOAL

Vocational Certificate of Education (National Certificate)

Licensees – Level 2
Awarding body:
  BII

Vocationally Related Qualification

Conflict Handling – Level 1
Awarding body:
  HAB

Essentials of Catering – Level 1
Awarding body:
  BII

Vocationally Related Qualification (Advanced Certificate)

Licensed Hospitality – Level 3
Awarding body:
  BII

Vocationally Related Qualification (BTEC Certificate)

Front Office Operations – Level 3
Awarding body:
  EDEXCEL

Hospitality Customer Relations – Level 3
Awarding body:
  EDEXCEL

Hospitality Small Business Operations – Level 3
Awarding body:
  EDEXCEL

Vocationally Related Qualification (BTEC First Diploma)

Hospitality – Level 2
Awarding body:
  EDEXCEL

Vocationally Related Qualification (BTEC National Certificate)

Hospitality Supervision – Level 3
Awarding body:
  EDEXCEL

Vocationally Related Qualification (BTEC National Diploma)

Hospitality Supervision – Level 3
Awarding body:
  EDEXCEL

Vocationally Related Qualification (Certificate)

Event and Match Day Stewarding – Level 2
Awarding body:
  1ST4SPORT

Event Management – Level 3
Awarding body:
   NCFE

Event Planning – Level 2
Awarding body:
   EDI
   NCFE

Event Stewarding – Level 2
Awarding body:
   NCFE

Food Safety in Catering – Level 2
Awarding body:
   EDI

Healthier Foods and Special Diets – Level 2
Awarding body:
   EDI

Hospitality and Catering Skills – Level 1
Awarding body:
   ABC

Organising Conferences, Leisure or Hospitality Events – Level 2
Awarding body:

Practical Food Safety in Catering – Level 2
Awarding body:
   EDI

Practical Supervision of Food Safety in Catering – Level 3
Awarding body:
   EDI

Professional Cookery – Level 2
Awarding body:
   EDI

Providing a Healthier School Meals Service – Level 1
Awarding body:
   EDI

Visitor Attraction Operations – Level 2
Awarding body:
   EDI

Vocationally Related Qualification (Diploma)

Licensed Hospitality – Level 3
Awarding body:
   BIIAB

Vocationally Related Qualification (Introductory Certificate)

Hospitality Conflict Handling – Level 1
Awarding body:
   HAB

Hospitality Customer Service – Level 1
Awarding body:
   HAB

Hospitality Selling – Level 1
Awarding body:
   HAB

Vocationally Related Qualification (National Certificate)

Entertainment Licensees – Level 2
Awarding body:
   BII

Licensees (Drugs Awareness) – Level 2
Awarding body:
   BII

Personal Licence Holders – Level 2
Awarding body:
   EDI

Vocationally Related Qualification (National Diploma)

Designated Premises Supervisors – Level 3
Awarding body:
   EDI

Vocationally Related Qualification (Scottish Certificate)

Personal Licence Holders – Level 2

Awarding body:
EDI

Chemical and Biochemical Engineering

APPRENTICESHIPS

Apprenticeships available in Chemical, Pharmaceutical, Petrochemical Manufacturing and Refining Industries
www.cogent-ssc.com

VOCATIONAL QUALIFICATIONS

National Vocational Qualification

Chemical, Pharmaceutical and Petro-Chemical Manufacture – Level 1
Awarding body:
C&G
PAA/VQSET

Chemical, Pharmaceutical and Petro-Chemical Manufacture – Level 2
Awarding body:
C&G
PAA/VQSET

Chemical, Pharmaceutical and Petro-Chemical Manufacture – Level 3
Awarding body:
C&G
PAA/VQSET

Scottish Vocational Qualification

Analytical Chemistry – Level 5
Awarding body:
PAA/VQSET/SQA

Chemical, Pharmaceutical and Petro-Chemical Manufacture – Level 1
Awarding body:
PAA/VQSET/SQA

Chemical, Pharmaceutical and Petro-Chemical Manufacture (Control Room Operations) – Level 2
Awarding body:
PAA/VQSET/SQA

Chemical, Pharmaceutical and Petro-Chemical Manufacture (Controlling Process Operations) – Level 3
Awarding body:
PAA/VQSET/SQA

Chemical, Pharmaceutical and Petro-Chemical Manufacture (Process Operations) – Level 2
Awarding body:
PAA/VQSET/SQA

Chemical, Pharmaceutical and Petro-Chemical Manufacture (Process Support Services) – Level 2
Awarding body:
PAA/VQSET/SQA

Chemical, Pharmaceutical and Petro-Chemical Manufacture (Technical Support) – Level 4
Awarding body:
PAA/VQSET/SQA

Children and Child Care

APPRENTICESHIPS

Apprenticeships available in Early Years Care and Education
www.skillsforhealth.org.uk

VOCATIONAL QUALIFICATIONS

BTEC Certificate

Early Years Care and Education – Level 2
Awarding body:
EDEXCEL

BTEC Higher National Certificate

Advanced Practice in Work with Children and Families – Level 5
Awarding body:
EDEXCEL

BTEC Higher National Diploma

Advanced Practice in Work with Children and Families – Level 5
Awarding body:
EDEXCEL

BTEC National Award

Early Years – Level 3
Awarding body:
EDEXCEL

BTEC National Certificate

Early Years – Level 2
Awarding body:
EDEXCEL

BTEC National Diploma

Early Years – Level 3
Awarding body:
EDEXCEL

BTEC Professional Diploma

Specialised Play for Sick Children and Young People – Level 4
Awarding body:
EDEXCEL

Certificate

Child Development – Entry Level
Awarding body:
OCR

Childcare – Entry Level
Awarding body:
CCEA
WJEC

Home Economics: Child Development (Entry 1, 2 and 3) – Entry Level
Awarding body:
AQA

Preparation for Childcare – Entry Level
Awarding body:
CACHE

Higher Level Certificate

Early Years Practice – Level 4
Awarding body:
OU

Management of Quality Standards in Children's Services – Level 4
Awarding body:
CACHE

National Vocational Qualification

Children's Care, Learning and Development – Level 2
Awarding body:
C&G
CACHE
EDEXCEL
EDI
EDI

Children's Care, Learning and Development – Level 3
Awarding body:
C&G
CACHE
EDEXCEL
EDI
EDI

Children's Care, Learning and Development – Level 4
Awarding body:
EDI

Early Years Care and Education – Level 2
Awarding body:
C&G
CACHE
EDEXCEL

Early Years Care and Education – Level 3
Awarding body:
CACHE
EDEXCEL

Playwork – Level 2
Awarding body:
C&G
CACHE
EDEXCEL

Playwork – Level 3
Awarding body:
C&G
CACHE
EDEXCEL

Scottish Vocational Qualification

Child Care and Education – Level 3
Awarding body:
C&G
CACHE

Childcare – Level 2
Awarding body:
C&G
CACHE
EDEXCEL

Childminding Practice – Level 3
Awarding body:
C&G
CACHE
EDEXCEL

Children's Care, Learning and Development – Level 2
Awarding body:
C&G

Children's Care, Learning and Development – Level 3
Awarding body:
SQA

Children's Care, Learning and Development – Level 4
Awarding body:
SQA

Playwork – Level 2
Awarding body:
SQA

Playwork – Level 3
Awarding body:
SQA

Playwork – Level 4
Awarding body:
SQA

Vocationally Related Qualification (Award)

Childcare – Level 2
Awarding body:
NOCN

Playwork – Level 2
Awarding body:
  NOCN

Playwork – Level 3
Awarding body:
  CACHE

Vocationally Related Qualification (BTEC Certificate)

Children's Care, Learning and Development – Level 3
Awarding body:
  EDEXCEL

Vocationally Related Qualification (BTEC National Certificate)

Early Years – Level 3
Awarding body:
  CACHE

Vocationally Related Qualification (Certificate of Professional Development)

Work with Children and Young People – Level 3
Awarding body:
  CACHE

Vocationally Related Qualification (Certificate)

Certificate in Children's Care, Learning and Development – Level 2
Awarding body:
  CACHE

Child Care and Education – Level 2
Awarding body:
  CACHE

Childminding Practice – Level 3
Awarding body:
  CACHE

Children's Care, Learning and Development – Level 2
Awarding body:
  C&G
  EDI
  EDI

Children's Care, Learning and Development – Level 3
Awarding body:
  C&G
  CACHE
  EDI
  EDI

Developing Skills for Early Years Practice – Level 3
Awarding body:
  NCFE

Developing Skills for Working with Children and Young People – Level 2
Awarding body:
  NCFE

Early Years Care and Education (Welsh Medium) – Level 2
Awarding body:
  CACHE

Early Years Practice – Level 2
Awarding body:
  CACHE

First Aid for those Caring for Children – Level 2
Awarding body:
  EDI

Implementing the High/Scope Approach – Level 3
Awarding body:
  CACHE

Playwork – Level 2
Awarding body:
  CACHE

Playwork – Level 3
Awarding body:
  CACHE

Pre-School Practice – Level 2
Awarding body:
  CACHE

**Promoting Children's Social and
Emotional Development – Level 3**
Awarding body:
   CACHE

Supporting Playwork Practice – Level 2
Awarding body:
   CACHE

Work with Children – Level 3
Awarding body:
   C&G
   CACHE

Vocationally Related Qualification (Diploma)

Child Care and Education – Level 3
Awarding body:
   CACHE

**Early Years Care and Education (Welsh
Medium) – Level 3**
Awarding body:
   CACHE

Early Years Practice – Level 3
Awarding body:
   CACHE

Home-based Childcare – Level 3
Awarding body:
   CACHE

**Playgroup Practice in Wales (DPPW) –
Level 3**
Awarding body:
   CACHE

Pre-School Practice – Level 3
Awarding body:
   CACHE

Supporting Playwork Practice – Level 3
Awarding body:
   CACHE

Vocationally Related Qualification (Foundation Award)

Caring for Children – Level 1
Awarding body:
   CACHE

Vocationally Related Qualification (Progression Award)

**Early Years Care and Education –
Level 2**
Awarding body:
   C&G

**Early Years Care and Education –
Level 3**
Awarding body:
   C&G

Cleaning, Laundry and Dry Cleaning

APPRENTICESHIPS

Apprenticeships and Advanced
Apprenticeships in Cleaning and Support
Services
www.assetskills.org

VOCATIONAL QUALIFICATIONS

National Vocational Qualification

Cleaning and Support Services – Level 1
Awarding body:
   C&G
   EDI
   HAB
   MTC
   WAMITAB

Cleaning and Support Services – Level 2
Awarding body:
   C&G
   EDI
   HAB
   MTC

**Cleaning and Support Services
(Highways and Land) – Level 2**
Awarding body:
   WAMITAB

Scottish Vocational Qualification

Cleaning and Support Services – Level 1
Awarding body:
   SQA & BICS
   SQA & HAB

Cleaning and Support Services – Level 2
Awarding body:
   SQA & BICS

**Cleaning and Support Services (Building
Interiors) – Level 2**
Awarding body:
   SQA & BICS
   SQA & HAB

**Cleaning and Support Services
(Caretaking) – Level 2**
Awarding body:
   SQA & BICS

**Cleaning and Support Services (Carpets)
– Level 2**
Awarding body:
   SQA & BICS

**Cleaning and Support Services (Food
Premises) – Level 2**
Awarding body:
   SQA & BICS
   SQA & HAB

**Cleaning and Support Services
(Highways and Land) – Level 2**
Awarding body:
   SQA & BICS
   SQA & WAMITAB

**Cleaning and Support Services
(Passenger Transport Vehicles) – Level 2**
Awarding body:
   SQA & BICS

**Cleaning and Support Services
(Windows) – Level 2**
Awarding body:
   SQA & BICS

Vocationally Related Qualification (Certificate)

Cleaning Science – Level 2
Awarding body:
   C&G

Vocationally Related Qualification (Diploma)

Cleaning Services Supervision – Level 3
Awarding body:
   C&G

Communications and Media

APPRENTICESHIPS

Apprenticeships in Arts and
Entertainment; and Media and Printing
www.ccskills.org.uk

VOCATIONAL QUALIFICATIONS

Advanced Vocational Certificate of Education

**Media: Communication and Production
– Level 3**
Awarding body:
AQA
EDEXCEL
OCR

Advanced Vocational Certificate of Education (Double Award)

**Media: Communication and Production
– Level 3**
Awarding body:
AQA
EDEXCEL
OCR

BEC Professional Certificate

Video Journalism – Level 4
Awarding body:
EDEXCEL

BTEC Higher National Certificate

Interactive Media – Level 5
Awarding body:
EDEXCEL

Media – Level 5
Awarding body:
EDEXCEL

BTEC Higher National Diploma

Interactive Media – Level 5
Awarding body:
EDEXCEL

Media – Level 5
Awarding body:
EDEXCEL

BTEC Professional Certificate

Digital Audio Editing – Level 4
Awarding body:
EDEXCEL

Digital Video Editing – Level 4
Awarding body:
EDEXCEL

BTEC Professional Diploma

Audio Recording – Level 5
Awarding body:
EDEXCEL

Certificate

**Communication Tactics with Deaf
People – Level 1**
Awarding body:
CACDP

Telematics – Level 1
Awarding body:
NCFE

Telematics – Level 2
Awarding body:
NCFE

Foundation Graded Examination

Communication Skills – Level 1
Awarding body:
TCL

Intermediate General National Vocational Qualification

Media: Communication and Production – Level 2
Awarding body:
AQA
EDEXCEL

Intermediate Graded Examination

Communication Skills – Level 2
Awarding body:
TCL

National Diploma

Professional Production Skills – Level 6
Awarding body:
TCL

National Vocational Qualification

Communication Technologies (Aerial Equipment) – Level 2
Awarding body:
EDEXCEL

Communication Technologies (Infrastructure) – Level 2
Awarding body:
EDEXCEL

Communication Technologies (Installation Team Leader) – Level 3
Awarding body:
EDEXCEL

Communication Technologies (Network Control) – Level 3
Awarding body:
EDEXCEL

Communication Technologies (Operating) – Level 2
Awarding body:
EDEXCEL

Communication Technologies (Planning) – Level 3
Awarding body:
EDEXCEL

Communication Technologies (Systems) – Level 3
Awarding body:
EDEXCEL

Communication Technologies (Work Quality Audit) – Level 3
Awarding body:
EDEXCEL

Grip for the Audio Visual Industries – Level 2
Awarding body:
C&G

Grip for the Audio Visual Industries – Level 3
Awarding body:
C&G

Installing Structured Cabling Systems – Level 3
Awarding body:
EAL

OG

Speech – Level 1
Awarding body:
TVU

Speech – Level 2
Awarding body:
TVU

Speech – Level 3
Awarding body:
TVU

Scottish Vocational Qualification

Communication Technologies (Work Quality Audit) – Level 3
Awarding body:
EDEXCEL

Vocationally Related Qualification (Award)

3D Digital Animation Techniques – Level 3
Awarding body:
ABC

3D Visual Thinking – Level 3
Awarding body:
ABC

Application of Visual Thinking – Level 3
Awarding body:
ABC

Data Management for Web Design – Level 3
Awarding body:
ABC

Digital Video Editing – Level 3
Awarding body:
ABC

Radio Production Skills – Level 3
Awarding body:
ABC

Visual Thinking – Level 3
Awarding body:
ABC

Vocationally Related Qualification (BTEC Certificate)

Interactive Use of Media – Level 1
Awarding body:
EDEXCEL

Interactive Use of Media – Level 2
Awarding body:
EDEXCEL

Interactive Use of Media – Level 3
Awarding body:
EDEXCEL

Vocationally Related Qualification (BTEC Diploma)

Interactive Use of Media – Level 1
Awarding body:
EDEXCEL

Interactive Use of Media – Level 2
Awarding body:
EDEXCEL

Interactive Use of Media – Level 3
Awarding body:
EDEXCEL

Vocationally Related Qualification (BTEC First Certificate)

Media – Level 2
Awarding body:
EDEXCEL

Vocationally Related Qualification (BTEC First Diploma)

Media – Level 2
Awarding body:
EDEXCEL

Vocationally Related Qualification (BTEC National Award)

Communications Electronic Engineering – Level 3
Awarding body:
EDEXCEL

Media – Level 3
Awarding body:
EDEXCEL

Telecommunications – Level 3
Awarding body:
   EDEXCEL

Vocationally Related Qualification (BTEC National Certificate)

Communications Electronic Engineering – Level 3
Awarding body:
   EDEXCEL

Multimedia – Level 3
Awarding body:
   EDEXCEL

Telecommunications – Level 3
Awarding body:
   EDEXCEL

Vocationally Related Qualification (BTEC National Diploma)

Communications Electronic Engineering – Level 3
Awarding body:
   EDEXCEL

Media – Level 3
Awarding body:
   EDEXCEL

Multimedia – Level 3
Awarding body:
   EDEXCEL

Telecommunications – Level 3
Awarding body:
   EDEXCEL

Vocationally Related Qualification (Certificate)

Communication and Guiding Skills with DeafBlind People – Level 3
Awarding body:
   CACDP

Communications Cabling – Level 2
Awarding body:
   C&G

iMedia Users – Level 2
Awarding body:
   OCR

iMedia Users – Level 3
Awarding body:
   OCR

Media – Level 3
Awarding body:
   OCR

Video Production – Level 2
Awarding body:
   NCFE

Vocationally Related Qualification (Diploma)

Communications Systems – Level 3
Awarding body:
   C&G

Digital Media – Level 3
Awarding body:
   ABC

iMedia Users – Level 2
Awarding body:
   OCR

iMedia Users – Level 3
Awarding body:
   OCR

Media – Level 3
Awarding body:
   OCR

Media Techniques – Level 3
Awarding body:
   C&G

Vocationally Related Qualification (Double Award)

Experimental Digital Media – Level 3
Awarding body:
   ABC

Vocationally Related Qualification (National Certificate)

Media – Level 2
Awarding body:
OCR

Media – Level 3
Awarding body:
OCR

Vocationally Related Qualification (National Diploma)

Media – Level 3
Awarding body:
OCR

Vocationally Related Qualification (National Extended Diploma)

Media – Level 3
Awarding body:
OCR

Community Work

APPRENTICESHIPS

Apprenticeships in Community Justice
www.skillsforjustice.com

Apprenticeships in Health and Social
Care; Health Care and Public Service
www.skillsforhealth.org.uk

VOCATIONAL QUALIFICATIONS

BTEC Professional Diploma

**Community Music Management –
Level 5**
Awarding body:
  EDEXCEL

Higher Level Certificate

Community Justice – Level 4
Awarding body:
  C&G

National Vocational Qualification

**Community Development Work –
Level 2**
Awarding body:
  C&G

**Community Development Work –
Level 3**
Awarding body:
  C&G

**Community Justice: Community Safety –
Level 3**
Awarding body:
  C&G

**Community Justice: Work with
Offending Behaviour – Level 3**
Awarding body:
  C&G

**Community Justice: Work with Victims,
Survivors and Witnesses – Level 3**
Awarding body:
  C&G

Community Wardens – Level 2
Awarding body:
  C&G

Democratic Services – Level 3
Awarding body:
  OU

Youth Justice Services – Level 3
Awarding body:
  C&G
  EDEXCEL

Youth Work – Level 2
Awarding body:
  ABC
  C&G

Youth Work – Level 3
Awarding body:
  ABC
  C&G

Scottish Vocational Qualification

**Community Development Work –
Level 2**
Awarding body:
  SQA

**Community Development Work –
Level 3**
Awarding body:
  SQA

**Community Development Work –
Level 4**
Awarding body:
  SQA

**Community Justice: Work with
Offending Behaviour – Level 3**
Awarding body:
  SQA

**Community Justice: Work with
Offending Behaviour – Level 4**
Awarding body:
  SQA

**Community Justice: Work with Victims,
Survivors and Witnesses – Level 3**
Awarding body:
  SQA

**Community Justice: Work with Victims,
Survivors and Witnesses – Level 4**
Awarding body:
  SQA

**Community Justice: Work with Victims,
Survivors and Witnesses – Level 5**
Awarding body:
  C&G

**Community Mental Health Care –
Level 3**
Awarding body:
  C&G

**Community Music Management –
Level 4**
Awarding body:
  C&G

Community Safety – Level 3
Awarding body:
  SQA

Community Safety – Level 4
Awarding body:
  SQA

Community Sports Leadership – Level 1
Awarding body:
  C&G

Youth Justice Services – Level 3
Awarding body:
  SQA

Youth Justice Services – Level 4
Awarding body:
  SQA

Youth Work – Level 2
Awarding body:
  SQA

Youth Work – Level 3
Awarding body:
  SQA

Vocational Certificate of Education (Diploma)

Youth Work – Level 3
Awarding body:
  ABC

Vocationally Related Qualification

Community Development – Level 1
Awarding body:
  NOCN

Introduction to Youth Work – Level 1
Awarding body:
  ABC

Vocationally Related Qualification (Award)

Community Development – Level 1
Awarding body:
  NOCN

Community Sports Leadership – Level 1
Awarding body:
  Sports Leaders UK

Vocationally Related Qualification (Certificate)

Community Arts – Level 2
Awarding body:
  ABC

Community Development – Level 2
Awarding body:
  NOCN

Community Development – Level 3
Awarding body:
  NOCN

Community Mental Health Care (for people aged 18-65 years) – Level 3
Awarding body:
  C&G

Supporting the Development Needs of Homeless and Vulnerable People – Level 2
Awarding body:
  C&G

Supporting Youth Work – Level 2
Awarding body:
  C&G

Supporting Youth Work – Level 3
Awarding body:
  ASET

Working in the Community – Level 2
Awarding body:
  CCEA

Youth Work – Level 2
Awarding body:
  ABC
  C&G

Youth Work – Level 3
Awarding body:
  C&G
  NOCN

Vocationally Related Qualification (Diploma)

Youth Work – Level 3
Awarding body:
  ABC

Vocationally Related Qualification (National Award)

Community Arts Management – Level 2
Awarding body:
  EDI

Community Arts Management – Level 3
Awarding body:
  EDI

Vocationally Related Qualification (National Certificate)

Tenant Participation and Neighbourhood Renewal – Level 3
Awarding body:
  CIH

Complementary Therapies

APPRENTICESHIPS

Apprenticeships, Advanced
Apprenticeships in Health and Beauty
Therapy
www.habia.org

VOCATIONAL QUALIFICATIONS

Vocationally Related Qualification (Certificate)

Aromatherapy Massage – Level 3
Awarding body:
　VTCT

Body Massage – Level 3
Awarding body:
　C&G

Holistic Therapies – Level 2
Awarding body:
　VTCT

Reflexology Techniques – Level 3
Awarding body:
　VTCT

Swedish Massage – Level 3
Awarding body:
　VTCT

Vocationally Related Qualification (Diploma)

Aromatherapy – Level 3
Awarding body:
　ITEC
　VTCT

Body Massage – Level 3
Awarding body:
　VTCT

Holistic Body Therapies – Level 3
Awarding body:
　C&G

Holistic Therapies – Level 2
Awarding body:
　VTCT

Indian Head Massage – Level 3
Awarding body:
　ITEC
　VTCT

On-Site Massage – Level 3
Awarding body:
　ITEC

Reflexology – Level 3
Awarding body:
　ABC
　VTCT

Reflexology Techniques – Level 3
Awarding body:
　ITEC

Using Therapy Techniques as an Aid to Stress Management – Level 3
Awarding body:
　VTCT

Computing, Information Systems and Technology

APPRENTICESHIPS

Apprenticeships in Information
Technology and Electronic Services
www.e-skills.com

VOCATIONAL QUALIFICATIONS

Advanced Vocational Certificate of Education

**Information and Communication
Technology – Level 3**
Awarding body:
AQA

Advanced Vocational Certificate of Education (Double Award)

**Information and Communication
Technology – Level 3**
Awarding body:
AQA
EDEXCEL

Award

**Digital Applications for IT Users –
Level 2**
Awarding body:
EDEXCEL

Certificate

**Digital Applications for IT Users –
Level 2**
Awarding body:
EDEXCEL

ICT Skills for Life – Entry Level
Awarding body:
C&G
OCR

**Information and Communication
Technology – Level 1**
Awarding body:
ICAA
OCNW

**Information and Communication
Technology – Level 2**
Awarding body:
OCNW

**Information and Communication
Technology – Entry Level**
Awarding body:
AQA
CCEA
EDEXCEL
OCR

**Information and Communication
Technology (ICT) for Education and
Training – Entry Level**
Awarding body:
OCNW

**Information and Communication
Technology A – Entry Level**
Awarding body:
AQA

**Information and Communication
Technology B – Entry Level**
Awarding body:
AQA

Information Technology – Entry Level
Awarding body:
WJEC

IT Users (e-Citizen) – Entry 3
Awarding body:
BCS

Using ICT – Entry 3
Awarding body:
C&G
OCR

Diploma

**Digital Applications for IT Users –
Level 2**
Awarding body:
EDEXCEL

Higher Level Certificate

IT – Level 4
Awarding body:
BCS

Higher Level Diploma

IT – Level 5
Awarding body:
BCS

Higher Professional Diploma

**Information Management Using ICT –
Level 4**
Awarding body:
C&G

National Vocational Qualification

**Communication Technology
Practitioners – Level 2**
Awarding body:
EDEXCEL

**Communication Technology
Practitioners – Level 3**
Awarding body:
EDEXCEL

**Communication Technology
Professionals – Level 3**
Awarding body:
C&G
EDEXCEL

Contact Centre Operations – Level 1
Awarding body:
EDI
OCR

Contact Centre Operations – Level 2
Awarding body:
EDI
OCR

Contact Centre Professionals – Level 3
Awarding body:
EDEXCEL
EDI
OCR

IT Practitioners – Level 1
Awarding body:
C&G
OCR

IT Practitioners – Level 2
Awarding body:
C&G
OCR

IT Practitioners – Level 3
Awarding body:
C&G

IT Professionals – Level 3
Awarding body:
OCR

IT Users – Level 1
Awarding body:
BCS
C&G
EDEXCEL
EDI
OCR

IT Users – Level 2
Awarding body:
BCS
C&G
EDEXCEL
EDI
OCR

IT Users – Level 3
Awarding body:
  BCS
  C&G
  EDEXCEL
  EDI
  OCR

Technical Services – Level 2
Awarding body:
  C&G
  EAL

Professional Graduate Diploma

IT – Level 6
Awarding body:
  BCS

Qualifications and Credit Framework (Certificate)

IT Users (ITO) – Level 2
Awarding body:
  BCS

Scottish Vocational Qualification

Contact Centre Operations – Level 1
Awarding body:
  SQA

Contact Centre Operations – Level 2
Awarding body:
  SQA

Contact Centre Professionals – Level 3
Awarding body:
  SQA

Contact Centre Professionals – Level 4
Awarding body:
  SQA

Developing IT Programmes – Level 2
Awarding body:
  BCS

Educational Use of ICT – Level 3
Awarding body:
  BCS

Educational Use of the Internet – Level 3
Awarding body:
  C&G

Electronic Notetaking for Deaf People – Level 2
Awarding body:
  C&G

Information and Communication Technology – Level 1
Awarding body:
  C&G

Information and Communication Technology – Level 3
Awarding body:
  C&G

Information and Communication Technology (ICT) for Education and Training – Level 3
Awarding body:
  C&G

IT Practitioners – Level 1
Awarding body:
  SQA & e-Skills UK

IT Practitioners – Level 2
Awarding body:
  SQA & e-Skills UK

IT Professionals – Level 3
Awarding body:
  SQA & e-Skills UK

IT Professionals – Level 4
Awarding body:
  SQA & e-Skills UK

IT Professionals – Level 5
Awarding body:
  SQA & e-Skills UK

IT Users – Level 1
Awarding body:
  C&G
  SQA & e-Skills UK

IT Users – Level 2
Awarding body:
  C&G
  SQA & e-Skills UK

IT Users – Level 3
Awarding body:
  C&G
  SQA & e-Skills UK

Technical Services – Level 2
Awarding body:
  EAL

Vocationally Related Qualification

Digital Workflow – Level 3
Awarding body:
  ABC

Technical Services – Level 2
Awarding body:
  C&G

Vocationally Related Qualification (Advanced Diploma)

IT Practitioners (ICT Systems Support) – Level 3
Awarding body:
  C&G

IT Practitioners (Software Development) – Level 3
Awarding body:
  C&G

Vocationally Related Qualification (Award)

Information and Communication Technology – Level 2
Awarding body:
  IAM

Software Skills for 3D Modelling – Level 3
Awarding body:
  ABC

Using ICT as a Tool for Learning – Level 2
Awarding body:
  NOCN

Vector-Based Image Generation – Level 3
Awarding body:
  ABC

Web Production Skills – Level 3
Awarding body:
  ABC

Vocationally Related Qualification (BTEC Award)

Contact Centre Skills – Level 2
Awarding body:
  EDEXCEL

Introduction to Contact Centres – Level 1
Awarding body:
  EDEXCEL

Vocationally Related Qualification (BTEC First Certificate)

IT Practitioners – Level 2
Awarding body:
  EDEXCEL

Vocationally Related Qualification (BTEC First Diploma)

IT Practitioners (General) – Level 2
Awarding body:
  EDEXCEL

IT Practitioners (ICT Systems Support) – Level 2
Awarding body:
  EDEXCEL

IT Practitioners (Software Development) – Level 2
Awarding body:
EDEXCEL

Vocationally Related Qualification (BTEC Higher National Certificate)

Computing (ICT Systems Support) – Level 5
Awarding body:
EDEXCEL

Computing (Software Development) – Level 5
Awarding body:
EDEXCEL

Vocationally Related Qualification (BTEC Higher National Diploma)

Computing (ICT Systems Support) – Level 5
Awarding body:
EDEXCEL

Vocationally Related Qualification (BTEC Introductory Certificate)

IT @ Work – Level 1
Awarding body:
EDEXCEL

Vocationally Related Qualification (BTEC Introductory Diloma)

IT @ Work – Level 1
Awarding body:
EDEXCEL

Vocationally Related Qualification (BTEC National Award)

IT Practitioners (General) – Level 3
Awarding body:
EDEXCEL

IT Practitioners (ICT Systems Support) – Level 3
Awarding body:
EDEXCEL

Vocationally Related Qualification (BTEC National Certificate)

IT Practitioners (ICT Systems Support) – Level 3
Awarding body:
EDEXCEL

IT Practitioners (Software Development) – Level 3
Awarding body:
EDEXCEL

Vocationally Related Qualification (BTEC National Diploma)

IT Practitioners (General) – Level 3
Awarding body:
EDEXCEL

IT Practitioners (ICT Systems Support) – Level 3
Awarding body:
EDEXCEL

IT Practitioners (Software Development) – Level 3
Awarding body:
EDEXCEL

Vocationally Related Qualification (Certificate)

Computer Keyboarding – Level 1
Awarding body:
  ABC

Contact Centre Skills – Level 2
Awarding body:
  C&G

Contact Centre Skills – Level 3
Awarding body:
  C&G

Contact Centre Techniques – Level 2
Awarding body:
  NCFE

Contact Centre Techniques – Level 1
Awarding body:
  NCFE

Digital Applications for IT Users – Level 1
Awarding body:
  EDEXCEL

Electronic Notetaking for Deaf People – Level 2
Awarding body:
  CACDP

ICT Applications – Level 1
Awarding body:
  EDI

ICT Applications – Level 2
Awarding body:
  EDI

ICT Applications – Level 3
Awarding body:
  EDI

Introduction to the Contact Centre Industry – Level 1
Awarding body:
  C&G

IT Practitioners (General) – Level 2
Awarding body:
  NCFE

IT Practitioners (ICT Systems Support) – Level 3
Awarding body:
  OCR

IT Practitioners (Software Development) – Level 3
Awarding body:
  OCR

IT Professionals (EUCIP) – Level 4
Awarding body:
  BCS

IT Professionals (ICT Systems Support) – Level 4
Awarding body:
  OCR

IT Services: Customer Response Centre – Level 2
Awarding body:
  EDEXCEL

IT Services: Customer Response Centre – Level 3
Awarding body:
  EDEXCEL

IT Systems Support - PC Maintenance – Level 1
Awarding body:
  C&G

IT Users – Level 1
Awarding body:
  NCFE

IT Users – Level 2
Awarding body:
  ABC
  NCFE

IT Users – Level 3
Awarding body:
  NCFE

IT Users (CLAiT Advanced) – Level 3
Awarding body:
  OCR

IT Users (CLAiT Plus) – Level 2
Awarding body:
  OCR

IT Users (ECDL Part 1) – Level 1
Awarding body:
BCS

IT Users (ECDL Part 2) – Level 2
Awarding body:
BCS

IT Users (New CLAiT) – Level 1
Awarding body:
OCR

Technical Theatre – Level 1
Awarding body:
NCFE

**Technology for Colliery Officials –
Level 3**
Awarding body:
C&G

Using E-mail and the Internet – Level 1
Awarding body:
C&G

Using E-mail and the Internet – Level 2
Awarding body:
C&G

Using ICT – Level 3
Awarding body:
BCS

**Word Processing (Administration) –
Level 1**
Awarding body:
ABC

Vocationally Related Qualification (Diploma)

**Designing and Planning
Communications Networks – Level 3**
Awarding body:
C&G

**Digital Applications for IT Users –
Level 1**
Awarding body:
EDEXCEL

Digital Origination – Level 3
Awarding body:
ABC

**IT Practitioners (ICT Systems Support) –
Level 2**
Awarding body:
BTDA

**IT Practitioners (Software Development)
– Level 2**
Awarding body:
C&G

IT Users – Level 2
Awarding body:
C&G

IT Users (CLAiT Advanced) – Level 3
Awarding body:
OCR

IT Users (CLAiT Plus) – Level 2
Awarding body:
OCR

IT Users (New CLAiT) – Level 1
Awarding body:
OCR

Vocationally Related Qualification (Foundation Award)

**Information and Communication
Technology – Level 2**
Awarding body:
IAM

Vocationally Related Qualification (Higher Professional Diploma)

IT Practitioners – Level 4
Awarding body:
C&G

Vocationally Related Qualification (National Certificate)

Information Technology – Level 2
Awarding body:
OCR

Conservation

APPRENTICESHIPS

Apprenticeship in Environmental
Conservation
www.lantra.co.uk

VOCATIONAL QUALIFICATIONS

Scottish Vocational Qualification

Conservation Control – Level 4
Awarding body:
SQA/CIOB/ICE/COTAC

Construction Management

APPRENTICESHIPS

Apprenticeships in Building Service
Engineering - Construction
www.summitskills.org.uk

Apprenticeships in Construction (Craft)
www.bconstructive.co.uk

VOCATIONAL QUALIFICATIONS

National Vocational Qualification

Associated Industrial Services Occupations – Level 2
Awarding body:
C&G/CITB

Construction Operations – Level 2
Awarding body:
EDEXCEL

Decorative Finishing and Industrial Painting Occupations – Level 1
Awarding body:
C&G/CITB

Decorative Finishing and Industrial Painting Occupations – Level 2
Awarding body:
C&G/CITB

Decorative Finishing and Industrial Painting Occupations – Level 3
Awarding body:
C&G/CITB

Fitted Interiors – Level 2
Awarding body:
C&G/CITB

Floorcovering – Level 2
Awarding body:
C&G/CITB

Floorcovering – Level 3
Awarding body:
C&G/CITB

Occupational Work Supervision – Level 2
Awarding body:
C&G/CITB

Piling Operations – Level 2
Awarding body:
C&G/CITB

Scottish Vocational Qualification

Specialist Operations – Level 3
Awarding body:
SQA & CIOB & ICE

Crime Investigation and Police Work

APPRENTICESHIPS

Apprenticeships in Community Justice
www.skillsforjustice.com

VOCATIONAL QUALIFICATIONS

National Vocational Qualification

Intelligence Analysis – Level 3
Awarding body:
OU

Investigations – Level 3
Awarding body:
C&G
EDEXCEL

Scottish Vocational Qualification

Intelligence Analysis – Level 3
Awarding body:
ITEC
VTCT

Intelligence Analysis – Level 4
Awarding body:
ITEC
VTCT

Vocationally Related Qualification (Certificate)

Parking Attendants – Level 2
Awarding body:
C&G

Customer Services

APPRENTICESHIPS

Apprenticeships in Customer Service,
Retailing and Wholesaling
enquiries@icsmail.com

VOCATIONAL QUALIFICATIONS

BTEC First Diploma

Public Services – Level 2
Awarding body:
 EDEXCEL

BTEC Higher National Diploma

Public Services – Level 5
Awarding body:
 EDEXCEL

Certificate

Customer Service Advisors – Level 2
Awarding body:
 C&G

National Vocational Qualification

Customer Service – Level 1
Awarding body:
 C&G
 EDEXCEL
 EDI
 HAB
 OCR
 VTCT

Customer Service – Level 2
Awarding body:
 CABWI
 EDEXCEL
 EDI
 HAB
 IMI
 OCR
 QFI
 VTCT

Customer Service – Level 3
Awarding body:
 C&G
 CABWI
 EDEXCEL
 EDI
 HAB
 IMI
 OCR
 QFI
 VTCT

Porter Service – Level 1
Awarding body:
 C&G
 HAB

Public Services – Level 2
Awarding body:
 C&G
 EDEXCEL

Reception – Level 1
Awarding body:
 C&G
 HAB

Reception – Level 2
Awarding body:
 C&G
 EDI
 HAB

Scottish Vocational Qualification

Customer Service – Level 2
Awarding body:
  EDI
  SQA & HAB

Customer Service – Level 3
Awarding body:
  EDI
  SQA
  SQA & HAB

Customer Service – Level 3
Awarding body:
  C&G

Customer Service for the Motor Industry – Level 3
Awarding body:
  C&G
  SQA

Managing Call Handling – Level 4
Awarding body:
  C&G
  SQA & HAB

Porter Service – Level 1
Awarding body:
  C&G
  SQA & HAB

Public Services – Level 2
Awarding body:
  SQA

Vocationally Related Qualification (BTEC Award)

Delivery of Conflict Management Training – Level 2
Awarding body:
  EDEXCEL

Vocationally Related Qualification (BTEC Certificate)

Public Services – Level 1
Awarding body:
  EDEXCEL

Vocationally Related Qualification (BTEC First Certificate)

Public Services – Level 2
Awarding body:
  EDEXCEL

Vocationally Related Qualification (BTEC First Diploma)

Public Services – Level 2
Awarding body:
  EDEXCEL

Vocationally Related Qualification (BTEC National Award)

Public Services – Level 3
Awarding body:
  EDEXCEL

Vocationally Related Qualification (BTEC National Certificate)

Public Services – Level 3
Awarding body:
  EDEXCEL

Vocationally Related Qualification (BTEC National Diploma)

Public Services – Level 3
Awarding body:
  EDEXCEL

Vocationally Related Qualification (Certificate)

Conflict Management – Level 2
Awarding body:
  C&G

Customer Service – Level 2
Awarding body:
EDI
HAB

Customer Service – Level 3
Awarding body:
EDI

Salon Reception – Level 2
Awarding body:
C&G

Service Sector Receptionists – Level 2
Awarding body:
VTCT

Vocationally Related Qualification (National Certificate)

Public Services – Level 2
Awarding body:
OCR

Public Services – Level 3
Awarding body:
OCR

Vocationally Related Qualification (National Diploma)

Public Services – Level 3
Awarding body:
OCR

Vocationally Related Qualification (National Extended Diploma)

Public Services – Level 3
Awarding body:
OCR

Dentistry

VOCATIONAL QUALIFICATIONS

BTEC National Award

Dental Technology – Level 3
Awarding body:
  EDEXCEL

BTEC National Diploma

Dental Technology – Level 3
Awarding body:
  EDEXCEL

Electrical and Electronic Engineering

APPRENTICESHIPS

Apprenticeships in Electrical and
Electronic Servicing
www.enginuity.org.uk

VOCATIONAL QUALIFICATIONS

BTEC Higher National Certificate

**Electrical/Electronic Engineering –
Level 5**
Awarding body:
   EDEXCEL

BTEC Higher National Diploma

**Electrical/Electronic Engineering –
Level 5**
Awarding body:
   EDEXCEL

National Vocational Qualification

**Electrical and Electronic Engineering –
Level 3**
Awarding body:
   EAL
   ETCAL

**Electricity System Technology
Engineering Support – Level 2**
Awarding body:
   C&G

**Electricity System Technology
Engineering Support – Level 3**
Awarding body:
   C&G

**Installing and Commissioning
Electrotechnical Systems and Equipment
(Plant) – Level 3**
Awarding body:
   ECITB

Nuclear Decommissioning – Level 2
Awarding body:
   C&G

**Nuclear Technology Decommissioning –
Level 2**
Awarding body:
   C&G

Scottish Vocational Qualification

**Electrical and Electronics Engineering –
Level 3**
Awarding body:
   EAL

**Electrical and Electronics Servicing –
Level 2**
Awarding body:
   C&G
   EAL

**Electrical and Electronics Servicing –
Level 3**
Awarding body:
   C&G

**Electrical/Electronic Engineering –
Level 3**
Awarding body:
   C&G

**Electricity System Technology
Engineering – Level 3**
Awarding body:
   C&G

**Electricity Systems Technology
Engineering – Level 3**
Awarding body:
   C&G

Electricity Systems Technology Engineering Support – Level 2
Awarding body:
C&G

Installing and Commissioning Electrotechnical Services and Equipment – Level 3
Awarding body:
ECITB

Nuclear Technology Decommnissioning – Level 2
Awarding body:
C&G

Process Engineering Maintenance (Electrical) – Level 2
Awarding body:
PAA/VQSET
SQA & cogent

Process Engineering Maintenance (Electrical) – Level 3
Awarding body:
PAA/VQSET
SQA & cogent

Vocationally Related Qualification

Audio Electronics and Connectivity – Level 3
Awarding body:
C&G

Multi Track Recording and Automation – Level 3
Awarding body:
C&G

Vocationally Related Qualification (BTEC National Certificate)

Electrical/Electronic Engineering – Level 3
Awarding body:
EDEXCEL

Vocationally Related Qualification (BTEC National Diploma)

Electrical/Electronic Engineering – Level 3
Awarding body:
EDEXCEL

Vocationally Related Qualification (Certificate)

Complex Commercial Refrigeration and Air Conditioning Systems – Level 3
Awarding body:
C&G

Digital Television Aerial Installation – Level 2
Awarding body:
C&G

Domestic Electrical Installers – Level 2
Awarding body:
EAL

Knowledge of Electrical Installation Engineering – Level 3
Awarding body:
C&G

Management of Electrical Equipment Maintenance (Code of Practice for In-Service Inspection) – Level 3
Awarding body:
C&G

Requirements for Electrical Installations – Level 3
Awarding body:
C&G

Vocationally Related Qualification (Diploma)

Building Electrical Maintenance – Level 3
Awarding body:
EAL

Installation of Electrical Equipment – Level 3
Awarding body:
EAL

Sound Engineering – Level 3
Awarding body:
C&G

Electrical Power and Electronics

APPRENTICESHIPS

Apprenticeships in Electrical Industry
www.euskills.co.uk

VOCATIONAL QUALIFICATIONS

National Vocational Qualification

Electrical and Electronics Servicing – Level 2
Awarding body:
  C&G
  EAL

Electrical and Electronics Servicing – Level 3
Awarding body:
  C&G
  EAL

Electrical Machine Repair and Rewind – Level 3
Awarding body:
  C&G

Electrical Panel Building – Level 3
Awarding body:
  C&G

Electrotechnical Services – Level 3
Awarding body:
  EAL

Installing Electrotechnical Systems – Level 2
Awarding body:
  C&G
  EAL

Scottish Vocational Qualification

Electrical and Electronics Servicing – Level 3
Awarding body:
  EAL

Electrical Installation Theory Part One – Level 2
Awarding body:
  C&G

Electrical Installation Theory Part Two – Level 3
Awarding body:
  C&G

Electrical Machine Repair and Rewind – Level 3
Awarding body:
  C&G

Electrical Panel Building – Level 3
Awarding body:
  C&G

Electronics – Level 1
Awarding body:
  C&G

Electrotechnical Services (Electrical Installation - Building and Structures) – Level 3
Awarding body:
  SQA & SJIB

Electrotechnical Services (Installing Highway Electrical Systems) – Level 3
Awarding body:
  LANTRA

Installing Highway Electrical Systems (Installation) – Level 3
Awarding body:
  LANTRA

Installing Highway Electrical Systems (Maintenance) – Level 2
Awarding body:
  LANTRA

Installing Highway Electrical Systems (Surface Protection) – Level 2
Awarding body:
LANTRA

Vocationally Related Qualification (BTEC First Diploma)

Electronics – Level 2
Awarding body:
EDEXCEL

Vocationally Related Qualification (Certificate)

Electrotechnical Technology – Level 2
Awarding body:
C&G

Electrotechnical Technology – Level 3
Awarding body:
C&G

Inspection, Testing, Design and Certification of Electrical Installations – Level 3
Awarding body:
C&G

Instructing Circuit Sessions – Level 2
Awarding body:
PREMIER IQ

Vocationally Related Qualification (Foundation Certificate)

Electronics – Level 1
Awarding body:
EAL

Vocationally Related Qualification (Progression Award)

Electrical and Electronics Servicing – Level 3
Awarding body:
C&G

Electrical and Electronics Servicing: Domestic Electrical Appliances – Level 2
Awarding body:
C&G

Electrical/Electronics Servicing: Consumer/Commercial Electronics – Level 2
Awarding body:
C&G

Emergency Services

APPRENTICESHIPS

Apprenticeships in Emergency Fire
Services Operations
www.apprenticeships.org.uk

VOCATIONAL QUALIFICATIONS

BTEC Certificate

**Emergency Fire Services Operations in
the Community – Level 3**
Awarding body:
EDEXCEL

National Vocational Qualification

**Emergency Fire Services Control
Operations – Level 3**
Awarding body:
EDEXCEL

**Emergency Fire Services Operations in
the Community – Level 3**
Awarding body:
EDEXCEL

**Emergency Fire Services Watch
Management – Level 3**
Awarding body:
EDEXCEL

Fire Safety – Level 2
Awarding body:
EDEXCEL

Fire Safety – Level 3
Awarding body:
EDEXCEL

**Gas Emergency Service Operations
(ACS) – Level 3**
Awarding body:
C&G

Scottish Vocational Qualification

**Emergency Fire Services - Operations in
the Community – Level 3**
Awarding body:
SQA

**Emergency Fire Services - Watch
Management – Level 3**
Awarding body:
SQA

**Emergency Services: Control Operations
– Level 3**
Awarding body:
SQA

Vocationally Related Qualification (Certificate of Competence)

**Climb Trees and Perform Aerial Rescue
– Level 2**
Awarding body:
NPTC

Energy

APPRENTICESHIPS

Apprenticeships in Building Service
Engineering
www.summitskills.org.uk

VOCATIONAL QUALIFICATIONS

Vocationally Related Qualification (Certificate)

Energy Efficiency for Domestic Heating – Level 3
Awarding body:
  C&G

Engineering (General)

APPRENTICESHIPS

Engineering Apprenticeships
www.enginuity.uk.org

VOCATIONAL QUALIFICATIONS

Advanced Subsidiary Vocational Certificate of Education

Engineering – Level 3
Awarding body:
AQA
EDEXCEL
OCR

Advanced Vocational Certificate of Education

Engineering – Level 3
Awarding body:
AQA
EDEXCEL
OCR

Advanced Vocational Certificate of Education (Double Award)

Engineering – Level 3
Awarding body:
AQA
EDEXCEL

BTEC Higher National Certificate

Operations Engineering – Level 5
Awarding body:
EDEXCEL

BTEC Higher National Diploma

Operation Engineering – Level 5
Awarding body:
EDEXCEL

BTEC Professional Diploma

Live Sound – Level 5
Awarding body:
EDEXCEL

Foundation General National Vocational Qualification

Engineering – Level 1
Awarding body:
AQA
EDEXCEL
OCR

Intermediate General National Vocational Qualification

Engineering – Level 2
Awarding body:
AQA
EDEXCEL
OCR

National Vocational Qualification

Chimney Engineering/Cleaning – Level 2
Awarding body:
C&G/CITB

Engineering Leadership – Level 3
Awarding body:
EAL

Engineering Maintenance – Level 3
Awarding body:
C&G
EAL
ETCAL

Engineering Maintenance and Installation – Level 2
Awarding body:
C&G
EAL

Engineering Technical Support – Level 3
Awarding body:
C&G
EAL
ETCAL

Engineering Technology Maintenance – Level 3
Awarding body:
C&G

Engineering Technology Maintenance Support – Level 2
Awarding body:
C&G

Engineering Technology Operations – Level 3
Awarding body:
C&G

Engineering Technology Operations Foundation – Level 1
Awarding body:
C&G

Engineering Technology Operations Support – Level 2
Awarding body:
C&G

Engineering Toolmaking – Level 3
Awarding body:
EAL

Engineering Woodworking, Pattern and Model Making – Level 3
Awarding body:
C&G
EAL

Installation and Commissioning – Level 3
Awarding body:
C&G

Instrument Servicing – Level 2
Awarding body:
EAL

Instrument Servicing – Level 3
Awarding body:
EAL

Performing Engineering Operations – Level 1
Awarding body:
C&G
EAL
EDEXCEL
ETCAL

Performing Engineering Operations – Level 2
Awarding body:
C&G
EAL
EDEXCEL
ETCAL

Process Engineering Maintenance – Level 2
Awarding body:
PAA/VQSET

Process Engineering Maintenance – Level 3
Awarding body:
PAA/VQSET

Supporting Engineering Activities – Level 2
Awarding body:
ECITB

Transport Engineering and Maintenance – Level 1
Awarding body:
EDI

Transport Engineering and Maintenance – Level 2
Awarding body:
EDI

Transport Engineering and Maintenance (PCV Body) – Level 3
Awarding body:
   EDI

Scottish Vocational Qualification

Engineering Leadership – Level 3
Awarding body:
   EAL

Engineering Maintenance – Level 3
Awarding body:
   EAL

Engineering Maintenance and Installation – Level 2
Awarding body:
   EAL

Engineering Maintenance for Processing Industries – Level 3
Awarding body:
   C&G/CITB

Engineering Management – Level 4
Awarding body:
   EAL

Engineering Management – Level 5
Awarding body:
   EAL

Engineering Production – Level 2
Awarding body:
   C&G/ETA

Engineering Production – Level 3
Awarding body:
   C&G/ETA

Engineering Surveying of Equipment, Systems or Services – Level 4
Awarding body:
   C&G/OPITO

Engineering Technical Support – Level 3
Awarding body:
   EAL

Engineering Technology – Level 3
Awarding body:
   EAL

Engineering Technology Maintenance – Level 3
Awarding body:
   C&G
   EAL

Engineering Technology Maintenance Support – Level 2
Awarding body:
   C&G
   EAL

Engineering Technology Management – Level 4
Awarding body:
   EAL

Engineering Technology Operations – Level 3
Awarding body:
   EAL

Engineering Toolmaking (Jig and Fixture Manufacturing) – Level 3
Awarding body:
   EAL

Engineering Toolmaking (Mould, Tool and Die Equipment Maintenance) – Level 3
Awarding body:
   EAL

Engineering Toolmaking (Toolmaker) – Level 3
Awarding body:
   EAL

Engineering Toolmaking (Toolroom Manual Machining) – Level 3
Awarding body:
   EAL

Engineering Toolmaking (Toolroom NC/CNC Machining) – Level 3
Awarding body:
   EAL

Engineering Woodworking, Pattern and Model Making – Level 3
Awarding body:
   EAL

**Installation and Commissioning –
Level 3**
Awarding body:
EAL

**Installing Plant and Systems (Instrument
Pipefitting) – Level 3**
Awarding body:
ECITB

**Installing Plant and Systems
(Mechanical) – Level 3**
Awarding body:
ECITB

**Performing Engineering Operations –
Level 1**
Awarding body:
EAL
SQA

**Performing Engineering Operations –
Level 2**
Awarding body:
EAL
SQA

**Process Engineering Maintenance
(Mechanical) – Level 3**
Awarding body:
PAA/VQSET
SQA & cogent

**Supporting Engineering Activities –
Level 2**
Awarding body:
ECITB

**Transport Engineering and Maintenance
– Level 1**
Awarding body:
EDI

**Transport Engineering and Maintenance
– Level 2**
Awarding body:
EDI

**Transport Engineering and Maintenance
– Level 3**
Awarding body:
EDI

Scottish Vocational Qualifications

**Engineering Technology Operations –
Level 3**
Awarding body:
EAL

Vocationally Related Qualification

**Engineering Inspection and Quality
Control – Level 3**
Awarding body:
EAL

**Transport Engineering and Maintenance
– Level 3**
Awarding body:
EDI

Vocationally Related Qualification (Advanced Diploma)

Engineering and Technology – Level 3
Awarding body:
EAL

**Engineering and Technology
(Progressive) – Level 3**
Awarding body:
EAL

Vocationally Related Qualification (BTEC First Certificate)

Engineering – Level 2
Awarding body:
EDEXCEL

Vocationally Related Qualification (BTEC First Diploma)

Engineering – Level 2
Awarding body:
EDEXCEL

Vocationally Related Qualification (BTEC Introductory Certificate)

Engineering – Level 1
Awarding body:
EDEXCEL

Vocationally Related Qualification (BTEC Introductory Diploma)

Engineering – Level 1
Awarding body:
EDEXCEL

Vocationally Related Qualification (BTEC National Certificate)

Civil Engineering – Level 3
Awarding body:
EDEXCEL

Vocationally Related Qualification (Certificate)

Engineering – Level 3
Awarding body:
C&G

Engineering and Technology – Level 1
Awarding body:
EAL

Engineering Construction – Level 3
Awarding body:
C&G

Live Sound and Performance Technology – Level 3
Awarding body:
C&G

Multi Track Recording and Microphone Techniques – Level 3
Awarding body:
C&G

Multi Track Recording and Mixing – Level 3
Awarding body:
C&G

Transport Engineering and Maintenance – Level 2
Awarding body:
EDI

Vocationally Related Qualification (Diploma)

Engineering Inspection and Quality Control – Level 3
Awarding body:
EAL

Engineering Pattern Development Methods – Level 3
Awarding body:
EAL

General Engineering Maintenance Techniques – Level 3
Awarding body:
EAL

Maintenance of Fluid Power Systems and Components – Level 3
Awarding body:
EAL

Toolmaking, Presswork and Extrusion – Level 3
Awarding body:
EAL

Vocationally Related Qualification (Intermediate Certificate)

Clock and Watch Servicing – Level 2
Awarding body:
  EAL

Engineering and Technology – Level 2
Awarding body:
  EAL

Vocationally Related Qualification (Progression Award)

Applying Engineering Principles – Level 1
Awarding body:
  C&G

Applying Engineering Principles – Level 2
Awarding body:
  C&G

Engineering Maintenance – Level 2
Awarding body:
  C&G

Environmental Studies

APPRENTICESHIPS

Environmental Conservation
Apprenticeship
www.lantra.co.uk

VOCATIONAL QUALIFICATIONS

Certificate

Environmental Studies – Entry Level
Awarding body:
   C&G

Sustainable Development – Level 1
Awarding body:
   NCFE

National Vocational Qualification

Environmental Conservation – Level 2
Awarding body:
   EDEXCEL
   NPTC

Environmental Conservation – Level 3
Awarding body:
   NPTC

Meteorological Observing – Level 3
Awarding body:
   PAA/VQSET

Scottish Vocational Qualification

Environmental Conservation – Level 2
Awarding body:
   SQA

Environmental Conservation – Level 3
Awarding body:
   Sports Leaders UK

Meteorological Observing – Level 3
Awarding body:
   PAA/VQSET

Weather Forecasting – Level 4
Awarding body:
   PAA/VQSET

Specialist Diploma

Environmental Management – Level 6
Awarding body:
   NEBOSH

Vocational Certificate of Education (Certificate)

Practical Environmental Skills – Level 2
Awarding body:
   ABC

Vocationally Related Qualification (BTEC First Certificate)

Countryside and Environment – Level 2
Awarding body:
   EDEXCEL

Vocationally Related Qualification (BTEC First Diploma)

Countryside and Environment – Level 2
Awarding body:
   EDEXCEL

Vocationally Related Qualification (Certificate)

Environmental Conservation – Level 3
Awarding body:
NPTC

Environmental Practitioner – Level 3
Awarding body:
NCFE

Geographical Information Systems – Level 3
Awarding body:
ASET

Practical Environmental Studies – Level 1
Awarding body:
ABC

Practical Environmental Studies – Level 2
Awarding body:
ABC

Vocationally Related Qualification (National Certificate)

Environmental Conservation – Level 2
Awarding body:
NPTC

Extracting & Providing Natural Resources

APPRENTICESHIPS

Oil and Gas Extraction Advanced
Apprenticeship
gordon.mcneil@cogent-ssc.com

VOCATIONAL QUALIFICATIONS

National Vocational Qualification

Drilling Operations – Level 2
Awarding body:
   EMP

Scottish Vocational Qualification

Drilling Operations: Extractive and Mineral Processing Industries – Level 2
Awarding body:
   EMP

Land Drilling (Directional Drilling) – Level 2
Awarding body:
   SQA & CITB

Land Drilling (Driller) – Level 2
Awarding body:
   SQA & CITB

Land Drilling (Lead Driller) – Level 2
Awarding body:
   SQA & CITB

Safety Services: Oil and Gas Extraction – Level 2
Awarding body:
   SQA & cogent

Safety Services: Oil and Gas Extraction – Level 3
Awarding body:
   SQA & cogent

Fencing

VOCATIONAL QUALIFICATIONS

National Vocational Qualification

Fencing Business Management – Level 4
Awarding body:
    LANTRA

Scottish Vocational Qualification

Fencing – Level 2
Awarding body:
    LANTRA

Fencing – Level 3
Awarding body:
    LANTRA

Fencing (Vehicle Safety) – Level 2
Awarding body:
    LANTRA

Film, Video and Television

APPRENTICESHIPS

Broadcast, Film, Video and Multimedia
Apprenticeship
www.skillset.org/careers

VOCATIONAL QUALIFICATIONS

Vocationally Related Qualification (Award)

Multi-Camera Television Studio Skills – Level 3
Awarding body:
    ABC

Vocationally Related Qualification (Double Award)

Film and Video Directing Skills – Level 3
Awarding body:
    ABC

Film and Video Production – Level 3
Awarding body:
    ABC

Television News Reporting – Level 3
Awarding body:
    ABC

Financial Services

APPRENTICESHIPS

Providing Financial Services
Apprenticeships
www.fsc.org.uk

VOCATIONAL QUALIFICATIONS

National Vocational Qualification

Retail Financial Services – Level 2
Awarding body:
  EDI

Retail Financial Services – Level 3
Awarding body:
  EDI

Scottish Vocational Qualification

Financial Administration – Level 3
Awarding body:
  CII

Providing Financial Services (Banks and Building Societies) – Level 2
Awarding body:
  SQA & CIoBS

Providing Financial Services (Banks and Building Societies) – Level 3
Awarding body:
  SQA & CIoBS

Fishkeeping and Fishing

APPRENTICESHIPS

Sea Fishing Apprenticeships and
Advanced Apprenticeships
www.seafishing.co.uk

VOCATIONAL QUALIFICATIONS

Scottish Vocational Qualification

Aquaculture – Level 2
Awarding body:
   SQA

Aquaculture – Level 3
Awarding body:
   SQA

Fisheries Management – Level 2
Awarding body:
   SQA

Fisheries Management – Level 3
Awarding body:
   SQA

Vocationally Related Qualification (BTEC First Diploma)

Fish Husbandry – Level 2
Awarding body:
   EDEXCEL

Vocationally Related Qualification (BTEC National Award)

Fish Management – Level 3
Awarding body:
   EDEXCEL

Vocationally Related Qualification (BTEC National Diploma)

Fish Management – Level 3
Awarding body:
   EDEXCEL

Floristry

APPRENTICESHIPS

Apprenticeships and Advanced
Apprenticeships in Floristry
www.lantra.co.uk

VOCATIONAL QUALIFICATIONS

National Vocational Qualification

Floristry – Level 2
Awarding body:
  NPTC

Floristry – Level 3
Awarding body:
  NPTC

Scottish Vocational Qualification

Floristry – Level 2
Awarding body:
  SQA

Floristry – Level 3
Awarding body:
  SQA

Vocationally Related Qualification (Advanced National Certificate)

Floristry – Level 3
Awarding body:
  NPTC

Vocationally Related Qualification (BTEC National Award)

Floristry – Level 3
Awarding body:
  EDEXCEL

Vocationally Related Qualification (BTEC National Certificate)

Floristry – Level 2
Awarding body:
  EDEXCEL

Floristry – Level 3
Awarding body:
  EDEXCEL

Vocationally Related Qualification (BTEC National Diploma)

Floristry – Level 3
Awarding body:
  EDEXCEL

Vocationally Related Qualification (Certificate)

Floristry – Level 2
Awarding body:
  NPTC

Vocationally Related Qualification (Diploma)

Flower Design – Level 3
Awarding body:
  ABC

Vocationally Related Qualification (National Certificate)

Floristry – Level 2
Awarding body:
   NPTC

Food and Drink

APPRENTICESHIPS

Apprenticeships and Advanced
Apprenticeships in Food and Drink
Manufacturing Operations and Bakery
www.improveltd.co.uk

VOCATIONAL QUALIFICATIONS

National Vocational Qualification

**Food and Drink Manufacturing
Operations – Level 1**
Awarding body:
  C&G

**Food and Drink Manufacturing
Operations – Level 2**
Awarding body:
  C&G
  MTC

**Food and Drink Manufacturing
Operations – Level 3**
Awarding body:
  C&G
  MTC

Food and Drink Service – Level 1
Awarding body:
  C&G
  HAB

Food and Drink Service – Level 2
Awarding body:
  C&G
  EDI
  HAB

Food Manufacture – Level 3
Awarding body:
  FDQ

Food Preparation and Cooking – Level 1
Awarding body:
  C&G
  HAB

Food Preparation and Cooking – Level 2
Awarding body:
  C&G
  HAB

**Food Preparation and Cooking (General)
– Level 1**
Awarding body:
  HAB

**Food Preparation and Cooking (General)
– Level 3**
Awarding body:
  C&G

**Food Preparation and Cooking (Kitchen
and Larder) – Level 3**
Awarding body:
  C&G
  HAB

**Food Preparation and Cooking
(Patisserie and Confectionery) – Level 3**
Awarding body:
  C&G
  HAB

Food Processing and Cooking – Level 2
Awarding body:
  C&G
  EDI
  HAB

Food Service Advanced Craft – Level 3
Awarding body:
  HAB

Hospitality – Level 1
Awarding body:
  EDI

Hospitality Supervision – Level 2
Awarding body:
  EDI

Meat and Poultry Processing – Level 1
Awarding body:
  MTC

Meat and Poultry Processing – Level 2
Awarding body:
  MTC

Meat and Poultry Processing – Level 3
Awarding body:
  MTC

Multi-skilled Hospitality Services – Level 2
Awarding body:
  EDI

Preparing and Serving Food – Level 1
Awarding body:
  HAB

Professional Cookery – Level 2
Awarding body:
  C&G
  EDI
  HAB

Professional Cookery – Level 3
Awarding body:
  C&G
  EDI
  HAB

Scottish Vocational Qualification

Distilling Industry Operations – Level 1
Awarding body:
  SQA & DIVQ

Food and Drink Manufacturing Operations – Level 1
Awarding body:
  FDQ
  SQA & IMPROVE

Food and Drink Manufacturing Operations – Level 2
Awarding body:
  FDQ
  SQA & IMPROVE

Food and Drink Manufacturing Operations – Level 3
Awarding body:
  FDQ
  SQA & IMPROVE

Food and Drink Service – Level 2
Awarding body:
  C&G
  SQA & HAB

Food and Drink Service: Drink Service Only – Level 2
Awarding body:
  C&G
  SQA & HAB

Food and Drink Service: Food Service Only – Level 2
Awarding body:
  C&G
  SQA & HAB

Food Preparation and Cooking (Kitchen and Larder) – Level 3
Awarding body:
  C&G/HCIMA
  EDEXCEL
  EDI
  SQA & HAB

Food Preparation and Cooking (Patisserie and Confectionery) – Level 3
Awarding body:
  C&G/HCIMA
  EDEXCEL
  EDI
  HAB

Food Processing and Cooking – Level 2
Awarding body:
  C&G
  SQA & HAB

Food Science and Manufacturing Technology – Level 3
Awarding body:
  EDEXCEL

Food Service Advanced Craft – Level 3
Awarding body:
  EDEXCEL

HACCP Practice (Meat Plant) – Level 2
Awarding body:
EDEXCEL

International Cuisine – Level 3
Awarding body:
C&G/HCIMA
EDEXCEL
EDI
HAB
ITEC

Meat and Poultry Processing – Level 2
Awarding body:
FDQ & SQA

Meat and Poultry Processing (Abbatoirs) – Level 3
Awarding body:
FDQ & SQA

Meat and Poultry Processing (Despatch) – Level 3
Awarding body:
FDQ & SQA

Meat and Poultry Processing (Production) – Level 3
Awarding body:
FDQ & SQA

Meat and Poultry Processing (Retail) – Level 3
Awarding body:
FDQ & SQA

Meat and Poultry Processing (Supervisory) – Level 3
Awarding body:
FDQ & SQA

Meat and Poultry Processing (Technical) – Level 3
Awarding body:
FDQ & SQA

Professional Cookery – Level 2
Awarding body:
C&G
SQA & HAB

Professional Cookery – Level 3
Awarding body:
C&G
SQA & HAB

Professional Cookery (Patisserie and Confectionery) – Level 3
Awarding body:
C&G
SQA & HAB

Professional Cookery (Preparation and Cooking) – Level 2
Awarding body:
C&G
SQA & HAB

Professional Cookery (Preparation and Cooking) – Level 3
Awarding body:
C&G
SQA & HAB

Vocational Certificate of Education (Foundation Certificate)

Wines – Level 1
Awarding body:
WSET

Vocationally Related Qualification

Providing a Healthier School Meals Service – Level 1
Awarding body:
EDI

Vocationally Related Qualification (Advanced Certificate)

Wines and Spirits – Level 3
Awarding body:
WSET

Vocationally Related Qualification (Award)

Healthier Food and Special Diets – Level 2
Awarding body:
    CIEH

Vocationally Related Qualification (BTEC Award)

Healthy Eating – Level 1
Awarding body:
    EDEXCEL

Nutrition Awareness – Level 2
Awarding body:
    EDEXCEL

Vocationally Related Qualification (BTEC Certificate)

Food and Beverage Service – Level 3
Awarding body:
    EDEXCEL

International Cuisine – Level 3
Awarding body:
    EDEXCEL

Vocationally Related Qualification (BTEC Diploma)

International Cuisine – Level 3
Awarding body:
    EDEXCEL

Vocationally Related Qualification (BTEC National Award

Food Science and Manufacturing Technology – Level 3
Awarding body:
    EDEXCEL

Vocationally Related Qualification (BTEC National Certificate)

Food Science and Manufacturing Techology – Level 3
Awarding body:
    EDEXCEL

Vocationally Related Qualification (Certificate)

Food Safety in Catering – Level 2
Awarding body:
    EDI

Healthier Foods and Special Diets – Level 2
Awarding body:
    EDI

Nutrition and Health – Level 2
Awarding body:
    NCFE

Pan-Asian Cookery – Level 2
Awarding body:
    ABC

Practical Food Safety in Catering – Level 2
Awarding body:
    EDI

Practical Supervision of Food Safety in Catering – Level 3
Awarding body:
    EDI

Professional Cookery – Level 2
Awarding body:
    EDI

Vocationally Related Qualification (Diploma)

Diet and Nutrition for Complementary Therapists – Level 3
Awarding body:
    ITEC

Pastry Chefs and Patissiers – Level 3
Awarding body:
  ABC

Vocationally Related Qualification (Foundation Certificate)

Nutrition – Level 1
Awarding body:
  RSPH

Pastry Chefs and Patissiers – Level 2
Awarding body:
  ABC

Vocationally Related Qualification (Intermediate Certificate)

Nutrition – Level 2
Awarding body:
  RSPH

Wines and Spirits – Level 2
Awarding body:
  WSET

Vocationally Related Qualification (National Certificate)

Personal Licence Holders – Level 2
Awarding body:
  EDI

Vocationally Related Qualification (National Diploma)

Designated Premises Supervisors – Level 3
Awarding body:
  EDI

Vocationally Related Qualification (Professional Certificate)

Spirits – Level 2
Awarding body:
  WSET

Vocationally Related Qualification (Scottish Certificate)

Personal Licence Holders – Level 2
Awarding body:
  EDI

Footwear

APPRENTICESHIPS

Apprenticeships in Man-Made Fibre Manufacture and Textiles Manufacture
www.skillfast-uk.org

VOCATIONAL QUALIFICATIONS

National Vocational Qualification

Footwear and Leather Products Manufacture – Level 3
Awarding body:
C&G

Footwear Manufacture – Level 1
Awarding body:
C&G

Footwear Manufacture – Level 2
Awarding body:
C&G

Footwear Repair – Level 2
Awarding body:
C&G

Footwear Repair – Level 3
Awarding body:
C&G

Forestry and Arboriculture

APPRENTICESHIPS

Apprenticeships in Trees and Timber
www.lantra.co.uk

VOCATIONAL QUALIFICATIONS

National Vocational Qualification

Arboriculture – Level 2
Awarding body:
  NPTC

Forestry – Level 2
Awarding body:
  NPTC

Treework – Level 3
Awarding body:
  NPTC

Scottish Vocational Qualification

Arboriculture – Level 2
Awarding body:
  SQA

Fenestration Installation – Level 2
Awarding body:
  GQA

Forest Machine Operations – Level 2
Awarding body:
  EDEXCEL

Forestry - Establishment – Level 2
Awarding body:
  NPTC
  SQA

Forestry - Harvesting – Level 2
Awarding body:
  SQA

Treework (Arboriculture) – Level 3
Awarding body:
  SQA

Treework (Establishment) – Level 3
Awarding body:
  SQA

Treework (Harvesting) – Level 3
Awarding body:
  SQA

Vocational Certificate of Education (Certificate)

Arboriculture (Theory) – Level 2
Awarding body:
  ABC

Vocational Certificate of Education (Technicians Certificate)

Arboriculture – Level 3
Awarding body:
  ABC

Vocationally Related Qualification (BTEC National Award)

Forestry and Arboriculture – Level 3
Awarding body:
  EDEXCEL

Vocationally Related Qualification (BTEC National Certificate)

Forestry and Aboriculture – Level 3
Awarding body:
  EDEXCEL

Vocationally Related Qualification (BTEC National Diploma)

Forestry and Aboriculture – Level 3
Awarding body:
EDEXCEL

Vocationally Related Qualification (Certificate of Competence)

Forest Machine Operations – Level 2
Awarding body:
NPTC

Stump Grinding Operations – Level 2
Awarding body:
NPTC

Vocationally Related Qualification (Certificate)

Arboriculture (Theory) – Level 2
Awarding body:
ABC

Vocationally Related Qualification (Technicians Certificate)

Arboriculture – Level 3
Awarding body:
ABC

Furniture and Furnishings

APPRENTICESHIPS

Apprenticeships and Advanced
Apprenticeships in Furniture Industry
www.proskills.co.uk

VOCATIONAL QUALIFICATIONS

National Vocational Qualification

Making and Installing Furniture – Level 2
Awarding body:
   C&G

Making and Installing Production Furniture – Level 3
Awarding body:
   C&G

Making and Repairing Hand-Crafted Furniture and Furnishings – Level 3
Awarding body:
   C&G

Supporting the Production of Furniture and Furnishings – Level 1
Awarding body:
   C&G

Gas Supply

APPRENTICESHIPS

Apprenticeships and Advanced
Apprenticeship in Gas Industry
www.euskills.co.uk

VOCATIONAL QUALIFICATIONS

National Vocational Qualification

Gas Network Operations – Level 1
Awarding body:
  C&G

Gas Network Operations - Craft – Level 3
Awarding body:
  C&G

Gas Network Operations - Mainlaying – Level 2
Awarding body:
  C&G

Gas Network Operations - Servicelaying – Level 2
Awarding body:
  C&G

Scottish Vocational Qualification

Domestic Natural Gas Emergency Service Operations (ACS) – Level 3
Awarding body:
  SQA

Domestic Natural Gas Installation – Level 2
Awarding body:
  SQA

Domestic Natural Gas Installation – Level 3
Awarding body:
  SQA

Domestic Natural Gas Installation and Maintenance (ACS) – Level 2
Awarding body:
  SQA

Domestic Natural Gas Installation and Maintenance (ACS) – Level 3
Awarding body:
  SQA

Domestic Natural Gas Maintenance – Level 2
Awarding body:
  SQA

Domestic Natural Gas Maintenance – Level 3
Awarding body:
  SQA

Gas Network Operations - Mainlaying – Level 2
Awarding body:
  SQA

Gas Network Operations - Servicelaying – Level 2
Awarding body:
  SQA

Gas Networks Engineering Management – Level 4
Awarding body:
  SQA

Gas, Service Installation and Maintenance – Level 3
Awarding body:
  SQA

Vocationally Related Qualification (Certificate)

Complex Domestic Natural Gas Installation and Maintenance – Level 3
Awarding body:
  C&G

Gas Emergency Service Operations – Level 3
Awarding body:
  C&G

Glass Technology and Glazing

APPRENTICESHIPS

Apprenticeships and Advanced
Apprenticeships in Glass Industry
www.proskills.co.uk

VOCATIONAL QUALIFICATIONS

National Vocational Qualification

Automotive Glazing – Level 2
Awarding body:
  GQA

Automotive Glazing – Level 3
Awarding body:
  GQA

Glass Manufacturing – Level 2
Awarding body:
  GQA

Glass Manufacturing – Level 3
Awarding body:
  GQA

Glass Processing – Level 3
Awarding body:
  GQA

Glazing – Level 2
Awarding body:
  GQA

Glazing – Level 3
Awarding body:
  GQA

Scottish Vocational Qualification

Automotive Glazing – Level 2
Awarding body:
  GQA

Glass Manufacturing – Level 2
Awarding body:
  GQA

Glass Manufacturing – Level 3
Awarding body:
  GQA

Glass Operations (Automotive Glazing) – Level 3
Awarding body:
  GQA

Glass Operations (Fenestration Installation and Surveying) – Level 3
Awarding body:
  GQA

Glass Operations (Glass Manufacturing) – Level 3
Awarding body:
  GQA

Glass Operations (Glass Processing) – Level 3
Awarding body:
  GQA

Glass Operations (Production of Glass Supporting Fabrications) – Level 3
Awarding body:
  GQA

Glass Processing – Level 2
Awarding body:
  GQA

Glass Processing – Level 3
Awarding body:
  GQA

Glazing Installation and Maintenance – Level 2
Awarding body:
  GQA

Glazing Installation and Maintenance – Level 3
Awarding body:
  GQA

Guidance

APPRENTICESHIPS

Apprenticeships and Advanced
Apprenticeships in Advice and Guidance
www.ento.co.uk

VOCATIONAL QUALIFICATIONS

Advanced Diploma

**The Theory and Practice of Counselling
(Therapeutic Work) – Level 4**
Awarding body:
  ABC

BTEC Advanced Professional Certificate

Counselling – Level 7
Awarding body:
  EDEXCEL

BTEC Professional Diploma

Therapeutic Counselling – Level 5
Awarding body:
  EDEXCEL

Certificate

Counselling Concepts – Level 2
Awarding body:
  ABC

Entry Level Certificate

**Personal Progression through Practical
Life Skills – Entry 1**
Awarding body:
  C&G

**Personal Progression through Practical
Life Skills – Entry 2**
Awarding body:
  C&G

Skills for Working Life – Entry 3
Awarding body:
  VTCT

Higher Level Certificate

**Cognitive Behavioural Therapeutic Skills
and Theory – Level 5**
Awarding body:
  CPCAB

Working with Young People – Level 4
Awarding body:
  OU

Higher Level Diploma

Counselling Practice – Level 5
Awarding body:
  AQA

Psychotherapeutic Counselling – Level 5
Awarding body:
  CPCAB

**The Theory and Practice of Counselling
– Level 4**
Awarding body:
  ABC

Therapeutic Counselling – Level 4
Awarding body:
  CPCAB

**Therapeutic Counselling Supervision –
Level 6**
Awarding body:
  CPCAB

Higher Professional Diploma

Counselling – Level 3
Awarding body:
  C&G

Counselling – Level 4
Awarding body:
  AMSPAR

National Vocational Qualification

Advice and Guidance – Level 2
Awarding body:
  C&G
  EDEXCEL
  OCR
  OU

Advice and Guidance – Level 3
Awarding body:
  C&G
  EDEXCEL
  OCR

Counselling – Level 3
Awarding body:
  C&G
  OU

Scottish Vocational Qualification

Advice and Guidance – Level 2
Awarding body:
  SQA
  SQA & ICG

Advice and Guidance – Level 3
Awarding body:
  SQA
  SQA & ICG

Advice and Guidance – Level 4
Awarding body:
  SQA
  SQA & ICG

Careers Education and Guidance – Level 4
Awarding body:
  AQA

Careers Education and Preparation for Working Life – Level 1
Awarding body:
  AQA

Careers Education and Preparation for Working Life – Level 2
Awarding body:
  AQA

Counselling – Level 3
Awarding body:
  SQA

Counselling – Level 4
Awarding body:
  SQA

Counselling: Bereavement – Level 3
Awarding body:
  SQA

Counselling: Children and Young People – Level 3
Awarding body:
  SQA

Mediation – Level 4
Awarding body:
  SQA

Vocational Certificate of Education (Advanced Certificate)

Providing Advice and Guidance – Level 3
Awarding body:
  NOCN

Vocationally Related Qualification (Advanced Certificate)

Counselling – Level 3
Awarding body:
  AQA

**Information, Advice and Guidance –
Level 3**
Awarding body:
  NOCN

Vocationally Related Qualification (Advanced Diploma)

Counselling – Level 3
Awarding body:
  AQA

Vocationally Related Qualification (BTEC Award)

Skills for Industry – Level 2
Awarding body:
  EDEXCEL

Vocationally Related Qualification (BTEC Diploma)

Developing Counselling Skills – Level 3
Awarding body:
  EDEXCEL

Vocationally Related Qualification (Certificate)

Counselling Skills – Level 2
Awarding body:
  CPCAB

Counselling Skills – Level 3
Awarding body:
  ABC

Counselling Skills and Theory – Level 3
Awarding body:
  NCFE

Counselling Studies – Level 3
Awarding body:
  CPCAB

Drug Awareness – Level 1
Awarding body:
  NCFE

Drug Awareness Studies And Their Applications – Level 2
Awarding body:
  NCFE

**Introduction to Counselling Skills –
Level 2**
Awarding body:
  CPCAB

**Understanding Personal Therapies –
Level 1**
Awarding body:
  VTCT

Vocationally Related Qualification (Diploma)

**Non-Medical Nutritional Advice –
Level 3**
Awarding body:
  VTCT

Vocationally Related Qualification (Intermediate Certificate)

Counselling Skills – Level 2
Awarding body:
  AQA

**Introduction to Counselling Concepts –
Level 2**
Awarding body:
  AQA

Vocationally Related Qualification (Progression Award)

Counselling Skills – Level 3
Awarding body:
  C&G

Hairdressing

APPRENTICESHIPS

Apprenticeships and Advanced
Apprenticeships in Barbering and in
Hairdressing
www.habia.co.uk

VOCATIONAL QUALIFICATIONS

Certificate

Hairdressing – Entry Level
Awarding body:
OCR

National Vocational Qualification

Barbering – Level 2
Awarding body:
C&G
EDEXCEL
VTCT

Barbering – Level 3
Awarding body:
C&G
EDEXCEL
VTCT

Hairdressing – Level 1
Awarding body:
C&G
EDEXCEL
VTCT

Hairdressing – Level 2
Awarding body:
C&G
EDEXCEL
VTCT

Hairdressing – Level 3
Awarding body:
C&G
EDEXCEL
VTCT

Scottish Vocational Qualification

Barbering – Level 2
Awarding body:
C&G
SQA
VTCT

Barbering – Level 3
Awarding body:
C&G
SQA
VTCT

Creative Hair Styling – Level 3
Awarding body:
ABC

Hairdressing – Level 1
Awarding body:
C&G
SQA
VTCT

Hairdressing – Level 2
Awarding body:
C&G
SQA
VTCT

Hairdressing – Level 3
Awarding body:
C&G
SQA
VTCT

Vocationally Related Qualification (Award)

Creative Hair Styling – Level 3
Awarding body:
   ABC

Hair Styling Techniques: Fashion Image – Level 3
Awarding body:
   ABC

Historical Hair Styling Techniques – Level 3
Awarding body:
   ABC

Vocationally Related Qualification (BTEC Certificate)

Hairdressing – Level 1
Awarding body:
   EDEXCEL

Vocationally Related Qualification (BTEC National Award)

Hairdressing – Level 3
Awarding body:
   EDEXCEL

Vocationally Related Qualification (BTEC National Certificate)

Hairdressing – Level 3
Awarding body:
   EDEXCEL

Vocationally Related Qualification (Diploma)

Barbering – Level 3
Awarding body:
   C&G
   VTCT

Hair and Make-up Styling – Level 3
Awarding body:
   ABC

Hairdressing – Level 3
Awarding body:
   C&G
   VTCT

Specialist Hairdressing – Level 3
Awarding body:
   C&G

Health and Safety

APPRENTICESHIPS

Apprenticeships and Advanced
Apprenticeships in Occupational Health
and Safety
www.ento.co.uk

VOCATIONAL QUALIFICATIONS

Certificate of Competence

Personal Safety Awareness – Level 1
Awarding body:
EDI

Higher Level Diploma

**Occupational Health and Safety –
Level 6**
Awarding body:
NEBOSH

**Occupational Safety and Health –
Level 6**
Awarding body:
BSC

National Vocational Qualification

**Health, Safety and Environmental
Management in Quarries – Level 3**
Awarding body:
EMP

**Occupational Health and Safety –
Level 3**
Awarding body:
C&G
OCR

**Occupational Health and Safety –
Level 3**
Awarding body:
EAL

Radiation Protection Support – Level 2
Awarding body:
C&G

Scottish Vocational Qualification

**Hazard Analysis Critical Control Point –
Level 1**
Awarding body:
C&G
OCR

**Hazard Analysis Principles and Practice
– Level 2**
Awarding body:
CIEH

**Health and Safety in the Workplace –
Level 3**
Awarding body:
CIEH

Health and Safety Regulation – Level 5
Awarding body:
SQA

**Occupational Health and Safety –
Level 3**
Awarding body:
EAL
SQA

**Occupational Health and Safety
Practice – Level 4**
Awarding body:
SQA

**Occupational Health and Safety
Practice – Level 5**
Awarding body:
SQA

Radiation Protection – Level 4
Awarding body:
    SQA

Site Inspection – Level 3
Awarding body:
    SQA & ICoW

Site Inspection – Level 4
Awarding body:
    SQA & ICoW

Vocationally Related Qualification

Health and Safety at Work – Level 1
Awarding body:
    BSC

Moving and Handling – Level 2
Awarding body:
    EDI

Vocationally Related Qualification (Advanced Certificate)

Applied HACCP Principles – Level 3
Awarding body:
    RIPH

Food Safety – Level 3
Awarding body:
    CIEH
    RIPH
    RSPH

Health and Safety in the Workplace – Level 3
Awarding body:
    CIEH

Vocationally Related Qualification (Advanced Diploma)

Health and Safety in the Workplace – Level 2
Awarding body:
    OCNW

Vocationally Related Qualification (Award)

Food Safety for Retail – Level 2
Awarding body:
    CIEH

Risk Assessment Principles and Practice – Level 2
Awarding body:
    CIEH

Vocationally Related Qualification (Certificate of Competence)

Manual Handling Operations - Risk Assessment – Level 2
Awarding body:
    NPTC

Safe Manual Handling Operator – Level 1
Awarding body:
    NPTC

Safe Use and Operation of Mobile Elevated Work Platforms – Level 2
Awarding body:
    NPTC

Safe Use of Abrasive Wheel Machines – Level 2
Awarding body:
    NPTC

Safe Use of Hedge Trimmers – Level 2
Awarding body:
    NPTC

Safe Use of Mowers – Level 2
Awarding body:
    NPTC

Safe Use of Pesticides – Level 2
Awarding body:
    NPTC

Safe Use of Sheep Dips – Level 2
Awarding body:
    NPTC

**Safe Use of Turf Maintenance
Equipment – Level 2**
Awarding body:
  NPTC

Vertebrate Pest Control – Level 2
Awarding body:
  NPTC

*Vocationally Related
Qualification (Certificate)*

**Construction Health and Safety –
Level 3**
Awarding body:
  NEBOSH

Drugs Awareness – Level 2
Awarding body:
  EDI

**Emergency First Aid in the Workplace –
Level 2**
Awarding body:
  EDI

**First Aid for those Caring for Children –
Level 2**
Awarding body:
  EDI

**Health and Safety in the Workplace –
Level 2**
Awarding body:
  ABC
  EDI
  OCNW

**Occupational Health and Safety –
Level 2**
Awarding body:
  CCEA
  NCFE

**Occupational Health and Safety –
Level 3**
Awarding body:
  NEBOSH

**Occupational Safety and Health –
Level 3**
Awarding body:
  BSC

Off-Site Safety Management – Level 3
Awarding body:
  OCR

Pest Control – Level 2
Awarding body:
  RSPH

Principles of Aviation First Aid – Level 2
Awarding body:
  OCNW

**Safe Operation of Dumper Trucks –
Level 2**
Awarding body:
  NPTC

**Safe Use of Pedestrian Controlled
Two-Wheeled Tractors – Level 2**
Awarding body:
  NPTC

**Safe Use of Veterinary Medicines –
Level 2**
Awarding body:
  NPTC

**Safer Moving and Handling (including
People) – Level 2**
Awarding body:
  NCFE

Salon Hygiene – Level 2
Awarding body:
  RIPH

Supervising Health and Safety – Level 2
Awarding body:
  CIEH

Supervising Staff Safely – Level 2
Awarding body:
  BSC

**Swimming Pool and Spa Water
Treatment – Level 2**
Awarding body:
  STA

**Swimming Pool Supervision and Rescue
– Level 2**
Awarding body:
  IQL

Wild Game Meat Hygiene – Level 2
Awarding body:
  LA

Vocationally Related Qualification (Foundation Certificate)

Food Hygiene – Level 1
Awarding body:
  CIEH
  RIPH
  RSPH

Health and Safety in the Workplace – Level 1
Awarding body:
  CIEH
  RSPH

Swimming Pool and Spa Water Treatment – Level 1
Awarding body:
  STA

Vocationally Related Qualification (Intermediate Certificate)

Applied HACCP Principles – Level 2
Awarding body:
  RIPH

Food Safety – Level 2
Awarding body:
  CIEH
  RIPH
  RSPH

Hazard Analysis Principles and Practice – Level 2
Awarding body:
  CIEH

Vocationally Related Qualification (Progression Award)

Health and Safety in the Workplace – Level 2
Awarding body:
  C&G

Heating and Ventilation

APPRENTICESHIPS

Apprenticeships and Advanced
Apprenticeships in Heating, Ventilation,
Air Conditioning and Refrigeration
www.summitskills.org.uk

VOCATIONAL QUALIFICATIONS

Vocationally Related Qualification (Certificate)

**Heating and Ventilating - Maintenance
of System Components – Level 2**
Awarding body:
    C&G

**Heating and Ventilating Installation –
Level 2**
Awarding body:
    C&G

Horticulture

APPRENTICESHIPS

Apprenticeships and Advanced
Apprenticeships in Production
Horticulture and Amenity Horticulture
www.lantra.co.uk

VOCATIONAL QUALIFICATIONS

National Vocational Qualification

Production Horticulture – Level 2
Awarding body:
  NPTC

Production Horticulture – Level 3
Awarding body:
  NPTC

Scottish Vocational Qualification

Horticulture – Level 2
Awarding body:
  C&G

Horticulture – Level 3
Awarding body:
  C&G

Production Horticulture – Level 2
Awarding body:
  SQA

Production Horticulture – Level 3
Awarding body:
  SQA

Vocationally Related Qualification (Advanced National Certificate)

Horticulture – Level 3
Awarding body:
  NPTC

Vocationally Related Qualification (BTEC First Diploma)

Horticulture – Level 2
Awarding body:
  EDEXCEL

Vocationally Related Qualification (BTEC National Award)

Horticulture – Level 3
Awarding body:
  EDEXCEL

Vocationally Related Qualification (BTEC National Certificate)

Horticulture – Level 3
Awarding body:
  EDEXCEL

Vocationally Related Qualification (BTEC National Diploma)

Horticulture – Level 3
Awarding body:
  EDEXCEL

Vocationally Related Qualification (Certificate)

Gardening – Level 2
Awarding body:
  NPTC

Horticulture – Level 1
Awarding body:
  ASET

Horticulture Skills – Level 1
Awarding body:
  NPTC

Production Horticulture – Level 3
Awarding body:
  NPTC

Vocationally Related Qualification (National Certificate)

Horticulture – Level 2
Awarding body:
  NPTC

Human Resources and Personnel Management

VOCATIONAL QUALIFICATIONS

National Vocational Qualification

Personnel Support – Level 3
Awarding body:
CIPD

Recruitment – Level 3
Awarding body:
CIPD

Scottish Vocational Qualification

Personnel Support – Level 3
Awarding body:
CIPD
ILM

Scottish Vocational Qualifications

Personnel Management – Level 4
Awarding body:
CIPD
ILM

Personnel Strategy – Level 5
Awarding body:
CIPD
ILM

Information/Library Work

APPRENTICESHIPS

Apprenticeships and Advanced Apprenticeships in Information and Library Services (Administration and Professional) and Health Care and Public Services
www.ento.co.uk

VOCATIONAL QUALIFICATIONS

National Vocational Qualification

Information and Library Services – Level 2
Awarding body:
    C&G

Information and Library Services – Level 3
Awarding body:
    C&G

Vocationally Related Qualification (Award)

Library and Information Skills – Level 1
Awarding body:
    NOCN

Library and Information Skills – Level 2
Awarding body:
    NOCN

Vocationally Related Qualification (Progression Award)

Library and Information Services – Level 3
Awarding body:
    C&G

Insulation

APPRENTICESHIPS

Apprenticeship in Construction (Craft)
www.citb.co.uk

VOCATIONAL QUALIFICATIONS

Vocationally Related Qualification (Certificate)

Thermal Insulation – Level 2
Awarding body:
    C&G

Insurance

APPRENTICESHIPS

Apprenticeships and Advanced
Apprenticeships in Finance, Insurance
and Real Estate
www.fssc.org.uk

VOCATIONAL
QUALIFICATIONS

National Vocational
Qualification

**Insurance (General and Intermediaries)
– Level 2**
Awarding body:
   OCR

**Insurance (General and Intermediaries)
– Level 3**
Awarding body:
   OCR

Scottish Vocational Qualification

**Insurance (General and Intermediaries)
– Level 3**
Awarding body:
   SQA

Jewellery

APPRENTICESHIPS

Apprenticeships in Jewellery,
Silversmithing and Allied Trades
www.apprenticeships.org.uk

VOCATIONAL QUALIFICATIONS

Scottish Vocational Qualification

Gemmology – Level 3
Awarding body:
    EAL

**Gemmology Diamond Diploma –
Level 3**
Awarding body:
    GEM-A

Jewellery Manufacture – Level 2
Awarding body:
    GQA

Jewellery Manufacture – Level 3
Awarding body:
    SQA

Vocationally Related Qualification

**Gemmology Diamond Diploma –
Level 3**
Awarding body:
    GEM-A

Vocationally Related Qualification (Advanced Certificate)

**Repair, Restoration and Conservation of
Clocks and Watches – Level 3**
Awarding body:
    EAL

Vocationally Related Qualification (Certificate)

Gemmology – Level 2
Awarding body:
    GEM-A

Vocationally Related Qualification (Diploma)

Gemmology – Level 3
Awarding body:
    GEM-A

Land Administration

VOCATIONAL QUALIFICATIONS

National Vocational Qualification

Local Land Charges – Level 3
Awarding body:
C&G

Vocationally Related Qualification (Advanced National Certificate)

Countryside Management – Level 3
Awarding body:
NPTC

Vocationally Related Qualification (BTEC National Award)

Countryside Management – Level 3
Awarding body:
EDEXCEL

Land-based Technology – Level 3
Awarding body:
EDEXCEL

Vocationally Related Qualification (BTEC National Certificate)

Countryside Management – Level 3
Awarding body:
EDEXCEL

Land-based Technology – Level 3
Awarding body:
EDEXCEL

Vocationally Related Qualification (BTEC National Diploma)

Countryside Management – Level 3
Awarding body:
EDEXCEL

Land-based Technology – Level 3
Awarding body:
EDEXCEL

Vocationally Related Qualification (Certificate)

Landbased Studies – Level 1
Awarding body:
NPTC

Rural Business Administration – Level 3
Awarding body:
NPTC

Land and Countryside Studies

APPRENTICESHIPS

Apprenticeships and Advanced
Apprenticeships in Land Based Service
Engineering
www.lantra.co.uk

VOCATIONAL QUALIFICATIONS

Certificate

Land Studies – Entry Level
Awarding body:
   CCEA
   WJEC

Higher Professional Diploma

Landbased Management – Level 4
Awarding body:
   C&G

Intermediate General National Vocational Qualification

Land and Environment – Level 2
Awarding body:
   EDEXCEL

National Vocational Qualification

Land Drilling – Level 1
Awarding body:
   C&G/CITB

Land Drilling – Level 2
Awarding body:
   C&G/CITB

Land-based Service Engineering – Level 2
Awarding body:
   C&G

Land-based Service Engineering – Level 3
Awarding body:
   C&G

Landbased Operations – Level 1
Awarding body:
   NPTC

Scottish Vocational Qualification

Land Based Operations – Level 1
Awarding body:
   SQA

Land Registration – Level 2
Awarding body:
   SQA

Land Registration – Level 3
Awarding body:
   SQA

Land-Based Service Engineering – Level 2
Awarding body:
   SQA & BAGMA

Land-Based Service Engineering – Level 3
Awarding body:
   SQA & BAGMA

Vocationally Related Qualification

Land-based Service Engineering – Level 3
Awarding body:
   C&G

Vocationally Related Qualification (BTEC Introductory Certificate)

Land and Environment – Level 1
Awarding body:
  EDEXCEL

Vocationally Related Qualification (BTEC Introductory Diploma)

Land and Environment – Level 1
Awarding body:
  EDEXCEL

Vocationally Related Qualification (BTEC National Certificate)

Land Based Technology – Level 3
Awarding body:
  EDEXCEL

Vocationally Related Qualification (BTEC National Diploma)

Land Based Technology – Level 3
Awarding body:
  EDEXCEL

Vocationally Related Qualification (Certificate)

Land-based Service Engineering – Level 2
Awarding body:
  C&G

Law

VOCATIONAL QUALIFICATIONS

Vocationally Related Qualification (Certificate)

Vocational Paralegal Studies – Level 2
Awarding body:
   C&G

Vocationally Related Qualification (Diploma)

Vocational Paralegal Studies – Level 3
Awarding body:
   C&G

Vocationally Related Qualification (Professional Diploma)

Law – Level 3
Awarding body:
   ILEX

Linguistics, Languages and Translation

VOCATIONAL QUALIFICATIONS

Award

Languages – Level 1
Awarding body:
C&G
EDEXCEL
GOAL
OCR

Languages – Level 2
Awarding body:
C&G
EDEXCEL
GOAL
OCR

Languages – Level 3
Awarding body:
C&G
EDEXCEL
GOAL
OCR

Languages – Level 4
Awarding body:
OCR

Languages for Travel and Leisure (Reading and Writing) – Level 1
Awarding body:
OCNW

Certificate

British Sign Language – Level 1
Awarding body:
CACDP

British Sign Language – Level 2
Awarding body:
CACDP

English Language and Literature – Level 3
Awarding body:
OCNW

ESOL Skills for Life – Level 1
Awarding body:
EDI

ESOL Skills for Life – Level 2
Awarding body:
EDI

ESOL Subject Specialists – Level 4
Awarding body:
CAMBRIDGE ESOL
TCL

Irish Sign Language – Level 1
Awarding body:
CACDP

Irish Sign Language – Level 2
Awarding body:
CACDP

Japanese – Level 1
Awarding body:
WJEC

Language Proficiency (Using Welsh) – Level 4
Awarding body:
WJEC

Languages for Travel and Leisure (Speaking and Listening, Reading and Writing) – Level 1
Awarding body:
OCNW

Languages for Travel and Leisure (Speaking and Listening) – Level 1
Awarding body:
OCNW

The Living History of British Sign Language – Level 2
Awarding body:
CACDP

Welsh Second Language – Level 3
Awarding body:
  WJEC

Welsh Second Language (Using Welsh) – Level 1
Awarding body:
  WJEC

Welsh Second Language: The Use of Welsh – Level 3
Awarding body:
  WJEC

Diploma

Public Service Interpreting – Level 6
Awarding body:
  IoL

Translation – Level 7
Awarding body:
  IoL

Entry Level Certificate

ESOL for Work – Entry 3
Awarding body:
  EDEXCEL
  NOCN

ESOL Skills for Life – Level 3
Awarding body:
  EDI

ESOL Skills for Life – Entry 1
Awarding body:
  EDI

ESOL Skills for Life – Entry 2
Awarding body:
  EDI

ESOL Certificate

ESOL for Work – Level 1
Awarding body:
  EDEXCEL
  NOCN

Foundation Award

Welsh Second Language – Level 1
Awarding body:
  WJEC

National Vocational Qualification

British Sign Language – Level 3
Awarding body:
  CACDP
  CACDP

Interpreting – Level 4
Awarding body:
  C&G

Irish Sign Language – Level 3
Awarding body:
  CACDP

Other General Qualification (Certificate)

French (FCSE) – Level 1
Awarding body:
  AQA

SL Language Ab Initio – Level 2
Awarding body:
  IBO

Vocationally Related Qualification (Certificate)

Lipspeaking – Level 2
Awarding body:
  CACDP

Maintenance

APPRENTICESHIPS

Apprenticeships and Advanced Apprenticeships in Chemical, Pharmaceuticals Petrochemical Manufacture and Refining Industries and in Transport Engineering and Maintenance
www.cogent-ssc.com
www.goskills.org

VOCATIONAL QUALIFICATIONS

National Vocational Qualification

Highways Maintenance – Level 2
Awarding body:
   C&G/CITB

Maintaining Plant and Systems - Electrical – Level 3
Awarding body:
   ECITB

Maintaining Plant and Systems - Instrument and Control – Level 3
Awarding body:
   ECITB

Maintaining Plant and Systems - Mechanical – Level 3
Awarding body:
   ECITB

Plant Maintenance – Level 2
Awarding body:
   EDEXCEL

Plant Maintenance – Level 3
Awarding body:
   EDEXCEL

Scottish Vocational Qualification

Highways Maintenance – Level 2
Awarding body:
   SQA & CITB

Maintaining Plant and Systems - Instrument & Controls – Level 3
Awarding body:
   ECITB

Maintaining Plant and Systems - Mechanical – Level 3
Awarding body:
   ECITB

Maintaining Plant and Systems (Mechanical) – Level 3
Awarding body:
   ECITB

Maintenance Operations – Level 2
Awarding body:
   EDEXCEL

Vocationally Related Qualification

Maintenance of Refrigeration Systems – Level 3
Awarding body:
   EAL

Vocationally Related Qualification (Award)

Basic Pool Plant Operations – Level 2
Awarding body:
   Active IQ

Vocationally Related Qualification (BTEC First Diploma)

Operations and Maintenance Engineering – Level 2
Awarding body:
    EDEXCEL

Vocationally Related Qualification (BTEC National Certificate)

Operations and Maintenance Engineering – Level 3
Awarding body:
    EDEXCEL

Vocationally Related Qualification (BTEC National Diploma)

Operations and Maintenance Engineering – Level 3
Awarding body:
    EDEXCEL

Vocationally Related Qualification (Certificate of Competence)

Machine Maintenance and Related Operations – Level 2
Awarding body:
    NPTC

Vocationally Related Qualification (Foundation Certificate)

Plant Maintenance – Level 1
Awarding body:
    C&G/CITB

Vocationally Related Qualification (Intermediate Certificate)

Plant Maintenance – Level 2
Awarding body:
    C&G/CITB

Management

APPRENTICESHIPS

Advanced Apprenticeship in
Management and Apprenticeship in
Management; Admin and Professional
www.managementstandards.org.uk

VOCATIONAL QUALIFICATIONS

BTEC Professional Diploma

Front of House Management – Level 5
Awarding body:
  EDEXCEL

Certificate

Contributing to a Project – Level 2
Awarding body:
  EDI

Management – Level 3
Awarding body:
  EDI

Project Management – Level 3
Awarding body:
  EDI

Team Leading – Level 2
Awarding body:
  EDI

Higher Level Award

Executive Management – Level 7
Awarding body:
  ILM

Management – Level 6
Awarding body:
  ILM

Higher Level Certificate

Executive Management – Level 7
Awarding body:
  ILM

Higher Professional Certificate

Technical Salon Management – Level 4
Awarding body:
  C&G

Higher Professional Diploma

Technical Salon Management – Level 4
Awarding body:
  C&G

National Vocational Qualification

Management – Level 3
Awarding body:
  CIPD
  CMI
  EDEXCEL
  EDI
  ILM
  OCR
  OU

Team Leading – Level 2
Awarding body:
  CIPD
  CMI
  EDEXCEL
  EDI
  ILM
  OCR
  OU

Utilities Control Centre Operations – Level 2
Awarding body:
  CABWI

Utilities Metering Operations – Level 2
Awarding body:
  CABWI

Scottish Vocational Qualification

Management – Level 3
Awarding body:
  CMI
  EAL
  ILM
  SQA/CMI/MSC

Management – Level 4
Awarding body:
  CMI
  EAL
  ILM
  SQA/CMI/MSC

Management – Level 5
Awarding body:
  CMI
  ILM
  SQA/CMI/MSC

Operational Management – Level 5
Awarding body:
  CMI
  EAL
  ILM
  SQA/CMI/MSC

Operational Services – Level 2
Awarding body:
  CMI
  ILM

Planning Supervision (CDM) – Level 4
Awarding body:
  CMI
  ILM

Quality Management – Level 4
Awarding body:
  CMI

Team Leading – Level 2
Awarding body:
  CMI
  ILM
  SQA

Vocationally Related Qualification (Certificate)

Handling Violence in the Workplace – Level 2
Awarding body:
  ABC

On-Tour Managers – Level 3
Awarding body:
  NCFE

Personal Effectiveness (Seven Habits) – Level 2
Awarding body:
  QNUK

Vocationally Related Qualification (Higher Level Certificate)

Strategic Leadership – Level 7
Awarding body:
  ILM

Vocationally Related Qualification (Higher Level Diploma)

Executive Management – Level 7
Awarding body:
  ILM

Strategic Leadership – Level 7
Awarding body:
  ILM

Strategic Leadership and Executive Management – Level 7
Awarding body:
  ILM

Manufacturing and Designing

APPRENTICESHIPS

Apprenticeships and Advanced Apprenticeships available in most manufacturing industries

VOCATIONAL QUALIFICATIONS

Foundation General National Vocational Qualification

Manufacturing – Level 1
Awarding body:
AQA
EDEXCEL
OCR

Intermediate General National Vocational Qualification

Manufacturing – Level 2
Awarding body:
AQA
EDEXCEL
OCR

National Vocational Qualification

Carton Manufacture – Level 3
Awarding body:
C&G

Envelope Manufacture – Level 2
Awarding body:
C&G

Envelope Manufacture – Level 3
Awarding body:
C&G

Manufacturing Ceramic Products – Level 2
Awarding body:
C&G

Packaging Operations – Level 1
Awarding body:
C&G

Packaging Operations – Level 2
Awarding body:
PAA/VQSET

Performing Manufacturing Operations – Level 1
Awarding body:
C&G
EAL
EDI
PAA/VQSET
QFI

Performing Manufacturing Operations – Level 2
Awarding body:
C&G
EAL
EDI
ETCAL
PAA/VQSET

National Vocational Qualifications

Optical Manufacturing – Level 2
Awarding body:
C&G

Optical Manufacturing – Level 3
Awarding body:
C&G

Scottish Vocational Qualification

Carton Manufacture – Level 3
Awarding body:
SQA & SPEF

Manufacturing Engineering – Level 3
Awarding body:
C&G

Packaging Operations – Level 1
Awarding body:
PAA/VQSET/SQA

Packaging Operations – Level 2
Awarding body:
PAA/VQSET/SQA

Performing Manufacturing Operations – Level 1
Awarding body:
C&G
EAL
SQA

Performing Manufacturing Operations – Level 2
Awarding body:
C&G
EAL
SQA

Scottish Vocational Qualifications

Optical Manufacturing – Level 2
Awarding body:
C&G

Optical Manufacturing – Level 3
Awarding body:
C&G

Vocationally Related Qualification

Advanced Manufacture Techniques - Computer Numerical Control (CNC) – Level 3
Awarding body:
C&G

Model Making and Presentation – Level 3
Awarding body:
ABC

Vocationally Related Qualification (BTEC Higher National Certificate)

Manufacturing Engineering – Level 5
Awarding body:
EDEXCEL

Vocationally Related Qualification (BTEC Higher National Diploma)

Manufacturing Engineering – Level 5
Awarding body:
EDEXCEL

Vocationally Related Qualification (Certificate)

Manufacturing – Entry 3
Awarding body:
OCR

Vocationally Related Qualification (Diploma)

Packaging Technology – Level 4
Awarding body:
PIABC

Vocationally Related Qualification (Double Award)

Prop Making – Level 3
Awarding body:
ABC

Vocationally Related Qualification (Progression Award)

Production Engineering: Casting – Level 2
Awarding body:
  C&G

Production Engineering: Casting – Level 3
Awarding body:
  C&G

Production Engineering: CNC Manufacturing – Level 2
Awarding body:
  C&G

Production Engineering: Composites – Level 2
Awarding body:
  C&G

Production Engineering: Composites – Level 3
Awarding body:
  C&G

Production Engineering: Electrical Assembly – Level 2
Awarding body:
  C&G

Production Engineering: Fabrication – Level 2
Awarding body:
  C&G

Production Engineering: Finishing – Level 2
Awarding body:
  C&G

Production Engineering: Fitting – Level 2
Awarding body:
  C&G

Production Engineering: Machining – Level 2
Awarding body:
  C&G

Production Engineering: Machining – Level 3
Awarding body:
  C&G

Production Engineering: Mechanical Assembly – Level 2
Awarding body:
  C&G

Production Engineering: Refurbishment – Level 2
Awarding body:
  C&G

Maritime Engineering

APPRENTICESHIPS

Marine Engineering Apprenticeships and
Advanced Apprenticeships available
www.senta.org.uk

VOCATIONAL QUALIFICATIONS

BTEC Higher National Certificate

Marine Engineering – Level 5
Awarding body:
EDEXCEL

BTEC Higher National Diploma

Marine Engineering – Level 4
Awarding body:
EDEXCEL

National Vocational Qualification

Marine Engineering – Level 2
Awarding body:
EAL

Marine Engineering – Level 3
Awarding body:
EAL

Scottish Vocational Qualification

Marine Engineering – Level 3
Awarding body:
SQA

**Marine Engineering (Composites) –
Level 2**
Awarding body:
EAL

**Marine Engineering (Electrical
Installation and Maintenance) – Level 2**
Awarding body:
EAL

**Marine Engineering (Interior Finishing) –
Level 2**
Awarding body:
EAL

**Marine Engineering (Manual Welding) –
Level 2**
Awarding body:
EAL

**Marine Engineering (Mechanical
Installation and Maintenance) – Level 2**
Awarding body:
EAL

**Marine Engineering (Paint Application) –
Level 2**
Awarding body:
EAL

Marine Engineering (Pipework) – Level 2
Awarding body:
EAL

Marine Engineering (Rigging) – Level 2
Awarding body:
EAL

**Marine Engineering (Sheet Metalwork) –
Level 2**
Awarding body:
EAL

**Marine Engineering (Structural
Steelwork) – Level 2**
Awarding body:
EAL

**Marine Engineering (Surface
Preparation) – Level 3**
Awarding body:
EAL

Marine Engineering (Welding Machine Operating) – Level 2
Awarding body:
　EAL

Marine Engineering (Woodworking/Outfitting) – Level 2
Awarding body:
　EAL

Marine Engineering Operations (Chief Engineer (Fishing) - Unlimited) – Level 4
Awarding body:
　SQA

Marine Engineering Operations (Engineer (Fishing)) – Level 3
Awarding body:
　SQA

Marine Engineering Operations (Engineer (Tug) - Inshore) – Level 3
Awarding body:
　SQA

Marine Engineering Operations (Engineer Officer of the Watch (MN) Over 750KW) – Level 3
Awarding body:
　SQA

Marine Engineering Operations (Marine Engine Operator (Meol) Less than 750KW) – Level 3
Awarding body:
　SQA

Marine Engineering Operations (Second Engineer (MN) - Under 300KW) – Level 4
Awarding body:
　SQA

Marine Engineering Operations (Second Engineer (MN) - Unlimited) – Level 4
Awarding body:
　SQA

Marine Vessel Operations (Bridge Watchkeeper - (Tugs) Inshore) – Level 3
Awarding body:
　SQA

Marine Vessel Operations (Bridge Watchkeeper - (Tugs) Near Coastal) – Level 3
Awarding body:
　SQA

Marine Vessel Operations (Chief Mate (MN) - Unlimited) – Level 4
Awarding body:
　SQA

Marine Vessel Operations (Master (Tug) - Inshore) – Level 4
Awarding body:
　SQA

Marine Vessel Operations (Mate (Fishing) - (Limited) – Level 3
Awarding body:
　SQA

Marine Vessel Operations (Mate (Fishing) - Unlimited) – Level 3
Awarding body:
　SQA

Marine Vessel Operations (Officer of the Watch (MN) - Under 500 GT Near Coastal) – Level 3
Awarding body:
　SQA

Marine Vessel Operations (Officer of the Watch (MN) - Unlimited) – Level 3
Awarding body:
　SQA

Marine Vessel Operations (Skipper (Fishing) - Inshore) – Level 3
Awarding body:
　SQA

Marine Vessel Operations (Skipper (Fishing) - Limited) – Level 4
Awarding body:
　SQA

Marine Vessel Operations (Skipper (Fishing) - Unlimited) – Level 4
Awarding body:
　SQA

Marine Vessel Support (Assistant Engineer (Fishing)) – Level 4
Awarding body:
  SQA

Marine Vessel Support (Deck (MN)) – Level 2
Awarding body:
  SQA

Marine Vessel Support (Deck Hand (Fishing)) – Level 2
Awarding body:
  SQA

Marine Vessel Support (Engine Room (MN)) – Level 2
Awarding body:
  SQA

Marine Vessel Support (Inshore Tug Hand) – Level 2
Awarding body:
  SQA

Offshore Crane Operations – Level 2
Awarding body:
  SQA & cogent

Offshore Deck Operations – Level 2
Awarding body:
  SQA & cogent

Offshore Drilling Operations – Level 1
Awarding body:
  SQA/cogent

Offshore Drilling Operations – Level 2
Awarding body:
  SQA/cogent

Offshore Drilling Operations – Level 3
Awarding body:
  SQA/cogent

Materials

APPRENTICESHIPS

Apprenticeships and Advanced Apprenticeships in Polymer Processing and in Man-Made Fibre Manufacture
www.cogent-ssc.com

VOCATIONAL QUALIFICATIONS

National Vocational Qualification

Formwork – Level 1
Awarding body:
  C&G/CITB

Formwork – Level 2
Awarding body:
  C&G/CITB
  EDEXCEL

Formwork – Level 3
Awarding body:
  C&G/CITB

Materials Processing and Finishing – Level 2
Awarding body:
  EAL
  ETCAL

Materials Processing and Finishing – Level 3
Awarding body:
  C&G
  EAL
  ETCAL

Scottish Vocational Qualification

Materials Processing and Finishing – Level 2
Awarding body:
  EAL

Materials Processing and Finishing – Level 3
Awarding body:
  EAL

Polymer Processing and Materials Technology – Level 3
Awarding body:
  EDEXCEL

Polymer Processing and Related Operations – Level 1
Awarding body:
  SASL

Polymer Processing and Related Operations – Level 2
Awarding body:
  SASL

Polymer Processing and Related Operations – Level 3
Awarding body:
  SASL

Mechanical Engineering

APPRENTICESHIPS

Apprenticeships and Advanced Apprenticeships in a range of Mechanical Engineering occupations are available
www.enginuity.org.uk

VOCATIONAL QUALIFICATIONS

BTEC Higher National Certificate

Mechanical Engineering – Level 5
Awarding body:
   EDEXCEL

BTEC Higher National Diploma

Mechanical Engineering – Level 5
Awarding body:
   EDEXCEL

National Vocational Qualification

Mechanical Engineering Services - Plumbing – Level 2
Awarding body:
   EAL

Mechanical Manufacturing Engineering – Level 2
Awarding body:
   C&G
   ETCAL

Mechanical Manufacturing Engineering – Level 3
Awarding body:
   C&G

Scottish Vocational Qualification

Mechanical Engineering Services: Domestic Plumbing – Level 3
Awarding body:
   SQA & SNIJIB

Mechanical Engineering Services: Heating and Ventilating Installation - Maintenance of Systems Components – Level 3
Awarding body:
   SQA & SummitSkills

Mechanical Engineering Services: Heating and Ventilating Installation - Rectification of Systems – Level 3
Awarding body:
   SQA & SummitSkills

Mechanical Engineering Services: Heating and Ventilating Installation (Domestic) – Level 3
Awarding body:
   SQA & SummitSkills

Mechanical Engineering Services: Heating and Ventilating Installation (Ductwork) – Level 2
Awarding body:
   SQA & SummitSkills

Mechanical Engineering Services: Heating and Ventilating Installation (Industrial/Commercial) – Level 2
Awarding body:
   SQA & SummitSkills

Mechanical Engineering Services: Heating and Ventilating Installation (Industrial/Commercial) – Level 3
Awarding body:
   SQA & SummitSkills

Mechanical Engineering Services: Heating and Ventilating Installation(Domestic) – Level 2
Awarding body:
   SQA & SummitSkills

Mechanical Engineering Services: Refrigeration and Air Conditioning Systems (Commercial and Industrial Air Conditioning Systems) – Level 3
Awarding body:
    SQA/SummitSkills/ACRIB

Mechanical Engineering Services: Small Commercial Refrigeration and Air Conditioning Systems – Level 2
Awarding body:
    SQA/SummitSkills/ACRIB

Mechanical Manufacturing Engineering – Level 2
Awarding body:
    EAL

Mechanical Manufacturing Engineering – Level 3
Awarding body:
    EAL

Transport Engineering and Maintenance (PCV Mechanical) – Level 2
Awarding body:
    EDI

Transport Engineering and Maintenance (PCV Mechanical) – Level 3
Awarding body:
    EDI

Vocationally Related Qualification

Mechanical Engineering – Level 3
Awarding body:
    EDEXCEL

Vocationally Related Qualification (BTEC National Certificate)

Mechanical Engineering – Level 3
Awarding body:
    EDEXCEL

Vocationally Related Qualification (Diploma)

Advanced Mechanical Engineering Principles – Level 3
Awarding body:
    EAL

Building Mechanical Maintenance Systems & Services – Level 3
Awarding body:
    EAL

Medical Technology

VOCATIONAL QUALIFICATIONS

Scottish Vocational Qualification

Dialysis Support – Level 3
Awarding body:
  C&G
  SQA

Medicine

VOCATIONAL QUALIFICATIONS

Higher Level Diploma

The Assessment and Management of Low Vision – Level 7
Awarding body:
  NEBOSH

Scottish Vocational Qualification

Operating Department Practice – Level 3
Awarding body:
  C&G
  SQA

Operating Department Support – Level 2
Awarding body:
  C&G
  SQA

Vocationally Related Qualification (Award)

Medical Terminology for Non-Clinical Professionals – Level 2
Awarding body:
  AMSPAR

Vocationally Related Qualification (BTEC Award)

The Control and Administration of Medicines – Level 3
Awarding body:
  EDEXCEL

Vocationally Related Qualification (Certificate)

Managing and Safe Handling of Medicines – Level 2
Awarding body:
  EDI

Red Vein Treatment – Level 3
Awarding body:
  ITEC

Safe Handling of Medicines – Level 2
Awarding body:
  CCEA
  NCFE

The Treatment and Management of Injury in Football – Level 3
Awarding body:
  1ST4SPORT

Treatment and Management of Injuries in Football – Level 2
Awarding body:
  1ST4SPORT

Vocationally Related Qualification (Diploma)

Lymphatic Drainage Massage – Level 2
Awarding body:
  ITEC

Metals and Metalwork

APPRENTICESHIPS

Apprenticeships and Advanced
Apprenticeships in Steel and Metals
Industry
www.qosg.org

VOCATIONAL QUALIFICATIONS

National Vocational Qualification

Fabricating of Steel Structures (Plating) – Level 3
Awarding body:
   ECITB

Steelfixing Occupations – Level 2
Awarding body:
   C&G/CITB
   EDEXCEL

Scottish Vocational Qualification

Metal Processing and Allied Operations (Fabricating Constructional Steelwork) – Level 2
Awarding body:
   EAL

Metal Processing and Allied Operations (Fabricating Constructional Steelwork) – Level 3
Awarding body:
   EAL

Metal Processing and Allied Operations (Laboratory and Associated Technical Activities) – Level 2
Awarding body:
   EAL

Metal Processing and Allied Operations (Laboratory and Associated Technical Activities) – Level 3
Awarding body:
   EAL

Metal Processing and Allied Operations (Metal Processing) – Level 2
Awarding body:
   EAL

Metal Processing and Allied Operations (Metal Processing) – Level 3
Awarding body:
   EAL

Steel Fixing – Level 2
Awarding body:
   OCR

Vocationally Related Qualification (BTEC National Award)

Blacksmithing and Metalworking – Level 3
Awarding body:
   EDEXCEL

Vocationally Related Qualification (BTEC National Certificate)

Blacksmithing and Metalworking – Level 3
Awarding body:
   EDEXCEL

Vocationally Related Qualification (BTEC National Diploma)

Blacksmithing and Metalworking – Level 3

Awarding body:
EDEXCEL

Museums, Galleries and Heritage

APPRENTICESHIPS

Apprenticeships in Cultural Heritage:
Recreation and Travel
www.chnto.co.uk

VOCATIONAL QUALIFICATIONS

National Vocational Qualification

Cultural Heritage Operations – Level 3
Awarding body:
EDI

Cultural Heritage Operations – Level 4
Awarding body:
EDI

Cultural Heritage Operations – Level 5
Awarding body:
EDI

Museums, Galleries and Heritage (Heritage Care and Visitor Services) – Level 2
Awarding body:
EDI

Occupational Qualification (National Award)

Cultural and Heritage Venue Operations – Level 2
Awarding body:
EDI

Cultural and Heritage Venue Operations – Level 3
Awarding body:
EDI

Scottish Vocational Qualification

Cultural Heritage Operations – Level 3
Awarding body:
SQA

Cultural Heritage Operations – Level 4
Awarding body:
SQA

Cultural Venue Support – Level 2
Awarding body:
SQA & CHNTO

Heritage Care and Visitor Services – Level 2
Awarding body:
SQA

Museums, Galleries and Heritage (Heritage Care and Visitor Services) – Level 2
Awarding body:
SQA & CHNTO

Music and Musical Instruments

APPRENTICESHIPS

Advanced Apprenticeships in Arts and Entertainment
www.metier.org.uk

VOCATIONAL QUALIFICATIONS

Advanced Graded Examination

Music Literacy – Level 3
Awarding body:
ABRSM
TCL
TVU

Music Performance – Level 3
Awarding body:
ABRSM
RSL
TCL
TVU

Associate

Music Literacy – Level 4
Awarding body:
TCL

Music Performance – Level 4
Awarding body:
TCL

Music Performance – Level 7
Awarding body:
GSMD

Music Practice: Composing – Level 4
Awarding body:
TCL

Music Practice: Directing – Level 4
Awarding body:
TCL

Music Practice: Mentoring – Level 4
Awarding body:
TCL

Music Practice: Performing – Level 4
Awarding body:
TCL

Associate Diploma

Music Facilitating – Level 4
Awarding body:
TCL

Award

Music Practitioners – Level 1
Awarding body:
RSL

Music Practitioners – Level 2
Awarding body:
RSL

Music Practitioners – Level 3
Awarding body:
RSL

BTEC Higher National Certificate

Music Performance – Level 5
Awarding body:
EDEXCEL

Music Production – Level 5
Awarding body:
EDEXCEL

BTEC Higher National Diploma

Music Performance – Level 5
Awarding body:
EDEXCEL

Music Production – Level 5
Awarding body:
  EDEXCEL

BTEC Professional Diploma

Creative Music Technology – Level 5
Awarding body:
  EDEXCEL

Music Composition – Level 5
Awarding body:
  EDEXCEL

Music Management – Level 5
Awarding body:
  EDEXCEL

Music Performance – Level 5
Awarding body:
  EDEXCEL

Music Science and Acoustics – Level 5
Awarding body:
  EDEXCEL

Songwriting – Level 5
Awarding body:
  EDEXCEL

Sound for the Media – Level 5
Awarding body:
  EDEXCEL

Sound Studio Management – Level 5
Awarding body:
  EDEXCEL

Certificate

Music Performance – Level 4
Awarding body:
  GSMD

Music Practitioners – Level 1
Awarding body:
  RSL

Music Practitioners – Level 2
Awarding body:
  RSL

Music Practitioners – Level 3
Awarding body:
  RSL

Diploma

Applied Music Practitioners – Level 3
Awarding body:
  RSL

Music Direction – Level 4
Awarding body:
  ABRSM

Music Performance – Level 4
Awarding body:
  ABRSM

Music Practitioners – Level 1
Awarding body:
  RSL

Music Practitioners – Level 2
Awarding body:
  RSL

Music Practitioners – Level 3
Awarding body:
  RSL

Fellowship

Directing – Level 7
Awarding body:
  TCL

Music Composition – Level 7
Awarding body:
  TCL

Music Direction – Level 7
Awarding body:
  ABRSM
  TCL

Music Education – Level 7
Awarding body:
  ABRSM
  TCL

Music Literacy – Level 7
Awarding body:
  TCL

Music Performance – Level 7
Awarding body:
ABRSM
TCL

Music Practice: Composing – Level 7
Awarding body:
TCL

Music Practice: Performing – Level 7
Awarding body:
TCL

Fellowship Diploma

Music Facilitating – Level 5
Awarding body:
TCL

Foundation Graded Examination

Music Literacy – Level 1
Awarding body:
ABRSM
TCL
TVU

Music Performance – Level 1
Awarding body:
ABRSM
RSL
TCL
TVU

Music Performance – Level 3
Awarding body:
TVU

Foundation Level Certificate

Music Performance – Level 1
Awarding body:
ABRSM

Graded Examination

Music Literacy – Level 1
Awarding body:
GSMD

Music Literacy – Level 2
Awarding body:
GSMD

Music Performance – Level 1
Awarding body:
GSMD

Music Performance – Level 2
Awarding body:
GSMD

Music Performance – Level 3
Awarding body:
GSMD

Music Theatre – Level 1
Awarding body:
TVU

Music Theatre – Level 2
Awarding body:
TVU

Music Theatre – Level 3
Awarding body:
TVU

Intermediate Graded Examination

Music Literacy – Level 2
Awarding body:
ABRSM
TCL
TVU

Music Performance – Level 2
Awarding body:
ABRSM
RSL
TCL

Intermediate Level Certificate

Music Performance – Level 2
Awarding body:
ABRSM

Licentiate

Music Composition – Level 6
Awarding body:
TCL

Music Direction – Level 6
Awarding body:
ABRSM

Music Literacy – Level 6
Awarding body:
TCL

Music Performance – Level 6
Awarding body:
ABRSM
GSMD
TCL

Music Practice: Composing – Level 6
Awarding body:
TCL

Music Practice: Directing – Level 6
Awarding body:
TCL

Music Practice: Mentoring – Level 6
Awarding body:
TCL

Music Practice: Performing – Level 6
Awarding body:
TCL

Performing – Level 6
Awarding body:
TCL

Licentiate Diploma

Music Facilitating (LTCL) – Level 4
Awarding body:
TCL

Other General Qualification (Award)

Music Educators – Level 3
Awarding body:
RSL

Other General Qualification (Certificate)

Music Educators – Level 3
Awarding body:
RSL

Other General Qualification (Diploma (Applied))

Music Educators – Level 3
Awarding body:
RSL

Other General Qualification (Graded Examination)

Music Performance – Level 1
Awarding body:
TCL

Music Performance – Level 2
Awarding body:
TCL

Music Performance – Level 3
Awarding body:
TCL

Music Theory/Literacy – Level 1
Awarding body:
TCL

Music Theory/Literacy – Level 2
Awarding body:
TCL

Qualifications and Credit Framework (Award)

Music Direction – Level 4
Awarding body:
ABRSM

Scottish Vocational Qualification

Keyboarding – Level 1
Awarding body:
ABRSM

Vocationally Related Qualification

Music Technology and Sound Production – Level 3
Awarding body:
  C&G

Sound and Music Technology – Level 3
Awarding body:
  C&G

Vocationally Related Qualification (BTEC First Certificate)

Music – Level 2
Awarding body:
  EDEXCEL

Vocationally Related Qualification (BTEC First Diploma)

Music – Level 2
Awarding body:
  EDEXCEL

Vocationally Related Qualification (BTEC National Award)

Music Practice – Level 3
Awarding body:
  EDEXCEL

Vocationally Related Qualification (BTEC National Certificate)

Music Practice – Level 3
Awarding body:
  EDEXCEL

Music Technology – Level 3
Awarding body:
  EDEXCEL

Vocationally Related Qualification (BTEC National Diploma)

Music Practice – Level 3
Awarding body:
  EDEXCEL

Music Technology – Level 3
Awarding body:
  EDEXCEL

Vocationally Related Qualification (Certificate)

Classical Musical Instrument Technology – Level 2
Awarding body:
  EDI

Classical Musical Instrument Technology – Level 3
Awarding body:
  EDI

Contemporary Music Practice – Level 1
Awarding body:
  NCFE

Multi Track Recording and Automation – Level 3
Awarding body:
  C&G

Music and Sound Composition – Level 3
Awarding body:
  C&G

Music Technology – Level 2
Awarding body:
  NCFE

Music Technology (Mix DJ Skills) – Level 2
Awarding body:
  NCFE

Popular Music Practice – Level 1
Awarding body:
  NOCN

Software Sound Manipulation and Composition – Level 3
Awarding body:
   C&G

Sound Facility Design – Level 3
Awarding body:
   C&G

Steel Stringed Fretted Instrument Construction – Level 2
Awarding body:
   EDI

Surround Sound and Composition – Level 3
Awarding body:
   C&G

Surround Sound and Film – Level 3
Awarding body:
   C&G

Vocationally Related Qualification (Diploma)

Music Technology and Sound Engineering – Level 3
Awarding body:
   C&G

Sound and Music Technology – Level 3
Awarding body:
   C&G

Office and Secretarial

APPRENTICESHIPS

Apprenticeships and Advanced
Apprenticeships in Business and
Administration
www.cfa.uk.com

VOCATIONAL QUALIFICATIONS

Entry Level Award

Speed Keying – Entry 3
Awarding body:
OCR

Higher Level Advanced Diploma

Administrative Management – Level 5
Awarding body:
IAM

Scottish Vocational Qualification

Administration – Level 1
Awarding body:
EDEXCEL

Administration – Level 2
Awarding body:
EDEXCEL

Administration – Level 3
Awarding body:
EDEXCEL

Administration – Level 4
Awarding body:
EDEXCEL

Vocationally Related Qualification (Certificate)

Audio Transcription – Level 1
Awarding body:
EDI
GOAL

Audio Transcription – Level 2
Awarding body:
EDI
GOAL

Audio Transcription – Level 3
Awarding body:
EDI
GOAL

Business Administration – Level 1
Awarding body:
EDI

Business Administration – Level 2
Awarding body:
EDI

Business Administration – Level 3
Awarding body:
EDI

Business Practice – Level 2
Awarding body:
EDI

Business Practice – Level 3
Awarding body:
EDI

Text Production – Level 1
Awarding body:
EDI

Text Production – Level 2
Awarding body:
EDI

Text Production – Level 3
Awarding body:
EDI

Painting and Decorating

APPRENTICESHIPS

Apprenticeships and Advanced
Apprenticeships in Construction (Craft)
www.citb.co.uk

VOCATIONAL QUALIFICATIONS

National Vocational Qualification

Wall and Floor Tiling – Level 2
Awarding body:
  C&G/CITB

Wall and Floor Tiling – Level 3
Awarding body:
  C&G/CITB

Scottish Vocational Qualification

Wall and Floor Tiling – Level 2
Awarding body:
  SQA & SBATC

Wall and Floor Tiling – Level 3
Awarding body:
  SQA & SBATC

Paper and Board

APPRENTICESHIPS

Apprenticeships and Advanced
Apprenticeships in Paper Manufacture
and in Fibre Board Packaging
www.paper.org.uk

VOCATIONAL QUALIFICATIONS

National Vocational Qualification

Fibreboard Operations – Level 2
Awarding body:
    PAA/VQSET

Fibreboard Operations – Level 3
Awarding body:
    PAA/VQSET

Scottish Vocational Qualification

Paper Manufacturing – Level 2
Awarding body:
    SQA & PETC

Paper Manufacturing – Level 3
Awarding body:
    SQA & PETC

Pensions

APPRENTICESHIPS

Apprenticeships and Advanced
Apprenticeships in Providing Financial
Services
www.fssc.org.uk

VOCATIONAL QUALIFICATIONS

Scottish Vocational Qualification

Pensions Administration – Level 4
Awarding body:
    PMI

Pensions Calculations – Level 4
Awarding body:
    PMI

**Public Sector Pensions Administration –
Level 3**
Awarding body:
    PMI

**Public Service Pensions Administration –
Level 3**
Awarding body:
    PMI

Performing Arts

APPRENTICESHIPS

Apprenticeships and Advanced
Apprenticeships in Arts and
Entertainment
www.metier.org.uk

VOCATIONAL QUALIFICATIONS

Advanced Graded Examination

Dance – Level 3
Awarding body:
  BBO
  ISTD
  RAD

Drama – Level 2
Awarding body:
  LAMDA

Drama – Level 3
Awarding body:
  TCL

Speech – Level 3
Awarding body:
  LAMDA
  TCL

Speech and Drama – Level 3
Awarding body:
  TCL

Theatre Dance – Level 3
Awarding body:
  BTDA

Advanced Vocational Certificate of Education

Performing Arts – Level 3
Awarding body:
  AQA
  OCR

Advanced Vocational Certificate of Education (Double Award)

Performing Arts – Level 3
Awarding body:
  AQA
  OCR

Associate

Performing – Level 4
Awarding body:
  TCL

BTEC National Award

Performing Arts (Acting) – Level 1
Awarding body:
  EDEXCEL

BTEC National Certificate

Performing Arts (Acting) – Level 1
Awarding body:
  EDEXCEL

BTEC National Diploma

Performing Arts (Acting) – Level 1
Awarding body:
  EDEXCEL

BTEC Professional Diploma

Light and Sound: Technical Theatre Management – Level 5
Awarding body:
  EDEXCEL

Performance and Making – Level 5
Awarding body:
  EDEXCEL

Performance: Acting – Level 5
Awarding body:
  EDEXCEL

Stage Sound – Level 5
Awarding body:
  EDEXCEL

Certificate

Performance Skills – Level 1
Awarding body:
  NCFE

Performance Skills – Level 2
Awarding body:
  NCFE

Speech and Drama (Performance Studies) – Level 3
Awarding body:
  LAMDA

Speech, Communication and Drama (Performance) – Level 4
Awarding body:
  GSMD

Diploma

Dance – Level 4
Awarding body:
  BTDA

Dance Teaching – Level 4
Awarding body:
  BBO

Fellowship

Performing – Level 7
Awarding body:
  TCL

Foundation Graded Examination

Dance – Level 1
Awarding body:
  BBO
  ISTD
  RAD

Drama – Level 1
Awarding body:
  LAMDA
  TCL

Speech – Level 1
Awarding body:
  LAMDA
  TCL

Speech and Drama – Level 1
Awarding body:
  TCL

Theatre Dance – Level 1
Awarding body:
  BTDA

Graded Examination

Acting Studies – Level 1
Awarding body:
  GSMD

Acting Studies – Level 2
Awarding body:
  GSMD

Acting Studies – Level 3
Awarding body:
  GSMD

Speech – Level 1
Awarding body:
  ESB

Speech – Level 2
Awarding body:
  ESB
  GSMD

Speech – Level 3
Awarding body:
  ESB
  GSMD

Speech and Drama – Level 1
Awarding body:
  GSMD
  TVU

Speech and Drama – Level 2
Awarding body:
  GSMD
  TVU

Speech and Drama – Level 3
Awarding body:
TVU

Intermediate General National Vocational Qualification

Performing Arts – Level 2
Awarding body:
AQA
OCR

Intermediate Graded Examination

Dance – Level 2
Awarding body:
BBO
ISTD
RAD

Drama – Level 2
Awarding body:
LAMDA
TCL

Speech – Level 2
Awarding body:
LAMDA

Speech and Drama – Level 2
Awarding body:
TCL

Theatre Dance – Level 2
Awarding body:
BTDA

Licentiate

Applied Drama – Level 6
Awarding body:
TCL

National Certificate

Professional Acting – Level 5
Awarding body:
TCL

Professional Classical Ballet – Level 5
Awarding body:
TCL

National Diploma

Professional Acting – Level 6
Awarding body:
TCL

Professional Dance – Level 6
Awarding body:
TCL

Professional Musical Theatre – Level 6
Awarding body:
TCL

Occupational Qualification (Certificate)

Creative and Cultural Practice – Level 2
Awarding body:
EDI

Creative and Cultural Practice – Level 3
Awarding body:
EDI

Occupational Qualification (National Award)

Live Events and Promotion – Level 2
Awarding body:
EDI

Live Events and Promotion – Level 3
Awarding body:
EDI

Music Business (Recording Industry) – Level 2
Awarding body:
EDI

Music Business (Recording Industry) – Level 3
Awarding body:
EDI

Technical Theatre – Level 2
Awarding body:
 EDI

Technical Theatre – Level 3
Awarding body:
 EDI

Scottish Vocational Qualification

Acting Studies – Level 1
Awarding body:
 ABC

Acting Studies – Level 2
Awarding body:
 ABC

Acting Studies – Level 3
Awarding body:
 AQA
 EDEXCEL

Lighting (Live Performance) – Level 2
Awarding body:
 SQA & METIER

Lighting (Live Performance) – Level 3
Awarding body:
 SQA & METIER

Sound (Live Performance) – Level 2
Awarding body:
 SQA & METIER

Sound (Live Performance) – Level 3
Awarding body:
 SQA & METIER

Stage Management – Level 2
Awarding body:
 SQA & METIER

Stage Management – Level 3
Awarding body:
 SQA & METIER

Stage Support (Live Performance) – Level 2
Awarding body:
 SQA & METIER

Vocationally Related Qualification (Advanced Vocational Graded Examination)

Dance – Level 3
Awarding body:
 BBO
 ISTD
 RAD

Vocationally Related Qualification (Award)

The Arts – Level 1
Awarding body:
 TCL

The Arts – Level 2
Awarding body:
 TCL

The Arts – Level 3
Awarding body:
 TCL

Vocationally Related Qualification (BTDA Advanced Vocational Graded Examination)

Theatre Dance – Level 3
Awarding body:
 BTDA

Vocationally Related Qualification (Certificate)

Foundation Dance Practice – Level 3
Awarding body:
 ISTD

Introduction to Dance Teaching – Level 3
Awarding body:
 BBO

Lifespan Development and Learning in Dance – Level 3
Awarding body:
 ISTD

Observation and Understanding of Learning Techniques in Dance – Level 3
Awarding body:
ISTD

Promotion of Health and Safety in Dance – Level 3
Awarding body:
ISTD

Vocationally Related Qualification (Diploma)

Image Styling for Performance – Level 3
Awarding body:
ABC

Theatrical And Media Make-Up – Level 3
Awarding body:
VTCT

Vocationally Related Qualification (Foundation)

Dance Instruction – Level 3
Awarding body:
ISTD

Vocationally Related Qualification (Intermediate Vocational Graded Examination)

Dance – Level 2
Awarding body:
BBO
RAD

Theatre Dance – Level 2
Awarding body:
BTDA

Petroleum, Oil and Gas Technology

APPRENTICESHIPS

Apprenticeships and Advanced
Apprenticeships in Oil and Gas
Extraction and in Chemical,
Pharmaceutical, Petrochemical
Manufacture and Refining Industries
www.cogent-scc.com

VOCATIONAL QUALIFICATIONS

National Vocational Qualification

Forecourt Operations – Level 2
Awarding body:
    C&G

Oil Fired Technical Services – Level 2
Awarding body:
    C&G

Oil Fired Technical Services – Level 3
Awarding body:
    C&G

Refinery Field Operations – Level 3
Awarding body:
    C&G

Scottish Vocational Qualification

Oil Fired Technical Services – Level 2
Awarding body:
    C&G

Oil Fired Technical Services – Level 3
Awarding body:
    C&G

Refinery Control Room Operations – Level 3
Awarding body:
    SQA & cogent

Refinery Field Operations – Level 3
Awarding body:
    SQA & cogent

Pharmaceutical Products

APPRENTICESHIPS

Apprenticeships and Advanced
Apprenticeships in Chemical,
Pharmaceutical, Petrochemical
Manufacture and Refining Industries
www.cogent-scc.com

VOCATIONAL QUALIFICATIONS

National Vocational Qualification

Pharmacy Services – Level 2
Awarding body:
    C&G

Pharmacy Services – Level 3
Awarding body:
    C&G
    EDEXCEL

Scottish Vocational Qualification

Pharmacy Services – Level 2
Awarding body:
    EDEXCEL
    SQA

Pharmacy Services – Level 3
Awarding body:
    C&G
    EDEXCEL

Vocationally Related Qualification (BTEC National Certificate)

Pharmacy Services – Level 3
Awarding body:
    C&G
    EDEXCEL

Photography and Photographic Services

APPRENTICESHIPS

Apprenticeships and Advanced
Apprenticeships in Photography and
Photographic Processes and in Photo
Imaging
www.phototraining.fsnet.co.uk

VOCATIONAL QUALIFICATIONS

BTEC Higher National Certificate

Photography – Level 5
Awarding body:
EDEXCEL

BTEC Higher National Diploma

Photography – Level 5
Awarding body:
EDEXCEL

Higher Professional Diploma

Photo Imaging – Level 4
Awarding body:
C&G

National Vocational Qualification

Photo Imaging – Level 2
Awarding body:
C&G

Photo Imaging – Level 3
Awarding body:
C&G

Photo Processing – Level 2
Awarding body:
C&G

Photo Processing – Level 3
Awarding body:
C&G

Scottish Vocational Qualification

Photo Imaging: Digital Imaging – Level 2
Awarding body:
SQA & SKILLSET

Photo Imaging: Digital Imaging – Level 3
Awarding body:
SQA & SKILLSET

Photo Imaging: Digital Imaging – Level 4
Awarding body:
SQA & SKILLSET

Photo Imaging: Digital Photography and Imaging – Level 3
Awarding body:
SQA & SKILLSET

Photo Imaging: Digital Photography and Imaging – Level 4
Awarding body:
SQA & SKILLSET

Photo Imaging: Photography – Level 2
Awarding body:
SQA & SKILLSET

Photo Imaging: Photography – Level 3
Awarding body:
SQA & SKILLSET

Photo Imaging: Photography – Level 4
Awarding body:
SQA & SKILLSET

Photo Processing: Laboratory Operations – Level 3
Awarding body:
SQA & SKILLSET

Photo Processing: Minilab Processing – Level 2
Awarding body:
SQA & SKILLSET

**Photo Processing: Minilab Processing –
Level 3**
Awarding body:
    SQA & SKILLSET

Vocationally Related Qualification (Award)

Large Format Photography – Level 3
Awarding body:
    ABC

Photojournalism – Level 3
Awarding body:
    ABC

Vocationally Related Qualification (BTEC Award)

Photography – Level 1
Awarding body:
    EDEXCEL

Photography – Level 2
Awarding body:
    EDEXCEL

Photography – Level 3
Awarding body:
    EDEXCEL

Vocationally Related Qualification (BTEC Certificate)

Photography – Level 1
Awarding body:
    EDEXCEL

Photography – Level 2
Awarding body:
    EDEXCEL

Photography – Level 3
Awarding body:
    EDEXCEL

Vocationally Related Qualification (BTEC Diploma)

Photography – Level 2
Awarding body:
    EDEXCEL

Photography – Level 3
Awarding body:
    EDEXCEL

Vocationally Related Qualification (BTEC National Certificate)

Photography – Level 3
Awarding body:
    EDEXCEL

Vocationally Related Qualification (BTEC National Diploma)

Photography – Level 3
Awarding body:
    EDEXCEL

Vocationally Related Qualification (Certificate)

**Photo Image Capture and Printing –
Level 2**
Awarding body:
    C&G

**Photo Image Capture, Printing and
Presentation – Level 2**
Awarding body:
    C&G

**Photo Image Management and Storage –
Level 2**
Awarding body:
    C&G

**Photo Image Printing, Management and
Storage – Level 2**
Awarding body:
    C&G

Photography – Level 1
Awarding body:
   NCFE

Photography – Level 2
Awarding body:
   NCFE

Studio and Location Photography – Level 3
Awarding body:
   ABC

Studio Photography, Image Printing and Presentation – Level 2
Awarding body:
   C&G

Vocationally Related Qualification (Diploma)

Press Photography – Level 3
Awarding body:
   ABC

Vocationally Related Qualification (Progression Award)

Photography – Level 2
Awarding body:
   C&G

Photography – Level 3
Awarding body:
   C&G

Plant Operations

APPRENTICESHIPS

Apprenticeships and Advanced
Apprenticeships in numerous industries
including Industrial Applications,
Manufacturing Textiles, Ceramics
Manufacture, Petrochemical and
associated industries
www.skillfirst.org.uk

VOCATIONAL QUALIFICATIONS

National Vocational Qualification

**Installing Plant & Systems - Instrument
Pipefitting – Level 3**
Awarding body:
  ECITB

**Installing Plant & Systems - Pipefitting –
Level 3**
Awarding body:
  ECITB

**Installing Plant and Systems -
Mechanical – Level 3**
Awarding body:
  ECITB

Plant Operations – Level 2
Awarding body:
  EDI

Scottish Vocational Qualification

**Specialised Plant and Machinery
Operations – Level 1**
Awarding body:
  LANTRA

**Specialised Plant and Machinery
Operations – Level 2**
Awarding body:
  EAL
  EMP
  LANTRA

Plumbing

APPRENTICESHIPS

Apprenticeships and Advanced Apprenticeships in Building Services and in Mechanical Engineering Services
www.summitskills.org.uk

VOCATIONAL QUALIFICATIONS

Vocationally Related Qualification (Certificate)

Basic Plumbing Studies – Level 2
Awarding body:
  C&G

Plumbing Studies – Level 3
Awarding body:
  C&G

Printing

APPRENTICESHIPS

Apprenticeships and Advanced
Apprenticeships in Print and Print
Packaging, Media and Printing, and
Photo Imaging
www.printnto.org

VOCATIONAL QUALIFICATIONS

National Vocational Qualification

Hand Binding – Level 3
Awarding body:
  C&G

Machine Printing – Level 2
Awarding body:
  C&G

Machine Printing – Level 3
Awarding body:
  C&G

Pre-Press – Level 2
Awarding body:
  C&G

Pre-Press – Level 3
Awarding body:
  C&G

Scottish Vocational Qualification

Hand Binding – Level 3
Awarding body:
  SQA & SPEF

Machine Printing – Level 2
Awarding body:
  SQA & SPEF

Machine Printing – Level 3
Awarding body:
  SQA & SPEF

**Mechanised Print Finishing and Binding
– Level 2**
Awarding body:
  SQA & SPEF

**Mechanised Print Finishing and Binding
– Level 3**
Awarding body:
  SQA & SPEF

Pre-Press – Level 2
Awarding body:
  SQA & SPEF

Pre-Press – Level 3
Awarding body:
  C&G
  SQA & SPEF

Print Administration – Level 3
Awarding body:
  SQA & SPEF

Vocationally Related Qualification (Award)

Bookbinding Conservation – Level 3
Awarding body:
  ABC

Creative Book Structures – Level 3
Awarding body:
  ABC

Digital Typography – Level 3
Awarding body:
  ABC

**Historical Print and Letterforms –
Level 3**
Awarding body:
  ABC

Lithographic Print Processes – Level 3
Awarding body:
  ABC

Print Buying – Level 3
Awarding body:
  ABC

Print Finishing and Paper Purchasing – Level 3
Awarding body:
  ABC

Print Production and Workflow Management – Level 3
Awarding body:
  ABC

Printmaking Skills – Level 3
Awarding body:
  ABC

Understanding Printing Technology Processes – Level 3
Awarding body:
  ABC

Vocationally Related Qualification (Certificate)

Experimental Photographic Printing – Level 3
Awarding body:
  ABC

Experimental Printmaking – Level 3
Awarding body:
  ABC

Graphic Printmaking – Level 3
Awarding body:
  ABC

Printing and Graphic Communications – Level 2
Awarding body:
  C&G

Printing and Graphic Communications – Level 3
Awarding body:
  C&G

Vocationally Related Qualification (Diploma)

Digital Pre-Press – Level 3
Awarding body:
  ABC

Print Media – Level 3
Awarding body:
  ABC

Vocationally Related Qualification (Double Award)

Experimental Typography – Level 3
Awarding body:
  ABC

Printmaking – Level 3
Awarding body:
  ABC

Process and Plant Engineering

APPRENTICESHIPS

Apprenticeships and Advanced Apprenticeships in numerous industries including Industrial Applications, Manufacturing Textiles, Ceramics Manufacture, Petrochemical and associated industries
www.skillfirst.org.uk

VOCATIONAL QUALIFICATIONS

National Vocational Qualification

Operating Process Plant – Level 2
Awarding body:
    CABWI

Plant Operations – Level 2
Awarding body:
    C&G/CITB
    EDEXCEL

Process Operations – Level 2
Awarding body:
    EMP

Process Operations (Man-made Fibre) – Level 2
Awarding body:
    PAA/VQSET

Processing Operations: Hydrocarbons – Level 1
Awarding body:
    C&G

Processing Operations: Hydrocarbons – Level 3
Awarding body:
    C&G

Processing Operations: Hydrocarbons (Control Room) – Level 3
Awarding body:
    C&G

Scottish Vocational Qualification

Operating Process Plant: Sludge – Level 2
Awarding body:
    SQA & CABWI

Operating Process Plant: Waste Water – Level 2
Awarding body:
    SQA & CABWI

Operating Process Plant: Water – Level 2
Awarding body:
    SQA & CABWI

Process Engineering Maintenance (Instrument and Control) – Level 2
Awarding body:
    PAA/VQSET
    SQA & cogent

Process Engineering Maintenance (Instrument and Control) – Level 3
Awarding body:
    PAA/VQSET
    SQA & cogent

Process Engineering Maintenance (Mechanical) – Level 2
Awarding body:
    PAA/VQSET
    SQA & cogent

Process Operations – Level 2
Awarding body:
    EMP

Process Operations: Hydrocarbons – Level 1
Awarding body:
    SQA & cogent

**Process Operations: Hydrocarbons –
Level 2**
Awarding body:
   SQA & cogent

**Processing Operations: Hydrocarbons –
Level 1**
Awarding body:
   SQA & CABWI

**Processing Operations: Hydrocarbons –
Level 2**
Awarding body:
   SQA & CABWI

**Processing Operations: Hydrocarbons –
Level 3**
Awarding body:
   SQA & CABWI
   SQA & cogent

**Processing Operations: Hydrocarbons
(Control Room) – Level 3**
Awarding body:
   SQA & cogent

Property

APPRENTICESHIPS

Apprenticeships and Advanced Apprenticeships in Property Services
www.assetskills.com

VOCATIONAL QUALIFICATIONS

Diploma

Commercial Property Agency – Level 5
Awarding body:
NAEA

Residential Estate Agency – Level 5
Awarding body:
NAEA

Residential Letting & Management – Level 5
Awarding body:
NAEA

Higher Level (Diploma)

Residential Service – Level 2
Awarding body:
NAEA

National Vocational Qualification

Property and Caretaking Supervision – Level 3
Awarding body:
ABBE

Residential Service – Level 2
Awarding body:
C&G
GOAL
HAB

Sale of Residential Property – Level 2
Awarding body:
OCR

Scottish Vocational Qualification

Property Management – Level 4
Awarding body:
SQA & ABBE
SQA & HAB

Residential Estate Agency – Level 4
Awarding body:
NAEA

Vocationally Related Qualification (Award)

Commercial Property Agency – Level 3
Awarding body:
NAEA

Residential Lettings and Property Management – Level 3
Awarding body:
NAEA

Sale of Residential Property – Level 3
Awarding body:
NAEA

Vocationally Related Qualification (Certificate)

Buying or Renting a Home – Level 1
Awarding body:
EDI

Providing Business Services

APPRENTICESHIPS

Apprenticeships and Advanced
Apprenticeships in Signmaking and in
Polymers/Signmaking
enquiries@polymernto.org.uk

VOCATIONAL QUALIFICATIONS

Scottish Vocational Qualification

Signmaking – Level 2
Awarding body:
SASL & BSGA

Signmaking – Level 3
Awarding body:
SASL & BSGA

Providing Goods and Services

APPRENTICESHIPS

Apprenticeships and Advanced
Apprenticeships in Procurement
www.apprenticeships.org.uk

VOCATIONAL QUALIFICATIONS

National Vocational Qualification

Procurement – Level 2
Awarding body:
EDEXCEL

Procurement – Level 3
Awarding body:
EDEXCEL

Scottish Vocational Qualification

Procurement – Level 2
Awarding body:
SQA

Procurement – Level 3
Awarding body:
SQA

Procurement – Level 4
Awarding body:
SQA

Vocationally Related Qualification (Certificate)

Small Commercial Refrigeration and Air Conditioning Systems – Level 2
Awarding body:
C&G

Providing Health, Social Care & Protective Services

APPRENTICESHIPS

Apprenticeships and Advanced Apprenticeships in Health and Social Care
www.skillsforhealth.org.uk

VOCATIONAL QUALIFICATIONS

Advanced Subsidiary Vocational Certificate of Education

Health and Social Care – Level 3
Awarding body:
AQA
EDEXCEL
OCR

Advanced Vocational Certificate of Education

Health and Social Care – Level 3
Awarding body:
AQA
EDEXCEL
OCR

Advanced Vocational Certificate of Education (Double Award)

Health and Social Care – Level 3
Awarding body:
AQA
EDEXCEL
OCR

BTEC Higher National Certificate

Health and Social Care – Level 5
Awarding body:
EDEXCEL

BTEC Higher National Diploma

Health and Social Care – Level 5
Awarding body:
EDEXCEL

BTEC Professional Diploma

Registered Managers (Adults) – Level 5
Awarding body:
EDEXCEL

Certificate

Deaf Awareness – Level 1
Awarding body:
CACDP

Deaf Community and Culture – Level 1
Awarding body:
CACDP

DeafBlind Awareness – Level 1
Awarding body:
CACDP

Drug and Substance Use and its Consequences in the Workplace – Level 1
Awarding body:
EDI

Introduction to Housing and Tenancy – Level 1
Awarding body:
EDI

Entry Level

Workplace Hazard Awareness – Entry 3
Awarding body:
  BSC

Entry Level Certificate

Personal, Social and Health Education – Entry 1
Awarding body:
  AQA

Higher Level

Health Emergency Planning – Level 4
Awarding body:
  RSPH

Higher Level Certificate

Contact Lens Practice – Level 6
Awarding body:
  ABDO

Housing – Level 4
Awarding body:
  CIH

Higher Level Diploma

Advanced Contact Lens Practice – Level 7
Awarding body:
  ABDO

Consultancy Supervision – Level 4
Awarding body:
  CPCAB

Counselling – Level 5
Awarding body:
  NCFE

Housing – Level 4
Awarding body:
  CIH

Ophthalmic Dispensing – Level 6
Awarding body:
  ABDO

Primary Care Management – Level 5
Awarding body:
  AMSPAR

The Geometric Optics of Ophthalmic Lens – Level 7
Awarding body:
  ABDO

Higher Level Professional Diploma

Health and Well-being – Level 4
Awarding body:
  C&G

Inspecting Learning Disability Services – Level 4
Awarding body:
  C&G

Learning Disability Services – Level 4
Awarding body:
  C&G

National Vocational Qualification

Custodial Care – Level 2
Awarding body:
  EDEXCEL

Custodial Care – Level 3
Awarding body:
  C&G
  EDEXCEL

Health – Level 2
Awarding body:
  C&G
  EDEXCEL

Health – Level 3
Awarding body:
  C&G
  EDEXCEL

Health and Social Care – Level 2
Awarding body:
 C&G
 EDEXCEL
 EDI
 OCR
 OU

Health and Social Care – Level 3
Awarding body:
 C&G
 CACHE
 EDEXCEL
 EDI
 OCR
 OU

Health and Social Care – Level 4
Awarding body:
 EDI

Housing – Level 2
Awarding body:
 C&G

Housing – Level 3
Awarding body:
 C&G

Housing and Council Tax Benefits – Level 3
Awarding body:
 IRRV

Leadership and Management for Care Services – Level 4
Awarding body:
 EDI

Learning, Development and Support Services for Children, Young People and Those who Care for Them – Level 3
Awarding body:
 EDEXCEL
 OCR

Medical Assistance – Level 2
Awarding body:
 C&G

Oral Healthcare Support – Level 2
Awarding body:
 C&G

Oral Healthcare: Dental Nursing – Level 3
Awarding body:
 C&G

Registered Managers (Adults) – Level 4
Awarding body:
 EDI

Support Services in Health Care – Level 2
Awarding body:
 C&G
 EDEXCEL
 EDI

National Vocational Qualification

Understanding Health Improvement – Level 2
Awarding body:
 RIPH

QCF Diploma

Support Work in Schools – Level 3
Awarding body:
 CACHE

Qualifications and Credit Framework (Award)

Work with Parents – Level 2
Awarding body:
 C&G

Work with Parents – Level 3
Awarding body:
 C&G

Qualifications and Credit Framework (Diploma)

Support Work in Schools – Level 3
Awarding body:
 CACHE

Scottish Vocational Qualification

**GP Referrals: Low Risk Conditions –
Level 3**
Awarding body:
C&G

**Health (Perioperative Care - Surgical
Support) – Level 3**
Awarding body:
SQA

**Health (Perioperative Care Support) –
Level 2**
Awarding body:
SQA

Health and Care – Level 2
Awarding body:
C&G

Health and Care – Level 3
Awarding body:
C&G

Health and Social Care – Level 2
Awarding body:
C&G
SQA

Health and Social Care – Level 3
Awarding body:
C&G

Health and Social Care – Level 4
Awarding body:
C&G

**Health and Social Care (Adults) –
Level 3**
Awarding body:
SQA

**Health and Social Care (Adults) –
Level 4**
Awarding body:
SQA

**Health and Social Care (Children and
Young People) – Level 3**
Awarding body:
SQA

**Health and Social Care (Children and
Young People) – Level 4**
Awarding body:
SQA

Housing – Level 2
Awarding body:
SQA & CIH

Housing – Level 3
Awarding body:
SQA & CIH

Housing – Level 4
Awarding body:
SQA & CIH

**Housing and Council Tax Benefits –
Level 3**
Awarding body:
IRRV

**Managers in Residential Health Care –
Level 4**
Awarding body:
SQA

Oral Healthcare Support – Level 2
Awarding body:
SQA/C&G/NEBDN

**Oral Healthcare: Dental Nursing –
Level 3**
Awarding body:
SQA/C&G/NEBDN

**Registered Manager in Health and Social
Care – Level 4**
Awarding body:
C&G
SQA

**Support Services in Health Care –
Level 2**
Awarding body:
SQA

Vocational Certificate of Education (Certificate)

Supporting Care Practice – Level 2
Awarding body:
C&G

Supporting Care Practice – Level 3
Awarding body:
    C&G

Vocational Certificate of Education (National Certificate)

Health and Social Care – Level 1
Awarding body:
    OCR

Vocational Certificate of Education (National First Award)

Health and Social Care – Level 1
Awarding body:
    OCR

Vocationallly Related Qualification (Certificate)

Health and Social Care – Level 3
Awarding body:
    EDI

Vocationally Related Qualification

Cervical Cytology – Level 3
Awarding body:
    C&G

Paediatric First Aid – Level 2
Awarding body:
    FAQ

Vocationally Related Qualification (Advanced Diploma)

Medical Secretaries – Level 3
Awarding body:
    AMSPAR

Vocationally Related Qualification (Award)

Disability Awareness – Level 1
Awarding body:
    EDI

Housing – Level 3
Awarding body:
    CIH

Tackling Substance Misuse – Level 3
Awarding body:
    NOCN

Vocationally Related Qualification (BTEC Award)

Infection Control – Level 2
Awarding body:
    EDEXCEL

Paediatric First Aid – Level 2
Awarding body:
    EDEXCEL

Vocationally Related Qualification (BTEC Certificate)

Health and Care – Level 2
Awarding body:
    EDEXCEL

Vocationally Related Qualification (BTEC Diploma)

Health and Care – Level 1
Awarding body:
    EDEXCEL

Vocationally Related Qualification (BTEC First Certificate)

Health and Social Care – Level 2
Awarding body:
    EDEXCEL

Vocationally Related Qualification (BTEC First Diploma)

Health and Social Care – Level 2
Awarding body:
EDEXCEL

Vocationally Related Qualification (BTEC Introductory Diploma)

Health and Social Care – Level 1
Awarding body:
EDEXCEL

Vocationally Related Qualification (BTEC National Certificate)

Health Studies – Level 3
Awarding body:
EDEXCEL

Vocationally Related Qualification (BTEC National Diploma)

Health Studies – Level 3
Awarding body:
EDEXCEL

Vocationally Related Qualification (Certificate)

Basic First Aid – Level 2
Awarding body:
FAQ

Communication with Deaf People – Level 2
Awarding body:
CACDP

Communication with Deafblind People – Level 2
Awarding body:
CACDP

Control of Infection and Contamination – Level 2
Awarding body:
EDEXCEL

DeafBlind Support Work – Level 2
Awarding body:
OCR

Diabetic Retinopathy Screening – Level 3
Awarding body:
C&G

Emergency First Aid in the Workplace – Level 2
Awarding body:
EDI

GP Referrals: Low Risk Conditions – Level 3
Awarding body:
CYQ

Health and Social Care – Level 2
Awarding body:
EDI

Health and Social Care – Level 3
Awarding body:
EDI

Housing – Level 2
Awarding body:
CIH

Infection Control – Level 2
Awarding body:
NCFE

Introduction to Caring for Adults – Level 1
Awarding body:
EDI

Medical Assistance – Level 2
Awarding body:
C&G

Mental Health Work – Level 2
Awarding body:
C&G

Moving and Handling – Level 1
Awarding body:
EDI

Note-taking for Deaf People – Level 2
Awarding body:
CACDP

**Providing Therapeutic Activities for
Older People – Level 3**
Awarding body:
C&G

Safe Use of Infusion Devices – Level 3
Awarding body:
C&G

**Supporting Users of Assistive
Technology – Level 2**
Awarding body:
C&G

Volunteering – Level 2
Awarding body:
NCFE

**Working with People who have Learning
Disabilities – Level 2**
Awarding body:
C&G
NOCN

**Working with People who have Learning
Disabilities – Level 3**
Awarding body:
C&G
NOCN

Vocationally Related Qualification (Diploma)

Anatomy and Physiology – Level 3
Awarding body:
ITEC

**Understanding the Health Care
Environment for Providers of
Complementary Therapies – Level 3**
Awarding body:
VTCT

Vocationally Related Qualification (Intermediate Diploma)

Medical Reception – Level 2
Awarding body:
AMSPAR

Vocationally Related Qualification (Introductory Certificate)

Housing – Level 2
Awarding body:
EDEXCEL
HAB

Housing – Level 3
Awarding body:
EDEXCEL

Housing – Level 4
Awarding body:
EDEXCEL
HAB

Vocationally Related Qualification (National Award)

Health and Social Care – Level 1
Awarding body:
OCR

Vocationally Related Qualification (National Certificate)

Health and Social Care – Level 2
Awarding body:
OCR

**Health, Social Care and Early Years –
Level 3**
Awarding body:
OCR

Housing – Level 3
Awarding body:
CIH
HAB

Housing – Level 4
Awarding body:
　HAB

Housing and Council Tax Benefits – Level 3
Awarding body:
　HCIMA

Vocationally Related Qualification (National Diploma)

Health, Social Care and Early Years – Level 3
Awarding body:
　OCR

Vocationally Related Qualification (National Extended Diploma)

Health, Social Care and Early Years – Level 3
Awarding body:
　OCR

Publishing

VOCATIONAL QUALIFICATIONS

BTEC Professional Certificate

Web Publishing – Level 4
Awarding body:
EDEXCEL

National Vocational Qualification

Desktop Publishing – Level 2
Awarding body:
C&G

Desktop Publishing – Level 3
Awarding body:
C&G

Newspaper Writing – Level 4
Awarding body:
EDI

Scottish Vocational Qualification

Desktop Publishing – Level 2
Awarding body:
SQA & SPEF

Desktop Publishing – Level 3
Awarding body:
SQA & SPEF

Newspaper Writing – Level 4
Awarding body:
NCFE

Vocationally Related Qualification

Desktop Publishing Skills – Level 3
Awarding body:
ABC

Vocationally Related Qualification (Award)

Desktop Publishing – Level 1
Awarding body:
C&G

Desktop Publishing – Level 2
Awarding body:
C&G

Features Journalism Skills – Level 3
Awarding body:
ABC

Library Materials Conservation – Level 3
Awarding body:
ABC

Teeline Shorthand for Journalists – Level 3
Awarding body:
ABC

Writing Skills for Journalism – Level 3
Awarding body:
ABC

Vocationally Related Qualification (Certificate)

Text Production – Level 1
Awarding body:
GOAL

Text Production – Level 2
Awarding body:
GOAL

Text Production – Level 3
Awarding body:
GOAL

Vocationally Related Qualification (Double Award)

News Journalism – Level 3
Awarding body:
   ABC

Retail

APPRENTICESHIPS

Apprenticeships and Advanced Apprenticeships in Retail
www.skillsmartretail.com

VOCATIONAL QUALIFICATIONS

Advanced Vocational Certificate of Education

Retail and Distributive Services – Level 3
Awarding body:
EDEXCEL
OCR

BTEC National Award

Retail – Level 3
Awarding body:
EDEXCEL

BTEC National Certificate

Retail – Level 3
Awarding body:
EDEXCEL

BTEC National Diploma

Retail – Level 3
Awarding body:
EDEXCEL

Certificate

Checkout Advisors – Level 2
Awarding body:
C&G

Retail – Entry 3
Awarding body:
OCR

Retail Credit Advisors – Level 2
Awarding body:
C&G

Retail Merchandisers – Level 2
Awarding body:
C&G

Retail Sales Advisors – Level 2
Awarding body:
C&G

Retail Stock Controller – Level 2
Awarding body:
C&G

Store Keepers (Goods in) – Level 2
Awarding body:
C&G

Store Keepers (Goods Out) – Level 2
Awarding body:
C&G

Entry Level Certificate

Retail – Entry 2
Awarding body:
OCNW

Retail – Entry 3
Awarding body:
OCNW

Foundation General National Vocational Qualification

Retail and Distributive Services – Level 1
Awarding body:
EDEXCEL

Higher Professional Diploma

Retail Management – Level 4
Awarding body:
  C&G

Intermediate General National Vocational Qualification

Retail and Distributive Services – Level 1
Awarding body:
  OCR

Retail and Distributive Services – Level 2
Awarding body:
  OCR

Retail and Distributive Services – Level 5
Awarding body:
  EDEXCEL

National Vocational Qualification

Optical Retailing – Level 2
Awarding body:
  C&G

Retail Operations – Level 2
Awarding body:
  C&G
  EDI
  OCR

Retail Operations – Level 3
Awarding body:
  C&G
  EDI
  OCR

Qualifications and Credit Framework (Award)

Retail Skills – Level 1
Awarding body:
  EDI
  OCR

Retail Skills – Level 2
Awarding body:
  EDI

Retail Skills – Level 3
Awarding body:
  C&G

Qualifications and Credit Framework (Certificate)

Retail Skills – Level 1
Awarding body:
  C&G
  EDI
  OCR

Qualifications and Credit Framework (Diploma)

Retail Skills – Level 1
Awarding body:
  C&G
  EDI
  OCR

Scottish Vocational Qualification

Optical Retailing – Level 2
Awarding body:
  SQA

Retail – Level 2
Awarding body:
  C&G

Retail – Level 3
Awarding body:
  C&G

Retail Operations – Level 2
Awarding body:
  C&G
  EDI
  SQA

Retail Operations – Level 3
Awarding body:
  C&G
  EDI
  SQA

Vocationally Related Qualification (BTEC Certificate)

Retail Beauty Consultancy – Level 2
Awarding body:
  EDEXCEL

Vocationally Related Qualification (BTEC Diploma)

Retail Beauty Consultancy – Level 2
Awarding body:
  EDEXCEL

Vocationally Related Qualification (BTEC First Certificate)

Retail – Level 2
Awarding body:
  EDEXCEL

Vocationally Related Qualification (BTEC First Diploma)

Retail – Level 2
Awarding body:
  EDEXCEL

Vocationally Related Qualification (BTEC National Award)

Retail – Level 3
Awarding body:
  EDEXCEL

Vocationally Related Qualification (BTEC National Certificate)

Retail – Level 3
Awarding body:
  EDEXCEL

Vocationally Related Qualification (BTEC National Diploma)

Retail – Level 3
Awarding body:
  EDEXCEL

Vocationally Related Qualification (Certificate)

Introducing Retail – Level 1
Awarding body:
  OCR

Introducing Retail – Level 2
Awarding body:
  OCR

Introduction to Retailing – Level 1
Awarding body:
  ASET
  EDI

Retail – Level 2
Awarding body:
  OCR

Retail – Level 3
Awarding body:
  OCR

Retail Operations – Level 2
Awarding body:
  EDI

Retail Operations – Level 3
Awarding body:
  EDI

Retail Principles – Level 2
Awarding body:
  C&G

Retailing – Level 2
Awarding body:
  C&G

Retailing – Level 3
Awarding body:
  C&G

Underage Sales Prevention – Level 2
Awarding body:
 EDI

Vocationally Related Qualification (Diploma)

Fashion Retail – Level 2
Awarding body:
 ABC

Fashion Retail – Level 3
Awarding body:
 ABC

Vocationally Related Qualification (National Certificate)

Licensed Retailing – Level 2
Awarding body:
 BIIAB

Licensing Practitioners – Level 2
Awarding body:
 BIIAB

Personal Licence Holders – Level 2
Awarding body:
 BIIAB
 EDI

Vocationally Related Qualification (Scottish Certificate)

Personal Licence Holders – Level 2
Awarding body:
 EDI

Roofing

APPRENTICESHIPS

Construction (Craft) Apprenticeships
www.bconstructive.co.uk

VOCATIONAL QUALIFICATIONS

National Vocational Qualification

Roofing Occupations – Level 1
Awarding body:
C&G/CITB

Roofing Occupations – Level 3
Awarding body:
C&G/CITB

Sales

APPRENTICESHIPS

Apprenticeships and Advanced
Apprenticeships in Sales and Telesales
www.cim.co.uk

VOCATIONAL QUALIFICATIONS

National Vocational Qualification

Sales – Level 2
Awarding body:
  C&G

Sales – Level 3
Awarding body:
  C&G

Telesales – Level 2
Awarding body:
  C&G

Telesales – Level 3
Awarding body:
  C&G

Vehicle Sales – Level 2
Awarding body:
  IMI

Vehicle Sales – Level 3
Awarding body:
  IMI

Scottish Vocational Qualification

Sales Management – Level 4
Awarding body:
  EDI

Vehicle Sales – Level 2
Awarding body:
  IMI

Vehicle Sales – Level 3
Awarding body:
  IMI

Sciences

APPRENTICESHIPS

Apprenticeships and Advanced Apprenticeships in Chemical, Pharmaceutical, Petrochemical Manufacture and Refining Industries
www.cogent-scc.com

Apprenticeships and Advanced Apprenticeships in Laboratory Technicians Working in Education and in Laboratory Technicians (Generic)
www.caats.com
www.semta.org.uk

VOCATIONAL QUALIFICATIONS

Advanced Vocational Certificate of Education

Science – Level 3
Awarding body:
AQA
EDEXCEL
OCR

Advanced Vocational Certificate of Education (Double Award)

Science – Level 3
Awarding body:
AQA
EDEXCEL
OCR

BTEC Higher National Certificate

Applied Biology – Level 5
Awarding body:
EDEXCEL

Applied Chemistry – Level 5
Awarding body:
EDEXCEL

Applied Physics – Level 5
Awarding body:
EDEXCEL

Biomedical Science – Level 5
Awarding body:
EDEXCEL

BTEC Higher National Diploma

Applied Biology – Level 5
Awarding body:
EDEXCEL

Applied Chemistry – Level 5
Awarding body:
EDEXCEL

Biomedical Science – Level 5
Awarding body:
EDEXCEL

BTEC National Certificate

Applied Science – Level 3
Awarding body:
EDEXCEL

BTEC National Diploma

Applied Science – Level 3
Awarding body:
EDEXCEL

Certificate

Biology – Level 3
Awarding body:
OCNW

Psychological Perspectives – Level 3
Awarding body:
OCNW

Psychology – Level 2
Awarding body:
OCNW

Foundation General National Vocational Qualification

Science – Level 1
Awarding body:
AQA
EDEXCEL
OCR

Intermediate General National Vocational Qualification

Science – Level 2
Awarding body:
AQA
EDEXCEL
OCR

National Vocational Qualification

Clinical Laboratory Support – Level 2
Awarding body:
C&G
EDEXCEL

Other General Qualification (Certificate)

Human Physiology – Level 2
Awarding body:
OCNW

Scottish Vocational Qualification

Applied Science – Level 3
Awarding body:
EDEXCEL

Clinical Laboratory Support – Level 2
Awarding body:
SQA

Laboratory and Associated Technical Activities – Level 1
Awarding body:
PAA/VQSET

Laboratory and Associated Technical Activities – Level 1
Awarding body:
SQA

Laboratory and Associated Technical Activities (Educational Pathway) – Level 4
Awarding body:
PAA/VQSET
SQA

Laboratory and Associated Technical Activities (Industrial Pathway) – Level 2
Awarding body:
PAA/VQSET
SQA

Laboratory and Associated Technical Activities (Industrial Pathway) – Level 3
Awarding body:
PAA/VQSET
SQA

Vocationally Related Qualification (BTEC First Certificate)

Applied Science – Level 2
Awarding body:
EDEXCEL

Vocationally Related Qualification (BTEC First Diploma)

Applied Science – Level 2
Awarding body:
EDEXCEL

Vocationally Related Qualification (BTEC National Award)

Applied Science – Level 3
Awarding body:
GEM-A

Vocationally Related Qualification (Certificate)

Laboratory Technical Skills – Level 1
Awarding body:
PAA/VQSET

Laboratory Technical Skills – Level 2
Awarding body:
PAA/VQSET

Laboratory Technical Skills – Level 3
Awarding body:
PAA/VQSET

Security

APPRENTICESHIPS

Apprenticeships and Advanced Apprenticeships in Safety, Security and Loss Prevention and Retails and Leisure Security, Security Sector and Security Systems
info@sito.co.uk

VOCATIONAL QUALIFICATIONS

Community Safety for Accredited Persons

Vocationally Related Qualification – Level 2
Awarding body:
EDEXCEL

National Vocational Qualification

Providing Security Services – Level 2
Awarding body:
C&G

Revenue Protection – Level 3
Awarding body:
C&G

Security Management (Supervisor) – Level 3
Awarding body:
C&G

Spectator Safety – Level 2
Awarding body:
EDI

Spectator Safety – Level 3
Awarding body:
EDI

Spectator Safety Management – Level 4
Awarding body:
EDI

Scottish Vocational Qualification

Fire, Security and Emergency Alarm Systems – Level 2
Awarding body:
SQA & SITO

Knowledge of Security and Emergency Alarm Systems – Level 3
Awarding body:
C&G

Providing Security Services – Level 2
Awarding body:
SQA & SITO

Providing Security Services (CCTV Operations) – Level 2
Awarding body:
SQA & SITO

Providing Security Services (Door Supervision) – Level 2
Awarding body:
SQA & SITO

Providing Security Services (Events Security) – Level 2
Awarding body:
SQA & SITO

Providing Security Services (Reception Security) – Level 2
Awarding body:
SQA & SITO

Providing Security Services (Retail Security) – Level 2
Awarding body:
SQA & SITO

Providing Security Services (Static and Patrol Guarding) – Level 2
Awarding body:
  SQA & SITO

Revenue Protection – Level 3
Awarding body:
  C&G

Security Systems: Technical Services – Level 3
Awarding body:
  SQA & SITO

Vocationally Related Qualification

Security Practitioners – Level 2
Awarding body:
  C&G

Vocationally Related Qualification (Award)

CCTV Operations (Public Space Surveillance) – Level 2
Awarding body:
  NOCN

Vocationally Related Qualification (BTEC Award)

CCTV Operations (Public Space Surveillance) – Level 2
Awarding body:
  EDEXCEL

Door Supervision – Level 2
Awarding body:
  EDEXCEL

Security Operations – Level 2
Awarding body:
  EDEXCEL

Vocationally Related Qualification (BTEC Certificate)

Close Protection Operations – Level 3
Awarding body:
  EDEXCEL

Vocationally Related Qualification (Certificate)

CCTV Operatives (Public Space Surveillance) – Level 2
Awarding body:
  EDI

Community Safety for Accredited Persons – Level 2
Awarding body:
  EDI

Developing Personal Safety and Security Skills – Level 2
Awarding body:
  EDI

Door Supervisors – Level 2
Awarding body:
  EDI
  NCFE

Introduction to Working in the Security Industry – Level 1
Awarding body:
  EDI

Knowledge for the Professional Security Officer – Level 2
Awarding body:
  C&G

Knowledge of Security and Emergency Alarm Systems – Level 3
Awarding body:
  C&G

Personal Safety Awareness – Level 1
Awarding body:
  EDI

Security Guards – Level 2
Awarding body:
  C&G
  EDI

Security Key Holding and Alarm Response – Level 3
Awarding body:
 EDI

Static and Patrol Security Skills – Level 1
Awarding body:
 SITO

Vocationally Related Qualification (National Certificate)

Door Supervisors – Level 2
Awarding body:
 BIIAB

Door Supervisors - Licensed Premises – Level 2
Awarding body:
 BIIAB

Sport, Leisure and Recreation

APPRENTICESHIPS

Apprenticeships and Advanced
Apprenticeships in Active Leisure and
Learning and in Cultural Heritage
Recreation and Learning
www.skillsactive.com
www.chuto.co.uk

VOCATIONAL QUALIFICATIONS

Advanced Vocational Certificate of Education

Leisure and Recreation – Level 3
Awarding body:
  AQA
  EDEXCEL
  OCR

Advanced Vocational Certificate of Education (Double Award)

Leisure and Recreation – Level 3
Awarding body:
  AQA
  EDEXCEL

Award

Active, Healthy Living – Level 1
Awarding body:
  PREMIER IQ

Certificate

Developing Personal Health and Fitness – Level 1
Awarding body:
  ABC

Developing Personal Health and Fitness – Level 2
Awarding body:
  ABC

Exercise Studies – Level 1
Awarding body:
  NCFE

National Vocational Qualification

Achieving Excellence in Sports Performance – Level 3
Awarding body:
  EDEXCEL

Activity Leadership – Level 2
Awarding body:
  EDEXCEL

Mechanical Ride Operations (Leisure Parks, Piers and Attractions) – Level 2
Awarding body:
  C&G

Outdoor Education, Development Training, Recreation – Level 3
Awarding body:
  C&G
  EDEXCEL

Sport, Recreation and Allied Occupations – Level 1
Awarding body:
  C&G
  EDEXCEL
  OCR

Sport, Recreation and Allied Occupations – Level 2
Awarding body:
  C&G

Sport, Recreation and Allied Occupations: Activity Leadership – Level 2
Awarding body:
CYQ

Sport, Recreation and Allied Occupations: Coaching, Teaching and Instructing – Level 2
Awarding body:
EDEXCEL
OCR

Sport, Recreation and Allied Occupations: Operational Services – Level 2
Awarding body:
C&G
CYQ
EDEXCEL
OCR

Sport, Recreation and Allied Occupations: Operations and Development – Level 3
Awarding body:
C&G
EDEXCEL
OCR

Sport, Recreation and Allied Occupations: Spectator Control – Level 2
Awarding body:
C&G

Sport, Recreation and Allied Occupations: Spectator Control – Level 3
Awarding body:
C&G

Scottish Vocational Qualification

Achieving Excellence in Sports Performance – Level 3
Awarding body:
SQA

Bingo Operations – Level 2
Awarding body:
SQA

Gym Instructing – Level 2
Awarding body:
C&G

Higher Sports Leadership – Level 3
Awarding body:
C&G

Leisure and Recreation – Level 3
Awarding body:
C&G
EDEXCEL

Match Officials in Football – Level 2
Awarding body:
C&G
EDEXCEL
OCR

Outdoor Education, Development Training, Recreation – Level 3
Awarding body:
EDEXCEL
OCR

Outdoor Education, Development Training, Recreation (Outdoor Education) – Level 3
Awarding body:
CYMCAQ
SQA

Outdoor Education, Development Training, Recreation: Recreation – Level 3
Awarding body:
SQA

Personal Development for the Outdoor Industry – Level 1
Awarding body:
CYMCAQ

Sport – Level 2
Awarding body:
CYMCAQ

Sport – Level 3
Awarding body:
CYMCAQ

Sport, Recreation and Allied Occupations – Level 1
Awarding body:
SQA

Sport, Recreation and Allied Occupations: Activity Leadership – Level 2
Awarding body:
SQA

Sport, Recreation and Allied Occupations: Instructing Exercise and Fitness – Level 2
Awarding body:
SQA

Sport, Recreation and Allied Occupations: Operational Services – Level 2
Awarding body:
SQA

Sport, Recreation and Allied Occupations: Operations and Development – Level 3
Awarding body:
SQA

Sport, Recreation and Allied Occupations: Teaching and Instruction – Level 2
Awarding body:
SQA

Vocational Certificate of Education (Certificate)

Understanding the Fitness, Leisure and Recreation Industry – Level 2
Awarding body:
CYQ

Vocationally Related Qualification

Motorsport Operations – Level 2
Awarding body:
NCFE

Vocationally Related Qualification (Award)

Activity Leadership – Level 2
Awarding body:
EDI

Circuit Training – Level 2
Awarding body:
CYQ

Healthy Living – Level 1
Awarding body:
EDI

Higher Sports Leadership – Level 3
Awarding body:
Sports Leaders UK

Sports Leadership – Level 1
Awarding body:
Sports Leaders UK

Vocationally Related Qualification (BTEC Certificate)

Sport and Leisure – Level 2
Awarding body:
EDEXCEL

Vocationally Related Qualification (BTEC First Certificate)

Sport – Level 2
Awarding body:
EDEXCEL

Vocationally Related Qualification (BTEC First Diploma)

Sport – Level 2
Awarding body:
EDEXCEL

Sport and Exercise Sciences – Level 2
Awarding body:
EDEXCEL

Vocationally Related Qualification (BTEC Higher National Certificate)

Sport and Exercise Sciences – Level 5
Awarding body:
EDEXCEL

Sport and Leisure Management – Level 5
Awarding body:
EDEXCEL

Vocationally Related Qualification (BTEC Higher National Diploma)

Sport and Leisure Management – Level 5
Awarding body:
EDEXCEL

Vocationally Related Qualification (BTEC Introductory Diploma)

Sport and Leisure – Level 1
Awarding body:
EDEXCEL

Vocationally Related Qualification (BTEC National Award)

Sport – Level 3
Awarding body:
EDEXCEL

Sport and Exercise Sciences – Level 3
Awarding body:
EDEXCEL

Vocationally Related Qualification (BTEC National Certificate)

Sport – Level 3
Awarding body:
EDEXCEL

Vocationally Related Qualification (BTEC National Diploma)

Sport – Level 3
Awarding body:
EDEXCEL

Sport and Exercise Sciences – Level 3
Awarding body:
EDEXCEL

Vocationally Related Qualification (Certificate)

Advanced Fitness Instructing – Level 3
Awarding body:
NCFE

Assessing in the Active Leisure Sector – Level 3
Awarding body:
CYQ

Development and Management of Swimming Programmes – Level 3
Awarding body:
ASA

Fitness Industry Studies – Level 2
Awarding body:
CCEA
NCFE

Fitness Instructing – Level 2
Awarding body:
CYQ
NCFE

Gym Instructing – Level 2
Awarding body:
PREMIER IQ

Internal Verifying in the Active Leisure Sector – Level 3
Awarding body:
CYQ

Match Officials in Football – Level 1
Awarding body:
1ST4SPORT

Match Officials in Football – Level 2
Awarding body:
 1ST4SPORT

Motorsports Incident Marshalling – Level 2
Awarding body:
 OCNW

Outdoor Activity Leadership – Level 2
Awarding body:
 NCFE

Personal Development for the Outdoor Industry – Level 1
Awarding body:
 NCFE

Personal Health and Lifestyle Awareness – Level 2
Awarding body:
 EDI

Sport and Leisure Studies – Level 1
Awarding body:
 NCFE

Sport and Recreation and Allied Occupations: Coaching, Teaching and Instructing – Level 3
Awarding body:
 C&G

Sport, Recreation and Allied Occupations: Industry and Organisational Awareness – Level 2
Awarding body:
 1ST4SPORT
 C&G

Sport, Recreation and Allied Occupations: Industry and Organisational Awareness – Level 3
Awarding body:
 1ST4SPORT

Sports and Fitness Therapies – Level 2
Awarding body:
 VTCT

Sports Coaching – Level 2
Awarding body:
 NCFE

Sports First Aid – Level 2
Awarding body:
 FAQ

Sports Massage – Level 3
Awarding body:
 PREMIER IQ

Sports Officials – Level 2
Awarding body:
 1ST4SPORT

Training and Development in the Active Leisure Sector – Level 3
Awarding body:
 CYQ

Trampoline Coaching – Level 1
Awarding body:
 BG

Understanding the Fitness, Leisure and Recreation Industry – Level 3
Awarding body:
 CYQ

Weight-Training for Sport (Free-weights) – Level 2
Awarding body:
 1ST4SPORT

Vocationally Related Qualification (Diploma)

Sports and Fitness Therapy Techniques – Level 3
Awarding body:
 VTCT

Sports Massage – Level 3
Awarding body:
 ITEC

Sports Massage Therapy – Level 3
Awarding body:
 VTCT

Vocationally Related Qualification (Higher Professional Diploma)

Sport and Exercise Sciences – Level 4
Awarding body:
    C&G

Vocationally Related Qualification (National Certificate)

Sport – Level 2
Awarding body:
    OCR

Sport – Level 3
Awarding body:
    OCR

Vocationally Related Qualification (National Diploma)

Sport – Level 3
Awarding body:
    OCR

Vocationally Related Qualification (National Extended Diploma)

Sport – Level 3
Awarding body:
    OCR

Vocationally Related Qualification (Progression Award)

Sport and Leisure – Level 1
Awarding body:
    C&G

Sport and Leisure – Level 2
Awarding body:
    C&G

Sport and Recreation – Level 3
Awarding body:
    C&G

Storage and Distribution

APPRENTICESHIPS

Apprenticeships and Advanced
Apprenticeships in Distribution,
Warehousing and Storage, Storage and
Warehousing and Traffic Office
www.skillsforlogistics.org

VOCATIONAL QUALIFICATIONS

BTEC Professional Diploma

Logistics – Level 4
Awarding body:
   EDEXCEL

National Vocational Qualification

Bulk Liquid Warehousing – Level 2
Awarding body:
   C&G
   PAA/VQSET

Carry and Deliver Goods – Level 2
Awarding body:
   C&G
   EDEXCEL
   EDI
   OCR

Distribution Control – Level 2
Awarding body:
   CABWI

Distribution, Warehousing and Storage Operations – Level 2
Awarding body:
   C&G
   EAL
   EDEXCEL
   OCR
   PAA/VQSET
   QFI

Distribution, Warehousing and Storage Operations – Level 3
Awarding body:
   C&G
   EAL
   OCR
   PAA/VQSET
   QFI

Distributive Operations – Level 1
Awarding body:
   C&G
   EAL
   EDEXCEL
   OCR
   PAA/VQSET
   QFI

Driving Goods Vehicles – Level 2
Awarding body:
   C&G
   EDEXCEL
   EDI
   OCR
   QFI

Driving Goods Vehicles – Level 3
Awarding body:
   C&G
   EDEXCEL
   EDI
   OCR
   QFI

Logistic Operations Management – Level 3
Awarding body:
   EDI

Mail Services – Level 2
Awarding body:
   C&G

Moving Loads – Level 3
Awarding body:
   ECITB

Storage and Warehousing – Level 2
Awarding body:
C&G

Storage and Warehousing – Level 3
Awarding body:
C&G

Traffic Office – Level 2
Awarding body:
C&G

Traffic Office – Level 3
Awarding body:
C&G

Warehousing and Storage – Level 1
Awarding body:
EDI

Warehousing and Storage – Level 2
Awarding body:
EDI

Scottish Vocational Qualification

Carry and Deliver Goods – Level 2
Awarding body:
SQA & Skills for Logistics

Distribution Control – Level 2
Awarding body:
SQA & CABWI

Distribution, Warehousing and Storage Operations – Level 2
Awarding body:
EAL
SQA

Distribution, Warehousing and Storage Operations – Level 3
Awarding body:
EAL
SQA

Distributive Operations – Level 1
Awarding body:
EAL
SQA

Driving Goods Vehicles – Level 2
Awarding body:
SQA & Skills for Logistics

Driving Goods Vehicles – Level 3
Awarding body:
SQA & Skills for Logistics

Forklift Truck Operations – Level 2
Awarding body:
EDEXCEL

Integrated Logistics Support Management – Level 4
Awarding body:
C&G
EDEXCEL
QFI

Logistics – Level 4
Awarding body:
EDEXCEL/RHDTC

Moving Loads – Level 3
Awarding body:
ECITB
OCR

Performing Road Haulage and Distribution Operations – Level 3
Awarding body:
SQA & CABWI

Stevedoring – Level 2
Awarding body:
SQA

Storage and Warehousing – Level 2
Awarding body:
SQA & Skills for Logistics

Storage and Warehousing – Level 3
Awarding body:
SQA & Skills for Logistics

Traffic Office – Level 2
Awarding body:
SQA & Skills for Logistics

Traffic Office – Level 3
Awarding body:
SQA & Skills for Logistics

Vocationally Related Qualification (BTEC First Diploma)

Logistics – Level 2
Awarding body:
  EDEXCEL

Vocationally Related Qualification (BTEC National Certificate)

Logistics – Level 3
Awarding body:
  EDEXCEL

Vocationally Related Qualification (BTEC National Award)

Logistics – Level 3
Awarding body:
  EDEXCEL

Vocationally Related Qualification (Certificate of Competence)

Forklift Truck Operations – Level 2
Awarding body:
  NPTC

Surveying

APPRENTICESHIPS

Advanced Apprenticeships in Property
Service Administration
www.assetskills.org

VOCATIONAL QUALIFICATIONS

National Vocational Qualification

Quantity Surveying Practice – Level 4
Awarding body:
ABBE

Scottish Vocational Qualification

Quantity Surveying Practice – Level 4
Awarding body:
ABBE

Surveying Support – Level 3
Awarding body:
SQA & ABBE

Surveying Support (Building Surveying) – Level 3
Awarding body:
ABBE

Surveying Support (General Practice) – Level 3
Awarding body:
SQA & ABBE

Valuation – Level 4
Awarding body:
SQA & ABBE

Teaching and Training

APPRENTICESHIPS

Apprenticeships and Advanced Apprenticeships in Teaching Assistants and Learning and Development /Direct Training and Support
supportstaffenquiry@tda.gov.uk
www.ento.co.uk

VOCATIONAL QUALIFICATIONS

Associate

Instrumental/Vocal Teaching – Level 4
Awarding body:
TCL

Principles of Instrumental/Vocal Teaching – Level 4
Awarding body:
TCL

Specialist Music Teaching – Level 4
Awarding body:
TCL

Teaching (ATCL) – Level 4
Awarding body:
TCL

BTEC Award

Instructional Techniques – Level 4
Awarding body:
EDEXCEL

BTEC Certificate

Instructional Techniques – Level 4
Awarding body:
EDEXCEL

Certificate

Adult Literacy – Level 1
Awarding body:
EDEXCEL

Adult Literacy – Level 2
Awarding body:
EDEXCEL

Adult Literacy – Entry Level
Awarding body:
EDEXCEL

Adult Numeracy – Level 1
Awarding body:
EDEXCEL

Adult Numeracy – Level 2
Awarding body:
EDEXCEL

Adult Numeracy – Entry Level
Awarding body:
EDEXCEL

Assessing and Teaching Learners with Specific Learning Difficulties (Dyslexia) – Level 5
Awarding body:
OCR

Assessing and Teaching Learners with Specific Learning Difficulties (Dyslexia) – Level 7
Awarding body:
OCR

FE Teaching for ESOL Subject Specialists – Level 7
Awarding body:
CAMBRIDGE ESOL

FE Teaching Stage 1 – Level 4
Awarding body:
ABC
C&G
OCNW

FE Teaching Stage 2 – Level 4
Awarding body:
 ABC
 C&G
 EDEXCEL
 OCR
 TCL

FE Teaching Stage 2 (TESOL) – Level 4
Awarding body:
 CAMBRIDGE ESOL

FE Teaching Stage 3 – Level 5
Awarding body:
 C&G
 CAMBRIDGE ESOL
 EDEXCEL
 OCNW
 TCL

Teaching English to Speakers of Other Languages – Level 4
Awarding body:
 TCL

Teaching English to Speakers of Other Languages (CELTA) – Level 4
Awarding body:
 CAMBRIDGE ESOL

Diploma

Assessing and Teaching Learners with Specific Learning Difficulties (Dyslexia) – Level 7
Awarding body:
 OCR

Principles of Instrumental/Vocal Teaching – Level 4
Awarding body:
 ABRSM

Speech and Drama Education – Level 5
Awarding body:
 LAMDA

Teaching English to Speakers of Other Languages – Level 7
Awarding body:
 TCL

Teaching English to Speakers of Other Languages (DELTA) – Level 7
Awarding body:
 CAMBRIDGE ESOL

Entry Level Certificate

ESOL for Work – Entry 3
Awarding body:
 C&G
 CAMBRIDGE ESOL
 ESB
 SQA

Skills for Working Life – Entry 2
Awarding body:
 NPTC

Skills for Working Life – Entry 3
Awarding body:
 NPTC

ESOL Certificate

ESOL for Work – Level 1
Awarding body:
 C&G
 CAMBRIDGE ESOL
 ESB
 OCNW
 SQA

Fellowship

Education Studies – Level 7
Awarding body:
 TCL

Higher Level Certificate

Higher Level Study Skills – Level 4
Awarding body:
 C&G

Supporting Learning in Primary Schools – Level 4
Awarding body:
 OU

Licentiate

Instrumental/Vocal Teaching – Level 6
Awarding body:
ABRSM
TCL

Specialist Music Teaching – Level 6
Awarding body:
TCL

Teaching – Level 6
Awarding body:
TCL

National Vocational Qualification

Co-ordination of Learning and Development Provision – Level 4
Awarding body:
EDI

Direct Training and Support – Level 3
Awarding body:
C&G
CIPD
EAL
EDEXCEL
EDI
OCR
PAA/VQSET

Direct Training and Support – Level 4
Awarding body:
EDI

Instructing Exercise and Fitness – Level 2
Awarding body:
C&G
CYQ
EDEXCEL
OCR

Instructing Physical Activity and Exercise – Level 3
Awarding body:
CYQ
OCR

Learning and Development – Level 3
Awarding body:
C&G
CIPD
EAL
EDEXCEL
EDI
OCR
OU
PAA/VQSET

Learning and Development – Level 4
Awarding body:
EDI

Learning and Development Provision – Level 4
Awarding body:
EDI

Teaching Assistants – Level 2
Awarding body:
C&G
CACHE
EDEXCEL
OCR

Teaching Assistants – Level 3
Awarding body:
C&G
CACHE
EDEXCEL
OCR

Other General Qualification (Award)

General Religious Education – Level 1
Awarding body:
NOCN

General Religious Education – Level 2
Awarding body:
NOCN

General Religious Education – Level 3
Awarding body:
NOCN

Other General Qualification (Certificate)

Learning Support – Level 2
Awarding body:
GQAL

QCF Diploma

Teaching English (ESOL) in the Lifelong Learning Sector – Level 5
Awarding body:
C&G

Teaching in the Lifelong Learning Sector – Level 5
Awarding body:
C&G
EDEXCEL

Teaching Mathematics (Numeracy) in the Lifelong Learning Sector – Level 5
Awarding body:
C&G

Qualifications and Credit Framework (Award)

Preparing to Teach in the Lifelong Learning Sector – Level 4
Awarding body:
CIPD

Support Work in Schools – Level 3
Awarding body:
CACHE

Qualifications and Credit Framework (BTEC Certificate)

Teaching in the Lifelong Learning Sector – Level 4
Awarding body:
EDEXCEL

Qualifications and Credit Framework (Certificate)

Support Work in Schools – Level 3
Awarding body:
CACHE

Teaching in the Lifelong Learning Sector – Level 4
Awarding body:
OCNW

Qualifications and Credit Framework (Diploma)

Support Work in Schools – Level 3
Awarding body:
CACHE

Teaching in the Lifelong Learning Sector – Level 5
Awarding body:
EDEXCEL

Scottish Vocational Qualification

Assessing and Teaching Learners with Specific Learning Difficulties (Dyslexia) – Level 5
Awarding body:
ASA

Assessing Candidates' Performance Through Observation – Level 3
Awarding body:
ASA
STA

Assessing Candidates' Performance Through Observation – Level 4
Awarding body:
BG

Assessing Candidates' Using a Range of Methods – Level 3
Awarding body:
BG

Classroom Assistants – Level 2
Awarding body:
C&G
SQA

Classroom Assistants – Level 3
Awarding body:
  C&G
  SQA

Coaching (Football) – Level 3
Awarding body:
  SQA

Coaching (Rugby Union) – Level 3
Awarding body:
  SQA

Coordination of Learning and Development Provision – Level 4
Awarding body:
  C&G
  CIPD
  SQA & CIPD

Direct Training and Support – Level 3
Awarding body:
  C&G
  CIPD
  SQA & CIPD

Learning and Development – Level 3
Awarding body:
  C&G
  CIPD
  EAL
  SQA & CIPD

Learning and Development – Level 4
Awarding body:
  C&G
  CIPD
  EAL
  SQA & CIPD

Learning and Development – Level 5
Awarding body:
  CIPD
  SQA & CIPD

Management of Learning and Development Provision – Level 4
Awarding body:
  C&G
  CIPD

Managing of Learning and Development Provision – Level 4
Awarding body:
  SQA & CIPD

Vocationally Related Qualification (Award)

Adapting Gym Instructions for Adolescents – Level 2
Awarding body:
  Active IQ

Coaching – Level 2
Awarding body:
  ASA

Delivering e-Testing – Level 3
Awarding body:
  EDI

Instructing Physical Activity for Ante/Post Natal Exercise – Level 3
Awarding body:
  CYQ

Preparing to Teach in the Lifelong Learning Sector – Level 3
Awarding body:
  EDI

Preparing to Teach in the Lifelong Learning Sector – Level 4
Awarding body:
  EDI

Vocationally Related Qualification (BTEC Certificate)

Training for Improved Sports Perfocmance – Level 3
Awarding body:
  EDEXCEL

Vocationally Related Qualification (Certificate)

Assistant Fitness Instructing – Level 1
Awarding body:
  CYQ

Coaching – Level 1
Awarding body:
  1ST4SPORT

Coaching – Level 2
Awarding body:
1ST4SPORT

Coaching Angling – Level 2
Awarding body:
1ST4SPORT

Coaching Football – Level 1
Awarding body:
1ST4SPORT

Coaching Football – Level 3
Awarding body:
1ST4SPORT

Coaching Golf – Level 2
Awarding body:
ASQ

Coaching Golf – Level 3
Awarding body:
ASQ

Coaching Hockey – Level 1
Awarding body:
1ST4SPORT

Coaching Hockey – Level 2
Awarding body:
1ST4SPORT

Coaching Orienteering – Level 2
Awarding body:
1ST4SPORT

Coaching Rugby Union – Level 1
Awarding body:
1ST4SPORT

Coaching Rugby Union – Level 2
Awarding body:
1ST4SPORT

Coaching Studies – Level 2
Awarding body:
1ST4SPORT

Deliverers of Conflict Management Training – Level 3
Awarding body:
EDEXCEL

Delivering Learning Using a Virtual Learning Environment (VLE) – Level 3
Awarding body:
EDI

Education Practice: ICT Advanced – Level 3
Awarding body:
EDI

Education Practice: ICT Skills – Level 3
Awarding body:
EDI

Education Principles and Practice – Level 3
Awarding body:
EDI

Educational Use of ICT – Level 3
Awarding body:
EDI

Instructing Health Related Exercise for Children – Level 2
Awarding body:
CYQ

Learning Support – Level 2
Awarding body:
C&G

Personal Training – Level 3
Awarding body:
CYQ
PREMIER IQ

Scuba Instruction – Level 3
Awarding body:
PADI

Speaking and Listening Skills for Adult Learners – Level 1
Awarding body:
ESB

Speaking and Listening Skills for Adult Learners – Level 2
Awarding body:
ESB

Speaking and Listening Skills for Adult Learners – Level 3
Awarding body:
ESB

Teaching Exercise and Fitness – Level 2
Awarding body:
OCR

Teaching in the Lifelong Learning Sector – Level 3
Awarding body:
   EDI

Teaching Swimming – Level 1
Awarding body:
   ASA
   STA

Teaching Swimming – Level 2
Awarding body:
   ASA

Vocationally Related Qualification (Diploma)

Education Practice: ICT Advanced – Level 4
Awarding body:
   EDI

Vocationally Related Qualification (Foundation Certificate)

Assistant Coaching – Level 1
Awarding body:
   BG

Vocationally Related Qualification (Intermediate Certificate)

Club Coaching – Level 2
Awarding body:
   BG

Testing/Quality Control

VOCATIONAL QUALIFICATIONS

National Vocational Qualification

Non-Destructive Testing – Level 3
Awarding body:
ECITB

Scottish Vocational Qualification

Non-Destructive Testing – Level 3
Awarding body:
ECITB

Textiles/Crafts/Fashion

APPRENTICESHIPS

Apprenticeships and Advanced
Apprenticeships in Textiles
enquiries@skillfast-uk.uk.org

VOCATIONAL QUALIFICATIONS

BTEC Professional Diploma

Costume Management – Level 5
Awarding body:
EDEXCEL

Certificate

Creative Craft – Level 1
Awarding body:
NCFE

Creative Craft – Level 2
Awarding body:
NCFE

Creative Craft – Level 3
Awarding body:
NCFE

National Vocational Qualification

Apparel Manufacturing Technology – Level 3
Awarding body:
C&G

Leather Production – Level 2
Awarding body:
C&G

Leather Production – Level 3
Awarding body:
C&G

Leathergoods – Level 2
Awarding body:
C&G

Manufacturing Sewn Products – Level 1
Awarding body:
C&G

Manufacturing Sewn Products – Level 2
Awarding body:
C&G

Manufacturing Textiles – Level 1
Awarding body:
C&G

Manufacturing Textiles – Level 2
Awarding body:
C&G

Manufacturing Textiles – Level 3
Awarding body:
C&G

Qualifications and Credit Framework (Award)

Distribution Services in the Textile Industry Working Practices – Level 2
Awarding body:
ABC

Qualifications and Credit Framework (Certificate)

Distribution Services in the Textile Industry Working Practices – Level 2
Awarding body:
ABC

Scottish Vocational Qualification

Costume (Live Performance) – Level 2
Awarding body:
SQA & METIER

Costume (Live Performance) – Level 3
Awarding body:
SQA & METIER

Costume Management – Level 4
Awarding body:
ABC

Manufacturing Textiles – Level 1
Awarding body:
SQA

Manufacturing Textiles – Level 2
Awarding body:
SQA

Manufacturing Textiles – Level 3
Awarding body:
SQA

Vocationally Related Qualification (BTEC Award)

Fashion and Clothing – Level 1
Awarding body:
EDEXCEL

Fashion and Clothing – Level 2
Awarding body:
EDEXCEL

Fashion and Clothing – Level 3
Awarding body:
EDEXCEL

Textiles – Level 1
Awarding body:
EDEXCEL

Textiles – Level 2
Awarding body:
EDEXCEL

Textiles – Level 3
Awarding body:
EDEXCEL

Vocationally Related Qualification (BTEC Certificate)

Fashion and Clothing – Level 1
Awarding body:
EDEXCEL

Fashion and Clothing – Level 2
Awarding body:
EDEXCEL

Fashion and Clothing – Level 3
Awarding body:
EDEXCEL

Textiles – Level 1
Awarding body:
EDEXCEL

Textiles – Level 3
Awarding body:
EDEXCEL

Vocationally Related Qualification (BTEC Diploma)

Fashion and Clothing – Level 1
Awarding body:
EDEXCEL

Fashion and Clothing – Level 2
Awarding body:
EDEXCEL

Fashion and Clothing – Level 3
Awarding body:
EDEXCEL

Textiles – Level 1
Awarding body:
EDEXCEL

Textiles – Level 2
Awarding body:
EDEXCEL

Textiles – Level 3
Awarding body:
EDEXCEL

Vocationally Related Qualification (BTEC National Certificate)

Fashion and Clothing – Level 3
Awarding body:
EDEXCEL

Vocationally Related Qualification (BTEC National Diploma)

Fashion and Clothing – Level 3
Awarding body:
EDEXCEL

Textiles – Level 3
Awarding body:
EDEXCEL

Vocationally Related Qualification (Certificate)

Aspects of Multi-Cultural Fashion – Level 2
Awarding body:
ABC

Creative Craft – Level 1
Awarding body:
CCEA

Creative Craft – Level 2
Awarding body:
CCEA

Creative Craft – Level 3
Awarding body:
CCEA

Vocationally Related Qualification (Diploma)

Fashion, Theatre and Media Make-Up – Level 3
Awarding body:
ITEC

Vocationally Related Qualification (Higher National Certificate)

Fashion and Textiles – Level 5
Awarding body:
EDEXCEL

Theology and Religious Studies

VOCATIONAL QUALIFICATIONS

Vocationally Related Qualification (Certificate)

Applied Christian Studies – Level 3
Awarding body:
    ABC

The Way of Faith (Beginnings) (Pilot) – Level 1
Awarding body:
    EDI

The Way of Faith (Horizons) – Level 3
Awarding body:
    EDI

The Way of Faith (Pathways) – Level 2
Awarding body:
    EDI

Town Planning

VOCATIONAL QUALIFICATIONS

Scottish Vocational Qualification

Town Planning Support (Administration) – Level 3
Awarding body:
SQA & ABBE

Town Planning Support (Development Control) – Level 3
Awarding body:
SQA & ABBE

Town Planning Support (Enforcement) – Level 3
Awarding body:
SQA & ABBE

Town Planning Support (Technical) – Level 3
Awarding body:
SQA & ABBE

Transport Studies

APPRENTICESHIPS

Apprenticeships in Traffic Office
www.skillsforlogistics.org

VOCATIONAL QUALIFICATIONS

Higher Level Advanced Diploma

Logistics and Transport – Level 6
Awarding body:
  CILT

National Vocational Qualification

Controlling Parking Areas – Level 2
Awarding body:
  C&G
  EDEXCEL

Parking Clerical – Level 3
Awarding body:
  C&G

PCV Driving (Bus and Coach) – Level 2
Awarding body:
  EDI

Road Passenger Transport – Level 2
Awarding body:
  EDEXCEL

Supervising Parking Control Activities – Level 3
Awarding body:
  C&G

Temporary Traffic Management – Level 2
Awarding body:
  C&G/CITB

Transportation – Level 3
Awarding body:
  OU

Professional Diploma

Logistics and Transport – Level 5
Awarding body:
  CILT

Scottish Vocational Qualification

Controlling Parking Areas – Level 2
Awarding body:
  SQA & SITO

Controlling Parking Areas (Barrier and Paystation Control) – Level 2
Awarding body:
  SQA & SITO

Controlling Parking Areas (Display Parking Control) – Level 2
Awarding body:
  SQA & SITO

Controlling Parking Areas (Vehicle Clamping) – Level 2
Awarding body:
  SQA & SITO

Controlling Parking Areas (Vehicle Removal) – Level 2
Awarding body:
  SQA & SITO

PCV Driving (Bus and Coach) – Level 2
Awarding body:
  EDI

Rail Transport Operations (Driving) – Level 2
Awarding body:
  SQA

Rail Transport Operations (Passenger Services) – Level 2
Awarding body:
  SQA

Rail Transport Operations (Shunting) – Level 2
Awarding body:
SQA

Rail Transport Operations (Signal Operations) – Level 2
Awarding body:
SQA

Road Passenger Transport (Coach) – Level 2
Awarding body:
EDI
SQA

Vocationally Related Qualification (BTEC Award)

Transporting Passengers by Taxi and Private Hire – Level 2
Awarding body:
EDEXCEL

Vocationally Related Qualification (BTEC Certificate)

Transporting Passengers by Bus and Coach – Level 2
Awarding body:
EDEXCEL

Vocationally Related Qualification (Certificate of Competence)

All Terrain Vehicle Handling – Level 2
Awarding body:
NPTC

Off Road Driving – Level 2
Awarding body:
NPTC

Transport of Livestock by Road – Level 2
Awarding body:
NPTC

Vocationally Related Qualification (Certificate)

Defensive Driving – Level 2
Awarding body:
EDI

Driving Instruction – Level 3
Awarding body:
EDI

Road Passenger Transport – Level 2
Awarding body:
EDI
GOAL

Vocationally Related Qualification (Higher Certificate)

Logistics and Transport – Level 3
Awarding body:
CILT

Vocationally Related Qualification (Introductory Certificate)

Logistics and Transport – Level 2
Awarding body:
CILT

Travel and Tourism

APPRENTICESHIPS

Apprenticeships and Advanced
Apprenticeships in Travel Services
Recreation and Travel and in Hospitality
www.people1st.co.uk

VOCATIONAL QUALIFICATIONS

Advanced Vocational Certificate of Education

Travel and Tourism – Level 3
Awarding body:
 AQA
 EDEXCEL
 OCR

Advanced Vocational Certificate of Education (Double Award)

Travel and Tourism – Level 3
Awarding body:
 AQA
 EDEXCEL
 OCR

Certificate

Travel and Tourism – Entry Level
Awarding body:
 AQA

Foundation General National Vocational Qualification

Leisure and Tourism – Level 1
Awarding body:
 AQA
 EDEXCEL

Higher Professional Diploma

Travel and Tourism – Level 4
Awarding body:
 C&G

Intermediate General National Vocational Qualification

Leisure and Tourism – Level 2
Awarding body:
 AQA
 EDEXCEL
 OCR

National Vocational Qualification

Aviation Operations in the Air - Cabin Crew – Level 2
Awarding body:
 C&G

Aviation Operations in the Air - Cabin Crew – Level 3
Awarding body:
 C&G

Port Operations – Level 2
Awarding body:
 EAL

Supervision of Port Operations – Level 3
Awarding body:
 EAL

Travel and Tourism – Level 2
Awarding body:
 C&G

Travel and Tourism – Level 3
Awarding body:
 C&G

Scottish Vocational Qualification

Port Passenger Operations – Level 2
Awarding body:
  C&G

Tourist Information Services – Level 2
Awarding body:
  SQA

Tourist Information Services – Level 3
Awarding body:
  SQA

Vocationally Related Qualification ((BTEC National Award)

Aviation Operations – Level 3
Awarding body:
  EDEXCEL

Vocationally Related Qualification (Advanced National Diploma)

Travel and Tourism – Level 3
Awarding body:
  C&G

Vocationally Related Qualification (Award)

Basic Expedition Leadership – Level 2
Awarding body:
  Sports Leaders UK

Vocationally Related Qualification (BTEC Certificate)

Preparation for Air Cabin Crew Service – Level 2
Awarding body:
  EDEXCEL

Preparation for Tourist Guiding – Level 2
Awarding body:
  EDEXCEL

Vocationally Related Qualification (BTEC Diploma)

Travel Operations – Level 2
Awarding body:
  EDEXCEL

Travel Operations – Level 3
Awarding body:
  EDEXCEL

Vocationally Related Qualification (BTEC First Certificate)

Travel and Tourism – Level 2
Awarding body:
  EDEXCEL

Vocationally Related Qualification (BTEC First Diploma)

Travel and Tourism – Level 2
Awarding body:
  EDEXCEL

Vocationally Related Qualification (BTEC Higher National Certificate)

Travel and Tourism Management – Level 5
Awarding body:
  EDEXCEL

Vocationally Related Qualification (BTEC Higher National Diploma)

Travel and Tourism Management – Level 5
Awarding body:
  EDEXCEL

Vocationally Related Qualification (BTEC Intermediate Diploma)

Overseas Resort Operations – Level 2
Awarding body:
  EDEXCEL

Vocationally Related Qualification (BTEC Introductory Certificate)

Hospitality, Travel and Tourism – Level 1
Awarding body:
  EDEXCEL

Vocationally Related Qualification (BTEC Introductory Diploma)

Hospitality, Travel and Tourism – Level 1
Awarding body:
  EDEXCEL

Vocationally Related Qualification (BTEC National Award)

Airline and Airport Operations – Level 3
Awarding body:
  EDEXCEL

Travel and Tourism – Level 3
Awarding body:
  EDEXCEL

Vocationally Related Qualification (BTEC National Certificate)

Airline and Airport Operations – Level 3
Awarding body:
  EDEXCEL

Aviation Operations – Level 3
Awarding body:
  EDEXCEL

Travel and Tourism – Level 3
Awarding body:
  EDEXCEL

Vocationally Related Qualification (BTEC National Diploma)

Airline and Airport Operations – Level 3
Awarding body:
  EDEXCEL

Aviation Operations – Level 3
Awarding body:
  EDEXCEL

Travel and Tourism – Level 3
Awarding body:
  EDEXCEL

Vocationally Related Qualification (Certificate)

Air Cabin Crew Skills – Level 2
Awarding body:
  OCNW

Airline Cabin Crew – Level 2
Awarding body:
  NCFE

Introducing Travel and Tourism – Level 1
Awarding body:
  OCR

Introducing Travel and Tourism – Level 2
Awarding body:
  OCR

Resort Representatives – Level 2
Awarding body:
  NCFE

Travel – Level 1
Awarding body:
  NCFE

Travel (Tour Operators) – Level 2
Awarding body:
C&G

Travel (Tour Operators) – Level 3
Awarding body:
C&G

Travel (Travel Agency) – Level 2
Awarding body:
C&G

Travel (Travel Agency) – Level 3
Awarding body:
C&G

Travel and Tourism – Level 1
Awarding body:
C&G

Travel and Tourism – Level 2
Awarding body:
C&G
NCFE

Travel and Tourism – Level 3
Awarding body:
C&G

Travel and Tourism Management – Level 3
Awarding body:
NCFE

Vocationally Related Qualification (First Award)

Travel and Tourism – Level 2
Awarding body:
C&G

Vocationally Related Qualification (First Diploma)

Travel and Tourism – Level 2
Awarding body:
C&G

Vocationally Related Qualification (Introductory Award)

Travel and Tourism – Level 1
Awarding body:
C&G

Vocationally Related Qualification (Introductory Diploma)

Travel and Tourism – Level 1
Awarding body:
C&G

Vocationally Related Qualification (National Award)

Travel and Tourism – Level 3
Awarding body:
C&G

Vocationally Related Qualification (National Certificate)

Travel and Tourism – Level 2
Awarding body:
OCR

Travel and Tourism – Level 3
Awarding body:
OCR

Vocationally Related Qualification (National Diploma)

Travel and Tourism – Level 3
Awarding body:
C&G

Vocationally Related Qualification (National Extended Diploma)

Travel and Tourism – Level 3
Awarding body:
OCR

Uniformed Services

APPRENTICESHIPS

Apprenticeships and Advanced
Apprenticeships in Community Justice
www.skillsforjustice.com

VOCATIONAL QUALIFICATIONS

National Vocational Qualification

Contribute to the Search and/or Disposal Function – Level 2
Awarding body:
EDEXCEL

Police Supervisory Management – Level 3
Awarding body:
C&G
OCR
OU

Policing – Level 3
Awarding body:
C&G
EDEXCEL
OCR
OU

Provide Support for Search or Munition Clearance Operations – Level 1
Awarding body:
EDEXCEL

Search for and Disposal of Munitions – Level 3
Awarding body:
EDEXCEL

Search for Munitions and/or Specified Targets – Level 3
Awarding body:
EDEXCEL

Shotfiring Operations – Level 3
Awarding body:
EMP

Supervisory Management of Munition Clearance and/or Search Operations – Level 3
Awarding body:
EDEXCEL

Scottish Vocational Qualification

Contribute to the Search and/or Disposal Function – Level 2
Awarding body:
SQA

Planning and Management of Munition Clearance Operations – Level 4
Awarding body:
SQA

Provide Support for Search or Munition Clearance Operations – Level 1
Awarding body:
SQA

Search for and Disposal of Munitions – Level 3
Awarding body:
SQA

Search for Munitions and/or Specified Targets – Level 3
Awarding body:
SQA

Shotfiring Operations – Level 3
Awarding body:
EMP

Supervisory Management of Munition Clearance and/or Search Operations – Level 3
Awarding body:
SQA

Vocationally Related Qualification (Certificate)

Entry to the Uniformed Services – Level 1
Awarding body:
  NCFE

Entry to the Uniformed Services – Level 2
Awarding body:
  NCFE

Entry to the Uniformed Services – Level 3
Awarding body:
  NCFE

Vehicle Maintenance

APPRENTICESHIPS

Apprenticeships and Advanced
Apprenticeships in Motor Industry
(Vehicle Maintenance and Repair) Land
Passenger Transportation: Maintenance
of Automatic Vehicles
www.automotiveskills.org.uk

VOCATIONAL QUALIFICATIONS

National Vocational Qualification

Automotive Engineering – Level 3
Awarding body:
   EAL

**Transport Engineering and Maintenance
– Level 1**
Awarding body:
   EDI

**Transport Engineering and Maintenance
– Level 2**
Awarding body:
   EDI

**Transport Engineering and Maintenance
– Level 3**
Awarding body:
   EDI

Scottish Vocational Qualification

Automotive Engineering – Level 3
Awarding body:
   EAL

**Roadside Assistance and Recovery –
Level 2**
Awarding body:
   C&G
   IMI

**Roadside Assistance and Recovery
(Recovery) – Level 3**
Awarding body:
   C&G
   IMI

**Roadside Assistance and Recovery
(Roadside Assistance) – Level 3**
Awarding body:
   C&G
   IMI

**Transport Engineering and Maintenance
– Level 1**
Awarding body:
   EDI

**Transport Engineering and Maintenance
– Level 2**
Awarding body:
   EDI

**Transport Engineering and Maintenance
– Level 3**
Awarding body:
   EDI

**Vehicle Body & Paint Operations (Body
Repair) – Level 2**
Awarding body:
   C&G
   IMI

**Vehicle Body & Paint Operations (Body
Repair) – Level 3**
Awarding body:
   C&G

**Vehicle Body & Paint Operations
(Met/Body Fitting) – Level 2**
Awarding body:
   C&G
   IMI

**Vehicle Body & Paint Operations
(Met/Body Fitting) – Level 3**
Awarding body:
   C&G
   IMI

Vehicle Body & Paint Operations (Refinishing) – Level 2
Awarding body:
C&G
IMI

Vehicle Body & Paint Operations (Refinishing) – Level 3
Awarding body:
C&G
IMI

Vehicle Body and Paint Operations – Level 3
Awarding body:
C&G
IMI

Vehicle Fitting – Level 1
Awarding body:
C&G
IMI

Vehicle Fitting – Level 2
Awarding body:
C&G
IMI

Vehicle Fitting (Fast Fit) – Level 1
Awarding body:
C&G
IMI

Vehicle Fitting (Fast Fit) – Level 2
Awarding body:
C&G
IMI

Vehicle Fitting (Tyres) – Level 1
Awarding body:
C&G
IMI

Vehicle Fitting (Tyres) – Level 2
Awarding body:
C&G
IMI

Vehicle Fitting Operations – Level 3
Awarding body:
C&G
IMI

Vehicle Fitting Operations (General Vehicle Fitting) – Level 2
Awarding body:
C&G
IMI

Vehicle Fitting Operations (Specialist Tyre Fitting) – Level 2
Awarding body:
C&G
IMI

Vehicle Fitting Operations (Tyre Fitting) – Level 1
Awarding body:
C&G
IMI

Vehicle Maintenance – Level 1
Awarding body:
C&G
IMI

Vehicle Maintenance (Light Vehicles) – Level 2
Awarding body:
IMI

Vehicle Maintenance (Vehicle Valeting) – Level 1
Awarding body:
EDEXCEL

Vehicle Maintenance and Repair – Level 1
Awarding body:
EDEXCEL

Vehicle Maintenance and Repair – Level 2
Awarding body:
EDEXCEL
IMI

Vehicle Maintenance and Repair – Level 3
Awarding body:
EDEXCEL
IMI

Vehicle Maintenance and Repair (Auto Electrical) – Level 2
Awarding body:
C&G
IMI

Vehicle Maintenance and Repair (Auto Electrical) – Level 3
Awarding body:
  C&G
  IMI

Vehicle Maintenance and Repair (Heavy Vehicles) – Level 2
Awarding body:
  C&G
  IMI

Vehicle Maintenance and Repair (Heavy Vehicles) – Level 3
Awarding body:
  C&G
  IMI

Vehicle Maintenance and Repair (Light Vehicles) – Level 2
Awarding body:
  C&G
  IMI

Vehicle Maintenance and Repair (Light Vehicles) – Level 3
Awarding body:
  C&G
  IMI

Vehicle Maintenance and Repair (Mobile Electronics and Security) – Level 2
Awarding body:
  C&G
  IMI

Vehicle Maintenance and Repair (Motorcycles) – Level 2
Awarding body:
  C&G
  IMI

Vehicle Maintenance and Repair (Motorcycles) – Level 3
Awarding body:
  C&G
  IMI

Vehicle Parts Operations – Level 1
Awarding body:
  C&G

Vehicle Parts Operations – Level 2
Awarding body:
  C&G

Vehicle Parts Operations – Level 3
Awarding body:
  C&G
  IMI

Vocationally Related Qualification (BTEC National Award)

Vehicle Technology – Level 3
Awarding body:
  EDEXCEL

Vocationally Related Qualification (BTEC National Certificate)

Vehicle Technology – Level 3
Awarding body:
  EDEXCEL

Vocationally Related Qualification (BTEC National Diploma)

Vehicle Technology – Level 3
Awarding body:
  EDEXCEL

Vocationally Related Qualification (Certificate)

Motorsport Scrutineering – Level 1
Awarding body:
  NCFE

Transport Engineering and Maintenance – Level 2
Awarding body:
  EDI

**Transport Engineering and Maintenance
– Level 3**
Awarding body:
EDI

Waste and Refuse

APPRENTICESHIPS

Apprenticeships and Advanced
Apprenticeships in Water Industry
(Process Operations) and in
Environmental Conservation
www.euskills.co.uk
www.lantra.co.uk

VOCATIONAL QUALIFICATIONS

National Vocational Qualification

**Managing Transfer Hazardous Waste –
Level 4**
Awarding body:
   WAMITAB

**Waste Management Operations –
Level 1**
Awarding body:
   C&G
   WAMITAB

**Waste Management Operations –
Level 2**
Awarding body:
   C&G
   WAMITAB

**Waste Management Operations: Civic
Amenity Site – Level 3**
Awarding body:
   C&G
   WAMITAB

**Waste Management Operations: Closed
Landfill – Level 3**
Awarding body:
   C&G
   WAMITAB

**Waste Management Operations: Inert
Waste – Level 3**
Awarding body:
   C&G
   WAMITAB

**Waste Management Supervision –
Level 3**
Awarding body:
   C&G
   WAMITAB

Scottish Vocational Qualification

**Managing Waste Collection Operations
– Level 4**
Awarding body:
   SQA & WAMITAB

**Waste Management Operations –
Level 3**
Awarding body:
   SQA & WAMITAB

**Waste Management Operations: Civic
Amenity Site – Level 3**
Awarding body:
   SQA & WAMITAB

**Waste Management Operations: Closed
Landfill – Level 3**
Awarding body:
   SQA & WAMITAB

**Waste Management Operations: Inert
Waste – Level 3**
Awarding body:
   SQA & WAMITAB

**Waste Management Operations:
Managing Incineration – Level 4**
Awarding body:
   SQA & WAMITAB

Waste Management Operations: Managing Landfill Hazardous Waste – Level 4
Awarding body:
SQA & WAMITAB

Waste Management Operations: Managing Landfill Non-Hazardous Waste – Level 4
Awarding body:
SQA & WAMITAB

Waste Management Operations: Managing Transfer Hazardous Waste – Level 4
Awarding body:
SQA & WAMITAB

Waste Management Operations: Managing Transfer Non-Hazardous Waste – Level 4
Awarding body:
SQA & WAMITAB

Waste Management Operations: Managing Treatment Hazardous Waste – Level 4
Awarding body:
SQA & WAMITAB

Waste Management Operations: Managing Treatment Non-Hazardous Waste – Level 4
Awarding body:
SQA & WAMITAB

Waste Management Supervision – Level 3
Awarding body:
SQA & WAMITAB

Water Byelaws Enforcement – Level 3
Awarding body:
SQA & CABWI

Water Treatment and Supply

APPRENTICESHIPS

Apprenticeships and Advanced
Apprenticeships in Water Industry
(Process Operations)
www.euskills.co.uk

VOCATIONAL QUALIFICATIONS

National Vocational Qualification

Controlling Water Operations (Process) – Level 3
Awarding body:
CABWI

Leakage Control – Level 2
Awarding body:
CABWI

Leakage Control – Level 3
Awarding body:
CABWI

Maintain Water Supply (Network) – Level 3
Awarding body:
CABWI

Monitoring the Water Environment – Level 2
Awarding body:
CABWI

Water Fittings Regulations Enforcement – Level 3
Awarding body:
CABWI

Water Industry Operations (Sewerage Maintenance) – Level 2
Awarding body:
CABWI

Scottish Vocational Qualification

Leakage Control – Level 2
Awarding body:
SQA & CABWI

Leakage Control – Level 3
Awarding body:
SQA & CABWI

Maintain Water Supply (Network) – Level 3
Awarding body:
SQA & CABWI

Water Industry Operations – Level 3
Awarding body:
SQA & CABWI

Well Services: Electric Logging (Cased Hole Services) – Level 2
Awarding body:
SQA & cogent

Well Services: Electric Logging (Cased Hole Services) – Level 3
Awarding body:
SQA & cogent

Well Services: Electric Logging (Open Hole Services) – Level 2
Awarding body:
SQA & cogent

Well Services: Electric Logging (Open Hole Services) – Level 3
Awarding body:
SQA & cogent

Well Services: Mechanical Wireline – Level 2
Awarding body:
SQA & cogent

Well Services: Tubing Operations – Level 2
Awarding body:
SQA & cogent

Vocationally Related Qualification (Certificate)

Protection of Water, Environment and Recommendations – Level 3
Awarding body:
    NPTC

Vocationally Related Qualification (Diploma)

Maintenance of Hydraulic Systems and Components – Level 3
Awarding body:
    EAL

Welding

APPRENTICESHIPS

Apprenticeships and Advanced
Apprenticeships in Engineering or Metal
Processing
www.enginuity.org.uk
www.metskills.co.uk

VOCATIONAL
QUALIFICATIONS

National Vocational Qualification

Fabrication and Welding – Level 3
Awarding body:
  EAL

Fabrication and Welding Engineering – Level 2
Awarding body:
  C&G
  EAL
  ETCAL

Fabrication and Welding Engineering – Level 3
Awarding body:
  C&G
  ETCAL

Welding - Pipework – Level 3
Awarding body:
  ECITB

Welding - Plate – Level 3
Awarding body:
  ECITB

Scottish Vocational Qualification

Fabrication and Welding – Level 3
Awarding body:
  EAL

Fabrication and Welding Engineering – Level 2
Awarding body:
  EAL

Production Engineering: Welding – Level 2
Awarding body:
  EAL

Production Engineering: Welding – Level 3
Awarding body:
  EAL

Welding - Pipework – Level 3
Awarding body:
  EAL
  ECITB

Welding - Plate – Level 3
Awarding body:
  ECITB

Welding (Pipework) – Level 3
Awarding body:
  ECITB

Welding (Plate) – Level 3
Awarding body:
  ECITB

Vocationally Related Qualification

Fabrication and Welding Practice – Level 3
Awarding body:
  ABC

Vocationally Related Qualification (Certificate)

Fabrication and Welding Practice – Level 1
Awarding body:
  ABC

**Fabrication and Welding Practice –
Level 2**
Awarding body:
ABC

*Vocationally Related
Qualification (Diploma)*

**Manual Metal-Arc (MMA) Welding
Process – Level 3**
Awarding body:
EAL

*Vocationally Related
Qualification (Progression
Award)*

**Production Engineering: Welding –
Level 2**
Awarding body:
C&G

**Production Engineering: Welding –
Level 3**
Awarding body:
C&G

Woodwork

APPRENTICESHIPS

Apprenticeships and Advanced
Apprenticeships in Construction (Craft)
www.citb.org.uk

VOCATIONAL QUALIFICATIONS

National Vocational Qualification

Wood Occupations – Level 2
Awarding body:
EDEXCEL

**Wood Preserving - Industrial Pre
Treatment (Construction) – Level 2**
Awarding body:
C&G/CITB

Woodmachining – Level 2
Awarding body:
C&G

Woodmachining – Level 3
Awarding body:
C&G

Scottish Vocational Qualification

Wood Occupations – Level 1
Awarding body:
SQA

Part 3

Sources of Information

Introduction

The acronyms listed at the beginning of this section are mainly quoted in those entries to be found in Part Two – The Directory of Vocational Qualifications – and the full addresses of most of these bodies will be found in the list that follows, together with other relevant useful addresses.

Acronyms

AAT	Association of Accounting Technicians
ABBE	Awarding Body for the Built Environment
ABC	Awarding Body Consortium
ABDO	Association of British Dispensing Opticians
ABRSM	Associated Board of the Royal Schools of Music
ACRIB	Air Conditioning and Refrigeration Industry Board
AFAQ-ETA	French Quality Assurance Assocation – Electricity Training Association
AMSPAR	Association of Medical Secretaries, Practice Managers, Administrators and Receptionists
AQA	Assessment and Qualifications Alliance
ASA	Amateur Swimming Association
ASDAN	Award Scheme Development and Accreditation Network
BG	British Gymnastics
BAGMA	British Agricultural and Garden Machinery Association
BBO	British Ballet Organisation
BCF	British Coatings Federation
BCS	British Computer Society
BHEST	British Horseracing Education and Standards Trust
BHS	British Horse Society
BII	British Institute of Innkeeping
BSC	British Safety Council
BSGA	British Sign and Graphics Association
BST	British Sports Trust
BTDA	British Theatre Dance Association
C&G	City and Guilds
CACDP	The Council for the Advancement of Communication between Deaf and Hearing People
CACHE	Council for Awards in Children's Care and Education
CAMBRIDGE ESOL	University of Cambridge ESOL Examinations
CCEA	Council for Curriculum, Examinations and Assessment
CIAT	Chartered Institute of Architectural Technologists
CIEH	Chartered Institute of Environmental Health
CIH	Chartered Institute of Housing
CII	Chartered Insurance Institute
CILT	Chartered Institute of Logistics and Transport (UK)
CIM	Chartered Institute of Marketing
CIOB	Chartered Institute of Building
CIoBS	Chartered Institute of Bankers In Scotland
CIPD	Chartered Institute of Personnel and Development
CIPR	Chartered Institute of Public Relations
CIPS	Chartered Institute of Purchasing and Supply
CITB	Construction Skills

CMI	Chartered Management Institute
COTAC	Conference on Training in Architectural Conservation
CPCAB	Counselling and Psychotherapy Central Awarding Body
CYMCAQ/ CYQ	Central YMCA Qualifications
DIVQ	Distilling Industry Vocational Qualifications Group
EAL	EMTA Awards Ltd
ECITB	Engineering Construction Industry Training Board
EDI	Education Development International Plc
EMP	Engineering Management Partnership
ESB	English Speaking Board (International) Ltd
ESTTL	Engineering Services Training Trust Ltd
ETCAL	Engineering Training Council Awards Ltd
FAQ	First Aid Qualifications
FDQ	Food and Drink Qualifications
GEM-A	Gemmological Association of Great Britain
GQA	Glass Qualifications Authority
GSMD	Guildhall School of Music and Drama Examination Service
HAB	Hospitality Awarding Body
IAB	International Association of Book-Keepers
ICAA	International Curriculum and Assessment Agency
ICE	Institution of Civil Engineers
ICG	Institute of Career Guidance
ICM	Institute of Credit Management
ICoW	Institute of Clerks of Works of Great Britain Incorporated
IDTA	International Dance Teachers Association
IFS	Institute of Financial Services
IH	Institute of Hospitality
ILEX	Institute of Legal Executives
ILM	Institute of Leadership and Management
IMI	Institute of the Motor Industry
IoL	Chartered Institute of Linguists
IOLET	Institute of Linguists Educational Trust
IOM	Institute of Operations Management
IQL	Institute of Qualified Lifeguards
IRRV	Institute of Revenues, Rating and Valuation
ISMM	Institute of Sales and Marketing Management
ISTD	Imperial Society of Teachers of Dancing
ITEC	International Therapy Examination Council
LA	Lantra
LAMDA	London Academy of Music and Dramatic Art
LANTRA	The Sector Skills Council for the Environmental and Land-based Sector

LCCI	London Chamber of Commerce and Industry Examinations Board
MOD	Ministry of Defence
MRS	Market Research Society
NAEA	National Association of Estate Agents
NEA	National Energy Action
NEBDN	National Examining Board for Dental Nurses
NEBOSH	National Examination Board in Occupational Safety and Health
NOCN	National Open College Network
NPTC	National Proficiency Tests Council
OCNW	Open College of the North West
OCR	Oxford, Cambridge and Royal School of Arts Examinations
OPITO	Offshore Petroleum Industry Training Organisation
OU	Open University
PAA/VQSET	Process Awards Authority/Vocational Qualifications in Science, Engineering and Technology
PADI	Professional Association of Dive Instructors
PIABC	Packaging Industry Awarding Body Company
PMI	The Pensions Management Institute
PREMIER TI	Premier Training International
RAD	Royal Academy of Dance
RCVS	The Royal College of Veterinary Surgeons
RHS	Royal Horticultural Society
RIPH	Royal Institute of Public Health
RSL	Rock School Ltd
RSPH	Royal Society for the Promotion of Health
SAMB	Scottish Association of Master Bakers
SBATC	Scottish Building Apprenticeship and Training Council
SfL	Skills for Logistics
SI	Securities & Investment Institute
SfS	Skills for Security
SJIB	Scottish Joint Industry Board for the Electrical Contracting Industry
SNIJIBPI	Scottish and Northern Ireland Joint Industry Board for the Plumbing Industry
SPEF	Scottish Print Employers Federation
SQA	Scottish Qualifications Authority
STA	Swimming Teachers Association
TCL	Trinity College London
TTF	Timber Trade Federation
TVU	Thames Valley University
UKSIP	UK Society of Investment Professionals
VTCT	Vocational Training Charitable Trust

WAMITAB	Waste Management Industry Training and Advisory Board
WCF	Worshipful Company of Farriers
WCSM	Worshipful Company of Spectacle Makers
WJEC	Welsh Joint Education Committee
WSET	Wine & Spirit Education Trust

Awarding Bodies and Sources of Further Information

1st4Sport Qualifications
Coachwise Ltd
Chelsea Close
Off Amberley Road
Armley
Leeds LS12 4HP
Tel: 0113 290 7610
Fax: 0113 231 9606
enquiries@1st4sportqualifications.com
www.1st4sportqualifications.com

ABDO College Distance Learning Institute
Godmersham Park
Godmersham
Canterbury
Kent CT4 7DT
Tel: 01227 733910
Fax: 01227 733900
general@abdo.org.uk
www.abdo.org.uk

Active IQ
Suite 3, Unit 4
Cromwell Business Centre
New Road
St Ives
Cambridgeshire
PE27 5BG
Tel: 01480 467950
Fax: 01480 467997
info@activeiq.co.uk

AFAQ-ETA
185 Park Street
Bankside
London SE1 9DY
Tel: 020 7922 1630
Fax: 020 7922 1627
www.eta.org.uk

Air Conditioning and Refrigeration Industry Board
Kelvin House
76 Mill Lane
Carshalton
Surrey SM5 2JR
Tel: 020 8254 7842
Fax: 020 8773 0165
www.acrib.org.uk

Amateur Swimming Association
Harold Fern House, Derby Square
Loughborough
Leicestershire LE11 5AL
Tel: 01509 618 700
Fax: 01509 618 701
customerservices@swimming.org
www.britishswimming.org

ASET
124 Micklegate
York YO1 6XJ
Tel: 0845 45 89 500
Fax: 01904 677042
customer.services@aset.ac.uk
www.aset.ac.uk

Assessment and Qualifications Alliance
Stag Hill House
Guildford
Surrey GU2 7XJ
Tel: 01483 506506
Fax: 01483 300152
mailbox@aqa.org.uk
www.aqa.org.uk

Associated Board of the Royal Schools of Music
24 Portland Place
London W1B 1LU
Tel: 020 7636 5400
Fax: 020 7637 0234
www.abrsm.org

Association of Accounting Technicians
140 Aldersgate Street
London
EC1A 4HY
Tel: 0845 863 0800 or 020 7397 3000
www.aat.org.uk

Association of Medical Secretaries, Practice Managers, Administrators and Receptionists
Tavistock House North
Tavistock Square
London WC1H 9LN
Tel: 020 7387 6005
Fax: 020 7388 2648
info@amspar.co.uk
www.amspar.co.uk

Awarding Body Consortium
Duxbury Park
Duxbury Hall Road
Chorley
Lancashire PR7 4AT
Tel: 01257 241428
Fax: 01257 260357
enquiries_chorley@abcawards.co.uk
www.abcawards.co.uk

Award Scheme Development and Accreditation Network (ASDAN)
Wainbrook House
Hudds Vale Road
St George
Bristol BS5 7HY
Tel: 0117 9411126
Fax: 0117 9351112
info@asdan.co.uk
www.asdan.co.uk

British Agricultural and Garden Machinery Association (BAGMA)
Entrance B, Level 1
Salamander Quay West
Park Lane
Harefield UB9 6NZ
Tel: 0870 205 2834
Fax: 0870 205 2835
info@bagma.com
www.bagma.com

British Ballet Organisation (BBO)
Woolborough House
39 Lonsdale Road
Barnes
London SW13 9JP
Tel: 020 8748 1241
Fax: 020 8748 1301
info@bbo.org.uk
www.bbo.org.uk

British Coatings Federation Ltd
James House
Bridge Street
Leatherhead
Surrey KT22 7EP
Tel: 01372 360660
Fax: 01372 376069
enquiry@bcf.co.uk
www.coatings.org.uk

British Computer Society
First Floor, Block D
North Star House
North Star Avenue
Swindon
Wiltshire SN2 1FA
Tel: 01793 417417
Fax: 01793 417444
www.bcs.org.uk

British Gymnastics
Ford Hall
Lilleshall National Sports Centre
Newport
Shropshire TF10 9NB
Tel: 0845 1297129
Fax: 0845 1249089
information@british-gymnastics.org
www.british-gymnastics.org

British Horse Society
Stoneleigh Deer Park
Kenilworth
Warwickshire CV8 2XZ
Tel: 0844 848 1666
Fax: 01926 707800
enquiry@bhs.org.uk
www.bhs.org.uk

British Horseracing Education and Standards Trust
Suite 16, Unit 8, Kings Court
Willie Snaith Road
Newmarket
Suffolk CB8 7SG
Tel: 01638 565130
Fax: 01638 660932
www.bhtb.co.uk

British Institute of Cleaning Science
9 Premier Court
Boarden Close
Moulton Park
Northampton NN3 6LF
Tel: 01604 678710
www.bics.org.uk

British Institute of Innkeeping Awarding Body
Wessex House
80 Park Street
Camberley
Surrey GU15 3PT
Tel: 01276 684449
Fax: 01276 23045
reception@bii.org
www.bii.org

British Safety Council
70 Chancellors Road
London W6 9RS
Tel: 020 8741 1231
Fax: 020 8741 4555
mail@britsafe.org
www.britishsafetycouncil.co.uk

British Sign and Graphics Association
5 Orton Enterprise Centre
Bakewell Road, Orton Southgate
Peterborough PE2 6XU
Tel: 01733 230033
info@bsga.co.uk
www.bsga.co.uk

British Theatre Dance Association
The International Arts Centre
Garden Street
Leicester LE1 3UA
Tel: 0845 166 2179
Fax: 0116 251 4781
info@btda.org.uk
www.btda.org.uk

CABWI Awarding Body
1 Queen Anne's Gate
London SW1H 9BT
Tel: 020 7957 4523
Fax: 020 7957 4641
enquiries@cabwi.co.uk
www.cabwi.co.uk

Cambridge, University of, ESOL Examinations
1 Hills Road
Cambridge CB1 2EU
Tel: 01223 553355
Fax: 01223 460278
esolhelpdesk@ucles.org.uk
www.cambridgeesol.org

Central YMCA Qualifications (CYQ)
112 Great Russell Street
London WC1B 3NQ
Tel: 020 7343 1800
Fax: 020 7436 2687
info@cyq.org.uk
www.cyq.org.uk

The CFA Society of the UK
4th Floor
90 Basinghall Street
London EC2V 5AY
Tel: 020 7796 3000
Fax: 020 7796 3333
info@cfauk.org
www.cfauk.org

Chartered Institute of Architectural Technologists
397 City Road
London EC1V 1NH
Tel: 020 7278 2206
Fax: 020 7837 3194
info@ciat.org.uk
www.ciat.org.uk

Chartered Institute of Bankers In Scotland
Drumsheugh House
38b Drumsheugh Gardens
Edinburgh EH3 7SW
Tel: 0131 473 7777
Fax: 0131 473 7788
info@ciobs.org.uk
www.ciobs.org.uk

Chartered Institute of Building
Englemere
Kings Ride
Ascot
Berks SL5 7TB
Tel: 01344 630700
Fax: 01344 630777
reception@ciob.org.uk
www.ciob.org.uk

Chartered Institute of Environmental Health
Chadwick Court
15 Hatfields
London SE1 8DJ
Tel: 020 7928 6006
Fax: 020 7827 5862
www.cieh.org

Chartered Institute of Housing
Octavia House
Westwood Way
Coventry CV4 8JP
Tel: 024 7685 1700
Fax: 024 7669 5110
customer.services@cih.org
www.cih.org

Chartered Institute of Logistics and Transport (UK)
Logistics and Transport Centre
Earlstrees Court
Earlstrees Road
Corby, Northants
NN17 4AX
Tel: 01536 740100
Fax: 01536 740101
enquiry@ciltuk.org.uk
www.ciltuk.org.uk

Chartered Institute of Marketing
Moor Hall
Cookham
Maidenhead
Berks SL6 9QH
Tel: 01628 427500
Fax: 01628 472499
membershipinfo@cim.co.uk
www.cim.co.uk

Chartered Institute of Personnel and Development (CIPD)
151 The Broadway
London SW19 1JQ
Tel: 020 8612 6200
Fax: 020 8612 6201
www.cipd.co.uk

Chartered Institute of Public Relations
CIPR PR Centre
32 St James's Square
London SW1Y 4JR
Tel: 020 7766 3333
Fax: 020 7766 3334
info@cipr.co.uk
www.cipr.co.uk

Chartered Institute of Purchasing and Supply
Easton House
Church Street
Easton on the Hill
Stamford
Lincolnshire PE9 3NZ
Tel: 01780 756777
Fax: 01780 751610
info@cips.org
www.cips.org

Chartered Insurance Institute
42–48 High Road
South Woodford
London E18 2JP
Tel: 020 8989 8464
Fax: 020 8530 3052
customer.serv@cii.co.uk
www.cii.co.uk

Chartered Management Institute
3rd Floor
2 Savoy Court
Strand
London WC2R 0EZ
Tel: 020 7497 0580
Fax: 020 7497 0463
enquiries@managers.org.uk
www.managers.org.uk

CILT (UK)
Earlstrees Court
Earlstrees Road
Corby
Northants NN17 4AX
Tel: 01536 740105
Fax: 01536 740101

CITB-ConstructionSkills
Bircham Newton
Kings Lynn
Norfolk PE31 6RH
Tel: 01485 577577
call.centre@skills.org
www.citb.co.uk

City and Guilds
1 Giltspur Street
London EC1A 9DD
Tel: 020 7294 2800
Fax: 020 7294 2400
www.cityandguilds.com

Conference on Training in Architectural Conservation
The Building Crafts College
Kennard Road
Stratford
London E15 1AH
Tel: 020 8522 1705
Fax: 020 8522 1309
cotac@thebcc.co.uk
www.cotac.org.uk

The Council for the Advancement of Communication between Deaf and Hearing People
Mersey House
Mandale Business Park
Belmont
Durham DH1 1TH
Tel: 0191 383 1155
Fax: 0191 383 7914
durham@cacdp.org.uk
www.cacdp.org.uk

Council for Awards in Children's Care and Education
Beaufort House
Grosvenor Road
St Albans
Herts AL1 3AW
Tel: 0845 347 2123
Fax: 01727 818618
info@cache.org.uk
www.cache.org.uk

Council for the Curriculum, Examinations and Assessment
29 Clarendon Road
Clarendon Dock
Belfast BT1 3BG
Tel: 028 9026 1200
Fax: 028 9026 1234
info@ccea.org.uk
www.ccea.org.uk

Counselling and Psychotherapy Central Awarding Body (CPCAB)
PO Box 1768
Glastonbury
Somerset BA6 8YP
Tel: 01458 850350
Fax: 01458 852055
admin@cpcab.co.uk
www.cpcab.co.uk

Distilling Industry Vocational Qualifications Group
20 Atholl Crescent
Edinburgh EH3 8HF
Tel: 0131 222 9200
Fax: 0131 222 9237
info@swa.org.uk
www.scotch-whisky.org.uk

Edexcel
One90 High Holborn
London WC1V 7BH
Tel: 0870 240 9800
Fax: 020 7190 5706
www.edexcel.org.uk

EDI Plc
International House
Siskin Parkway East
Middlemarch Business Park
Coventry CV3 4PE
Tel: 08707 202909
Fax: 024 7651 6505
enquiries@ediplc.com
www.ediplc.com

EMP Awarding Body Limited
Knowledge Centre
Wyboston Lane
Great North Road
Wyboston
Bedfordshire
MK44 3BY
Tel: 01480 479267
Fax: 01480 213854
info@empawards.com
www.empawards.com

EMTA Awards Ltd
SEMTA House
14 Upton Road
Watford
Hertfordshire WD18 OJT
Tel: 01923 652 400
Fax: 01923 652 401
customercare@eal.org.uk
www.eal.org.uk

Engineering Construction Industry Training Board
Blue Court
Church Lane
Kings Langley
Hertfordshire WD4 8JP
Tel: 01923 260000
Fax: 01923 270969
ecitb@ecitb.org.uk
www.ecitb.org.uk

Engineering Management Partnership
School of Management
University of Bath
Bath BA2 7AY
Tel: 01225 384245
Fax: 01225 386473
emp@management.bath.ac.uk
www.emp.ac.uk

Engineering Training Council Awards Ltd
Interpoint
20–24 York Street
Belfast BT15 1AQ
Tel: 028 9032 9878
Fax: 028 9031 0301
www.etcni.org.uk

English Speaking Board (International) Ltd
26a Princes Street
Southport PR8 1EQ
Tel: 01704 501730
Fax: 01704 539637
admin@esbuk.org
www.esbuk.org

First Aid Qualifications
EMP House
Telford Way
Coalville
Leicestershire
LE67 3HB
Tel: 0845 029 1905
Fax: 0845 029 1906
info@firstaidqualifications.com
www.firstaidqualifications.com

Food and Drink Qualifications
PO Box 141
Winterhill House
Snowdon Drive
Milton Keynes MK6 1YY
Tel: 01908 231 062
Fax: 01908 231 063
info@fdq.org.uk
www.fdq.org.uk

Gemmological Association of Great Britain
27 Greville Street
London EC1N 8TN
Tel: 020 7404 3334
Fax: 020 7404 8843
information@gem-a.info
www.gem-a.info

Glass Qualifications Authority Ltd
Provincial House
Solly Street
Sheffield S1 4BA
Tel: 0114 272 0033
Fax: 0114 272 0060
info@gqualifications.com
www.glassqualificationsauthority.com

Guildhall School of Music and Drama Examination Service
Silk Street
Barbican
London EC2Y 8DT
Tel: 020 7628 2571
Fax: 020 7256 9438
registry@gsmd.ac.uk
www.gsmd.ac.uk

Hospitality Awarding Body (HAB)
c/o City and Guilds
1 Giltspur Street
London EC1A 9DD
Tel: 0870 060 2556
Fax: 0870 060 2555
info@hab.org.uk
www.hab.org.uk

Imperial Society of Teachers of Dancing
22/26 Paul Street
London EC2A 4QE
Tel: 020 7377 1577
www.istd.org

Institute of Career Guidance
Third Floor, Copthall House
1 New Road
Stourbridge
West Midlands DY8 1PH
Tel: 01384 376464
www.icg-uk.org

Institute of Clerks of Works of Great Britain Incorporated
Equinox
28 Commerce Road
Lynch Wood
Peterborough PE2 6LR
Tel: 01733 405160
Fax: 01733 405161
info@icwgb.co.uk
www.icwgb.org

Institute of Credit Management
The Water Mill
Station Road
South Luffenham
Oakham
Leicestershire LE15 8NB
Tel: 01780 722900
Fax: 01780 721333
info@icm.org.uk
www.icm.org.uk

Institute of Financial Services (IFS)
4–9 Burgate Lane
Canterbury
Kent CT1 2XJ
Tel: 01227 818609
Fax: 01227 784331
customerservices@ifslearning.com
www.ifslearning.com

Institute of Hospitality
Trinity Court
34 West Street
Sutton
Surrey SM1 1SH
Tel: 020 8661 4900
Fax: 020 8661 4901
commdept@instituteofhospitality.org
www.instituteofhospitality.org

Institute of Leadership and Management
Stowe House
Netherstowe
Lichfield
Staffordshire WS13 6TJ
Tel: 01543 266 867
Fax: 01543 266 811
customer@i-l-m.com
www.i-l-m.com

Institute of Legal Executives
Kempston Manor
Kempston
Bedfordshire MK42 7AB
Tel: 01234 841000
Fax: 01234 840373
info@ilex.org.uk
www.ilex.org.uk

Institute of Linguists Educational Trust
Chartered Institute of Linguists
Saxon House
48 Southwark Street
London SE1 1UN
Tel: 020 7940 3100
Fax: 020 7940 3101
info@iol.org.uk
www.iol.org.uk

Institute of the Motor Industry
Fanshaws
Brickendon
Hertford SG13 8PQ
Tel: 01992 511 521
Fax: 01992 511 548
imi@motor.org.uk
www.motor.org.uk

Institute of Revenues, Rating and Valuation
41 Doughty Street
London WC1N 2LF
Tel: 020 7831 3505
www.irrv.org.uk

Institute of Sales and Marketing Management
Harrier Court
Lower Woodside
Bedfordshire LU1 4DQ
Tel: 01582 840001
Fax: 01582 849142
www.ismm.co.uk

Institution of Civil Engineers
One Great George Street
Westminster
London SW1P 3AA
Tel: 020 7222 7722
communications@ice.org.uk
www.ice.org.uk

International Association of Book-Keepers
Burford House
44 London Road
Sevenoaks
Kent TN13 1AS
Tel: 01732 458080
Fax: 01732 455848
mail@iab.org.uk
www.iab.org.uk

International Curriculum and Assessment Agency Ltd
The ICAA Education Centre
Bighton, Alresford
Hants SO24 9RE
Tel: 01962 735801
Fax: 01962 735597
info@icaa.com
www.icaag.com

International Dance Teachers Association
International House
76 Bennett Road
Brighton
East Sussex BN2 5JL
Tel: 01273 685652
Fax: 01273 674388
www.idta.co.uk

International Therapy Examination Council (ITEC)
2nd Floor, Chiswick Gate
598–608 Chiswick High Road
London W4 5RT
Tel: 020 8994 4141
Fax: 020 8994 7880
info@itecworld.co.uk
www.itecworld.co.uk

Lantra
Lantra House
Stoneleigh Park, Nr Coventry
Warwickshire CV8 2LG
Tel: 0845 707 8067
connect@lantra.co.uk
www.lantra.co.uk

Lifesavers The Royal Life Saving Society UK
River House
High Street
Broom, Alcester
Warwickshire B50 4HN
Tel: 01789 773994
Fax: 01789 773995
lifesavers@rlss.org.uk
www.lifesavers.org.uk

London Academy of Music and Dramatic Art (LAMDA)
155 Talgarth Road
London W14 9DA
Tel: 020 8834 0500
Fax: 020 8834 0501
enquiries@lamda.org.uk
www.lamda.org.uk

Market Research Society
15 Northburgh Street
London EC1V 0JR
Tel: 020 7490 4911
Fax: 020 7490 0608
info@mrs.org.uk
www.mrs.org.uk

Ministry of Defence
Whitehall
London SW1A 2HB
Tel: 0870 607 4455
www.mod.uk

National Association of Estate Agents
Arbon House
6 Tournament Court
Edgehill Drive
Warwick
CV34 6LG
Tel: 01926 496800
Fax: 01926 417788
info@naea.co.uk
www.naea.co.uk

National Energy Action
St Andrew's House
90–92 Pilgrim Street
Newcastle upon Tyne NE1 6SG
Tel: 0191 261 5677
Fax: 0191 261 6496
info@nea.org.uk
www.nea.org.uk

National Examination Board in Occupational Safety and Health
Dominus Way
Meridian Business Park
Leicester LE19 1QW
Tel: 0116 263 4700
Fax: 0116 282 4000
info@nebosh.org.uk
www.nebosh.org.uk

National Examining Board for Dental Nurses
110 London Street
Fleetwood
Lancashire FY7 6EU
Tel: 01253 778417
Fax: 01253 777268
info@nebdn.org

National Open College Network
The Quadrant
Parkway Business Park
99 Parkway Avenue
Sheffield S9 4WG
Tel: 0114 227 0500
Fax: 0114 227 0501
nocn@nocn.org.uk
www.nocn.org.uk

National Proficiency Tests Council
Stoneleigh Park
Stoneleigh
Warwickshire CV8 2LG
Tel: 024 7685 7300
Fax: 024 7669 6128
information@nptc.org.uk
www.nptc.org.uk

NCFE
Citygate
St James' Boulevard
Newcastle upon Tyne NE1 4JE
Tel: 0191 239 8000
Fax: 0191 239 8001
info@ncfe.org.uk
www.ncfe.org.uk

The Oil and Gas Academy
First Floor, Block 2
The Altec Centre
Minto Drive
Altens
Aberdeen AB12 3LW

Open College of the North West
West Lodge
Quernmore Road
Lancaster LA1 3JT
Tel: 01524 845046
Fax: 01524 388467
accreditation@ocnw.com
www.ocnw.com

Open University
PO Box 197
Milton Keynes MK7 6AA
Tel: 0845 300 6090
www.open.ac.uk

Oxford, Cambridge and Royal School of Arts Examinations (OCR)
(Vocational qualifications)
Progress House
Westwood Way
Coventry CV4 8JQ
Tel: 02476 851509
Fax: 02476 421944
vocationalqualifications@ocr.org.uk
(Head Office)
1 Hills Road
Cambridge CB1 2EU
Tel: 01223 553 998
Fax: 01223 552 627
general.qualifications@ocr.org.uk
www.ocr.org.uk

Packaging Industry Awarding Body Company
Springfield House
Springfield Business Park
Grantham
Lincolnshire NG31 7BG
Tel: 01476 514595
Fax: 01476 514591
info@piabc.org.uk
www.piabc.org.uk

The Pensions Management Institute
PMI House
4/10 Artillery Lane
London E1 7LS
Tel: 020 7247 1452
Fax: 020 7375 0603
enquiries@pensions-pmi.org.uk
www.pensions-pmi.org.uk

Premier Training International
Premier House
Willowside Park
Canal Road
Trowbridge
Wiltshire BA14 8RH
Tel: 0845 909090
www.premierglobal.co.uk

Process Awards Authority/Vocational Qualifications in Science, Engineering and Technology
Brooke House
24 Dam Street
Lichfield
Staffordshire WS13 6AA
Tel: 01543 254223
Fax: 01543 257848
info@paa-uk.org
www.paa-uk.org

Professional Association of Dive Instructors (PADI) International Ltd
Unit 7, St Philips Central
Albert Road
St Philips
Bristol BS2 0PD
Tel: 0117 300 7234
Fax: 0117 971 0400
general@padi.co.uk
www.padi.co.uk

Rock School Ltd
Evergreen House
2–4 King Street
Twickenham
Middlesex TW1 3RZ
Tel: 0845 460 4747
Fax: 0845 460 1960
info@rockschool.co.uk
www.rockschool.co.uk

Royal Academy of Dance
36 Battersea Square
London SW11 3RA
Tel: 020 7326 8000
Fax: 020 7924 3129
info@rad.org.uk
www.rad.org.uk

The Royal College of Veterinary Surgeons
Belgravia House
62–64 Horseferry Road
London SW1P 2AF
Tel: 020 7222 2001
Fax: 020 7222 2004
admin@rcvs.org.uk
www.rcvs.org.uk

Royal Horticultural Society
80 Vincent Square
London SW1P 2PE
Tel: 0845 260 5000
info@rhs.org.uk
www.rhs.org.uk

Royal Institute of Public Health
28 Portland Place
London W1B 1DE
Tel: 020 7580 2731
Fax: 020 7580 6157
examinations@riph.org.uk
www.riph.org.uk

Royal Society for the Promotion of Health
38A St George's Drive
London SW1V 4BH
Tel: 020 7630 0121
Fax: 020 7976 6847
rsph@rsph.org
www.rsph.org

Scottish Association of Master Bakers
Atholl House
4 Torphichen Street
Edinburgh EH3 8JQ
Tel: 0131 229 1401
Fax: 0131 229 8239
master.bakers@samb.co.uk
www.samb.co.uk

Scottish Building Apprenticeship and Training Council
Carron Grange
Carrongrange Avenue
Stenhousemuir FK5 3BQ
Tel: 01324 555550
Fax: 01324 555551
info@scottish-building.co.uk
www.sbatc.co.uk

Scottish Joint Industry Board of the Electrical Contracting Industry
The Walled Garden
Bush Estate
Midlothian EH26 0SB
Tel: 0131 445 9216
grading@sjib.org.uk
www.sjib.org.uk

Scottish and Northern Ireland Joint Industry Board for the Plumbing Industry
2 Walker Street
Edinburgh EH3 7LB
Tel: 0131 225 2255
info@snipef.org
www.snipef.org

Scottish Print Employers Federation
48 Palmerston Place
Edinburgh EH12 5DE
Tel: 0131 220 4353
Fax: 0131 220 4344
info@spef.org.uk
www.spef.org.uk

Scottish Qualifications Authority
The Optima Building
58 Robertson Street
Glasgow G2 8DQ
Tel: 0845 279 1000
Fax: 0845 213 5000
customer@sqa.org.uk
www.sqa.org.uk

Securities & Investment Institute
8 Eastcheap
London EC3M 1AF
Tel: 020 7645 0600
Fax: 020 7645 0601
clientservices@sii.org.uk
www.sii.org.uk

Single Subject Qualifications
1 Giltspur Street
London EC1A 9DD
Tel: 020 7294 2800
Fax: 020 7294 2400
www.cityandguilds.com

Skillset
Focus Point
21 Caledonian Road
London N1 9GB
Tel: 020 7713 9800
www.skillset.org

Skills for Logistics
12 Warren Yard
Warren Farm Office Village
Stratford Road
Milton Keynes MK12 5NW
Tel: 01908 313360
Fax: 01908 313006
info@skillsforlogistics.org
www.skillsforlogistics.org

Skills for Security
Security House
Barbourne Road
Worcester WR1 1RS
Tel: 08450 750111
Fax: 01905 724949
info@skillsforsecurity.org.uk
www.skillsforsecurity.org.uk

Sports Leaders UK
23–25 Linford Forum
Rockingham Drive
Linford Wood
Milton Keynes MK14 6LY
Tel: 01908 689180
Fax: 01908 393744
info@sportsleaders.org
www.sportsleaders.org

SummitSkills
Vega House
Opal Drive
Fox Milne
Milton Keynes MK15 0DF
Tel: 01908 303960
enquiries@summitskills.org.uk
www.summitskills.org.uk

Swimming Teachers Association
Anchor House
Birch Street
Walsall
West Midlands WS2 8HZ
Tel: 01922 645097
Fax: 01922 720628
sta@sta.co.uk
www.sta.co.uk

Thames Valley University
St Mary's Road
Ealing
London W5 5RF
Tel: 020 8579 5000
Fax: 020 8566 1353
www.tvu.ac.uk

Timber Trade Federation

The Building Centre
26 Store Street
London WC1E 7BT
Tel: 020 3205 0067
ttf@ttf.co.uk
www.ttf.co.uk

Trinity College London

89 Albert Embankment
London SE1 7TP
Tel: 020 7820 6100
Fax: 020 7820 6161
info@trinitycollege.co.uk
www.trinitycollege.co.uk

Vocational Training Charitable Trust

3rd Floor, Eastleigh House
Upper Market Street
Eastleigh
Hampshire SO50 9FD
Tel: 023 8068 4500
Fax: 023 8065 1493
customerservice@vtct.org.uk
www.vtct.org.uk

Waste Management Industry Training and Advisory Board

Peterbridge House
3 The Lakes
Northampton NN4 7HE
Tel: 01604 231950
Fax: 01604 232457
info.admin@wamitab.org.uk.
www.wamitab.org.uk

Welsh Joint Education Committee

245 Western Avenue
Cardiff CF5 2YX
Tel: 029 2026 5000
info@wjec.co.uk
www.wjec.co.uk

Wine & Spirit Education Trust

International Wine & Spirit Centre
39–45 Bermondsey Street
London SE1 3XF
Tel: 020 7089 3800
Fax: 020 7089 3845
wset@wset.co.uk
www.wset.co.uk

Worshipful Company of Farriers

19 Queen Street
Chipperfield
Kings Langley
Herts WD4 9BT
Tel: 01923 260747
Fax: 01923 261677
theclerk@wcf.org.uk
www.wcf.org.uk

Worshipful Company of Spectacle Makers

Apothecaries' Hall
Black Friars Lane
London EC4V 6EL
Tel: 020 7236 2932
Fax: 020 7329 3249
www.spectaclemakers.com

Part 4

Directory of Colleges Offering Vocational Qualifications

Introduction

Within the last decade the provision of vocational qualifications has been radically restructured. Qualifications are now offered in further education colleges, higher education institutions (see *British Qualifications* also published by Kogan Page), in the workplace and delivered by distance learning to students in their homes. To list the complete range of course providers within this book would not be possible. However, the addresses of active Further Education colleges have been included as a starting point for readers to identify providers of vocational qualifications. Awarding bodies may also provide details of the full range of different study opportunities (see Part Three for full contact details of Awarding Bodies).

Avon

Bristol Old Vic Theatre School
2 Downside Road
Clifton
Bristol
Avon BS8 2XF
Tel: 0117 9733535
Fax: 0117 9739371
enquiries@oldvic.ac.uk
www.oldvic.ac.uk

City of Bristol College
Marksbury Road
Bristol
Avon BS3 5JL
Tel: 0117 3125000
Fax: 0117 3125051
enquiries@cityofbristol.ac.uk
www.cityofbristol.ac.uk

Filton College
Filton Avenue
Filton
Bristol
Avon BS34 7AT
Tel: 0117 9312121
Fax: 0117 9312233
info@filton.ac.uk
www.filton.ac.uk

Bedfordshire

Barnfield College
New Bedford Road
Luton
Bedfordshire LU2 7BF
Tel: 01582 569600
enquiries@barnfield.ac.uk
www.barnfield.ac.uk

Bedford College
Cauldwell Street
Bedford
Bedfordshire MK42 9AH
Tel: 0800 074 0234
Fax: 01234 342674
info@bedford.ac.uk
www.bedford.ac.uk

Dunstable College
Kingsway
Dunstable
Bedfordshire LU5 4HG
Tel: 01582 477776
Fax: 01582 478801
enquiries@dunstable.ac.uk
www.dunstable.ac.uk

Belfast

Belfast Metropolitan College
Montgomery Road
Belfast BT6 9JD
Tel: 028 9026 5265
central-admissions@ belfastinstitute.ac.uk
www.belfastmet.ac.uk

Berkshire

Berkshire College of Agriculture
Hall Place
Burchetts Green
Maidenhead
Berkshire SL6 6QR
Tel: 01628 824444
Fax: 01628 824695
enquiries@bca.ac.uk
www.bca.ac.uk

Bracknell and Wokingham College
Church Road
Bracknell
Berkshire RG12 1DJ
Tel: 0845 330 3343
study@bracknell.ac.uk
www.bracknell.ac.uk

East Berkshire College
Langley Campus
Station Road
Langley
Berkshire SL3 8BY
Tel: 0845 373 2500
info@eastberks.ac.uk
www.eastberks.ac.uk

Newbury College
Monks Lane
Newbury
Berkshire RG14 7TD
Tel: 01635 845000
Fax: 01635 845312
info@newbury-college.ac.uk
www.newbury-college.ac.uk

Thames Valley University
St Mary's Road
Ealing
London W5 5RF
Tel: 020 8579 5000
Fax: 020 8566 1353
www.tvu.ac.uk

Buckinghamshire

Amersham and Wycombe College
Stanley Hill
Amersham
Buckinghamshire HP7 9HN
Tel: 0800 614 016
Fax: 01494 585566
www.amersham.ac.uk

Aylesbury College
Oxford Road
Aylesbury
Buckinghamshire HP21 8PD
Tel: 01296 588588
Fax: 01296 588589
customerservices@aylesbury.ac.uk
www.aylesbury.ac.uk

Buckingham Chilterns University College
Queen Alexandra Road
High Wycombe
Buckinghamshire HP11 2JZ
Tel: 0800 0565 660
Fax: 01494 524392
advice@bcuc.ac.uk
www.bcuc.ac.uk

Milton Keynes College
Woughton Campus West
Leadenhall
Milton Keynes
Buckinghamshire MK6 5LP
Tel: 01908 684444
Fax: 01908 684399
info@mkcollege.ac.uk
www.mkcollege.ac.uk

Cambridgeshire

Cambridge Regional College
Kings Hedges Road
Cambridge
Cambridgeshire CB4 2QT
Tel: 01223 532240
enquiry@camre.ac.uk
www.camre.ac.uk

Huntingdonshire Regional College
California Road
Huntingdon
Cambridgeshire PE29 1BL
Tel: 01480 379100
Fax: 01480 379127
college@huntingdon.ac.uk
www.huntingdon.ac.uk

Isle College
Ramnoth Road
Wisbech
Cambridgeshire PE13 2JE
Tel: 01945 582561
Fax: 01945 582706
courses@isle.ac.uk
www.isle.ac.uk

Peterborough Regional College
Park Crescent
Peterborough
Cambridgeshire PE1 4DZ
Tel: 0845 872 8722
Fax: 01733 767986
info@peterborough.ac.uk
www.peterborough.ac.uk

Cheshire

Cheadle & Marple Sixth Form College
Cheadle Campus
Cheadle Road
Cheadle Hulme
Cheshire SK8 5HA
Tel: 0161 486 4600
Fax: 0161 482 8129
info@camsfc.ac.uk
www.camsfc.ac.uk

Cheadle & Marple Sixth Form College
Marple Campus
Hibbert Lane
Marple
Stockport
Cheshire SK6 7PA
Tel: 0161 484 6600
Fax: 0161 484 6602
www.camsfc.ac.uk

Riverside College Halton
Kingsway
Widnes
Cheshire WA8 7QQ
Tel: 0151 257 2800
www.haltoncollege.ac.uk

Macclesfield College
Park Lane
Macclesfield
Cheshire SK11 8LF
Tel: 01625 410000
Fax: 01625 410001
info@macclesfield.ac.uk
www.macclesfield.ac.uk

Mid-Cheshire College
Hartford Campus
Chester Road
Northwich
Cheshire CW8 1LJ
Tel: 01606 74444
info@midchesh.ac.uk
www.midchesh.ac.uk

North Area College
Buckingham Road
Heaton Moor
Stockport
Cheshire SK4 4RA
Tel: 0161 442 7494
Fax: 0161 442 2166
www.nacstock.ac.uk

Priestley College
Loushers Lane
Warrington
Cheshire WA4 6RD
Tel: 01925 633591
Fax: 01925 413887
enquiries@priestley.ac.uk
www.priestleycollege.ac.uk

Reaseheath College
Nantwich
Cheshire CW5 6DF
Tel: 01270 625131
Fax: 01270 625665
enquiries@reaseheath.ac.uk
www.reaseheath.ac.uk

Sir John Deane's College
Monarch Drive
Northwich
Cheshire CW9 8AF
Tel: 01606 46011
Fax: 01606 353939
www.sjd.ac.uk

South Cheshire College
Dane Bank Avenue
Crewe
Cheshire CW2 8AB
Tel: 01270 654654
Fax: 01270 651515
info@s-cheshire.ac.uk
www.s-cheshire.ac.uk

South Trafford College
Manchester Rd
West Timperley
Altrincham
Cheshire WA14 5PQ
Tel: 0161 952 4600
Fax: 0161 952 4672
enquiries@stcoll.ac.uk
www.stcoll.ac.uk

Warrington Collegiate
Winwick Road Campus
Winwick Road
Warrington
WA2 8QA
Tel: 01925 494494
Fax: 01925 418328
learner.services@warrington.ac.uk
www.warrington.ac.uk

West Cheshire College

Handbridge Centre
Eaton Road
Handbridge
Chester CH4 7ER
Tel: 01244 670600
Fax: 01244 670676
info@west-cheshire.ac.uk
www.west-cheshire.ac.uk

Cleveland

Bede Sixth Form College

Hale Road
Billingham
Cleveland TS23 3ER
Tel: 01642 808285
Fax: 01642 808284
enquiries@bede.ac.uk

Hartlepool College of Further Education

Stockton Street
Hartlepool
Cleveland TS24 7NT
Tel: 01429 295000
Fax: 01429 292999
enquiries@hartlepoolfe.ac.uk
www.hartlepoolfe.ac.uk

Prior Pursglove College

Church Walk
Guisborough
Cleveland TS14 6BU
Tel: 01287 280800
Fax: 01287 280280
www.pursglove.ac.uk

Redcar and Cleveland College

Corporation Road
Redcar
Cleveland TS10 1EZ
Tel: 01642 473132
Fax: 01642 490856
webenquiry@cleveland.ac.uk
www.cleveland.ac.uk

Stockton Riverside College

Harvard Avenue
Stockton-on-Tees
Cleveland TS17 6FB
Tel: 01642 865400
Fax: 01642 865470
www.stockton.ac.uk

Cornwall

Cornwall College Camborne

Trevenson Road
Pool
Redruth
Cornwall TR15 3RD
Tel: 01209 616161
Fax: 01209 611612
enquiries@cornwall.ac.uk
www.camborne.ac.uk

Cornwall College, St Austell

Tregonnisey Road
St Austell
Cornwall PL25 4DJ
Tel: 01726 226626
Fax: 01726 226627
info@st-austell.ac.uk
www.st-austell.ac.uk

Duchy College

Rosewarne Campus
Camborne
Cornwall TR14 OAB
Tel: 01209 722100
Fax: 01209 722159
rosewarne.enquiries@duchy.ac.uk
www.cornwall.ac.uk/duchy

Duchy College

Stoke Campus
Stoke Climsland
Callington
Cornwall PL17 8PB
Tel: 01579 372233
Fax: 01579 372200
stoke.enquiries@duchy.ac.uk
www.cornwall.ac.uk/duchy

Falmouth Marine School

Killigrew Street
Falmouth
Cornwall TR11 3QS
Tel: 01326 310310
Fax: 01326 310300
falenquiries@cornwall.ac.uk
www.falmouthmarineschool.ac.uk

Penwith College

St Clare Street
Penzance
Cornwall TR18 2SA
Tel: 01736 335000
Fax: 01736 335100
enquire@penwith.ac.uk
www.itsgot2bpenwith.ac.uk

Truro College
College Road
Truro
Cornwall TR1 3XX
Tel: 01872 267000
enquiry@trurocollege.ac.uk
www.trurocollege.ac.uk

Cumbria

Carlisle College
Victoria Place
Carlisle
Cumbria CA1 1HS
Tel: 01228 822703
Fax: 01228 822710
info@carlisle.ac.uk
www.carlisle.ac.uk

Furness College
Channelside
Barrow-in-Furness
Cumbria LA14 2PJ
Tel: 01229 825017
Fax: 01229 870964
info@furness.ac.uk
www.furness.ac.uk

Kendal College
Milnthorpe Road
Kendal
Cumbria LA9 5AY
Tel: 01539 814700
Fax: 01539 814701
enquiries@kendal.ac.uk
www.kendal.ac.uk

Lakes College West Cumbria
Hallwood Road
Lillyhall Business Park
Workington
Cumbria CA14 4JN
Tel: 01946 839300
Fax: 01946 839302
info@lcwc.ac.uk
www.westcumbcoll.ac.uk

University of Central Lancashire
Preston
PR1 2HE
Tel: 01772 201201
www.uclan.ac.uk

Derbyshire

Chesterfield College
Infirmary Road
Chesterfield
Derbyshire S41 7NG
Tel: 01246 500500
advice@chesterfield.ac.uk
www.chesterfield.ac.uk

Derby College
Morley Ilkeston
Derbyshire DE7 6DN
Tel: 01332 520200
Fax: 01332 510548
enquiries@derby-college.ac.uk
www.derby-college.ac.uk

South East Derbyshire College
Field Road
Ilkeston
Derbyshire DE7 5RS
Tel: 0115 849 2000
Fax: 0115 849 2121
admissions@sedc.ac.uk
www.sedc.ac.uk

Devon

Bicton College
East Budleigh
Budleigh Salterton
Devon EX9 7BY
Tel: 01395 562400
Fax: 01395 567502
enquiries@bicton.ac.uk
www.bicton.ac.uk

East Devon College
Bolham Road
Tiverton
Devon EX16 6SH
Tel: 01884 235200
Fax: 01884 235262
enquiries@admin.eastdevon.ac.uk
www.edc.ac.uk

Exeter College
Victoria House
33–36 Queen Street
Exeter
Devon EX4 3SR
Tel: 01392 205223
Fax: 01392 205225
info@exe-coll.ac.uk
www.exe-coll.ac.uk

North Devon College
Old Sticklepath Hill
Barnstaple
Devon EX31 2BQ
Tel: 01271 345291
Fax: 01271 338121
postbox@ndevon.ac.uk
www.ndevon.ac.uk

Plymouth College of Art and Design
Tavistock Place
Plymouth
Devon PL4 8AT
Tel: 01752 203434
Fax: 01752 203444
enquiries@pcad.ac.uk
www.pcad.ac.uk

City College Plymouth
Kings Road Centre
Devonport
Plymouth
PL1 5QG
Tel: 01752 305300
Fax: 01752 305343
reception@cityplym.ac.uk
www.cityplym.ac.uk

South Devon College
Vantage Point
Long Road
Paignton
TQ4 7EJ
Tel: 01803 540540
enquiries@southdevon.ac.uk
www.southdevon.ac.uk

Dorset

Bournemouth and Poole College
North Road
Poole
Dorset BH14 0LS
Tel: 01202 205205
enquiries@thecollege.co.uk
www.thecollege.co.uk

Kingston Maurward College
Dorchester
Dorset DT2 8PY
Tel: 01305 215000
Fax: 01305 215001
administration@kmc.ac.uk
www.kmc.ac.uk

Weymouth College
Cranford Avenue
Weymouth
Dorset DT4 7LQ
Tel: 01305 761100
Fax: 01305 208892
igs@weymouth.ac.uk
www.weymouth.ac.uk

Durham

Bishop Auckland College
Woodhouse Lane
Bishop Auckland
County Durham DL14 6JZ
Tel: 01388 443000
Fax: 01388 609294
enquiries@bacoll.ac.uk
www.bacoll.ac.uk

Darlington College
Central Park
Haughton Road
Darlington
DL1 1DR
Tel: 01325 503030
Fax: 01325 503000
enquire@darlington.ac.uk
www.darlington.ac.uk

Derwentside College
Consett Campus
Front Street
Consett
County Durham DH8 5EE
Tel: 01207 585900
Fax: 01207 585991
www.derwentside.ac.uk

East Durham and Houghall Community College
Burnhope Way Centre
Burnhope Way
Peterlee
County Durham SR8 1NU
Tel: 0191 518 2000
Fax: 0191 586 7125
enquiries@edhcc.ac.uk
www.edhcc.ac.uk

New College Durham
Framwellgate Moor Campus
Framwellgate Moor
Durham
DH1 5ES
Tel: 0191 375 4000
Fax: 0191 375 4222
help@newdur.ac.uk
www.newdur.ac.uk

East Sussex

Bexhill College
Penland Road
Bexhill-on-Sea
East Sussex TN40 2LG
Tel: 01424 214545
Fax: 01424 215050
enquiries@bexhillcollege.ac.uk
www.bexhillcollege.ac.uk

City College Brighton and Hove
Pelham Street
Brighton
East Sussex BN1 4FA
Tel: 01273 667788
info@ccb.ac.uk
www.ccb.ac.uk

Hastings College of Arts & Technology
Archery Road
St. Leonards on Sea
East Sussex TN38 0HX
Tel: 01424 442222
Fax: 01424 721763
studentadvisers@hastings.ac.uk
www.hastings.ac.uk

Plumpton College
Ditchling Road
Nr Lewes
East Sussex BN7 3AE
Tel: 01273 890454
Fax: 01273 890071
enquiries@plumpton.ac.uk
www.plumpton.ac.uk

Sussex Downs College
Cross Levels Way
Eastbourne
East Sussex BN21 2UF
Tel: 01323 637637
Fax: 01323 637472
info@sussexdowns.ac.uk
www.sussexdowns.ac.uk

Varndean College
Surrenden Road
Brighton
East Sussex BN1 6WQ
Tel: 01273 508011
Fax: 01273 542950
www.varndean.ac.uk

Essex

Barking College
Dagen
Dagenham Road
Romford
Essex RM7 0XU
Tel: 01708 770000
Fax: 01708 770007
admissions@barkingcollege.ac.uk
www.barkingcollege.ac.uk

Braintree College
1 Church Lane
Braintree
Essex CM7 5SN
Tel: 01376 321711
Fax: 01376 340799
enquiries@braintree.ac.uk
www.braintree.ac.uk

Chelmsford College
Princes Road Campus
Princes Road
Chelmsford
Essex CM2 9DE
Tel: 01245 265611
Fax: 01245 346615
www.chelmsford-college.ac.uk

Colchester Institute
Sheepen Road
Colchester
Essex CO3 3LL
Tel: 01206 518777
www.colchester.ac.uk

Epping Forest College
Borders Lane
Loughton
Essex IG10 3SA
Tel: 020 8508 8311
informationcentre@ epping-forest.ac.uk
www.epping-forest.ac.uk

Harlow College
Velizy Avenue
Town Centre
Harlow
Essex CM20 3LH
Tel: 01279 868000
Fax: 01279 868260
full-time@harlow-college.ac.uk
www.harlow-college.ac.uk

Havering College
Ardleigh Green Campus
Ardleigh Green Road
Hornchurch
Essex RM11 2LL
Tel: 01708 455011
www.havering-college.ac.uk

Palmer's College
Chadwell Road
Grays
Essex RM17 5TD
Tel: 01375 370121
enquiries@palmers.ac.uk
www.palmers.ac.uk

Redbridge College
Little Heath
Barley Lane
Romford
Essex RM6 4XT
Tel: 020 8548 7400
Fax: 020 8599 8224
info@redbridge-college.ac.uk
www.redbridge-college.ac.uk

Seevic College
Runnymede Chase
Benfleet
Essex SS7 1TW
Tel: 01268 756 111
Fax: 01268 565 515
info@seevic-college.ac.uk
www.seevic-college.ac.uk

South East Essex College of Arts and Technology
Luker Road
Southend-on-Sea
Essex SS1 1ND
Tel: 01702 220400
Fax: 01702 432320
admissions@southend.ac.uk
www.southend.ac.uk

Thurrock and Basildon College
Nethermayne Campus
Nethermayne
Basildon
Essex SS16 5NN
Tel: 0845 6015746
Fax: 01375 373356
enquire@tab.ac.uk
www.tab.ac.uk

Writtle College
Chelmsford
Essex CM1 3RR
Tel: 01245 424200
Fax: 01245 420456
info@writtle.ac.uk
www.writtle.ac.uk

Gloucestershire

Cirencester College
Fosse Way Campus
Stroud Road
Cirencester
Gloucestershire GL7 1XA
Tel: 01285 640994
Fax: 01285 644171
student.services@cirencester.ac.uk
www.cirencester.ac.uk

Gloucestershire College of Arts and Technology
Gloucester Campus
Brunswick Road
Gloucester
Gloucestershire GL1 1HU
Tel: 01452 532000
Fax: 01452 563441
info@gloscat.ac.uk
www.gloscat.ac.uk

Hartpury College
Hartpury House
Gloucester
Gloucestershire GL19 3BE
Tel: 01452 702132
Fax: 01452 700629
enquire@hartpury.ac.uk
www.hartpury.ac.uk

Royal Forest of Dean College
Five Acres Campus
Berry Hill
Coleford
Gloucestershire GL16 7JT
Tel: 01594 883416
Fax: 01594 837497
enquiries@rfdc.ac.uk
www.rfdc.ac.uk

Stroud College in Gloucestershire
Stratford Road
Stroud
Gloucestershire GL5 4AH
Tel: 01453 763424
Fax: 01453 753543
enquire@stroudcol.ac.uk
www.stroud.ac.uk

Hampshire

Alton College
Old Odiham Road
Alton
Hampshire GU34 2LX
Tel: 01420 592200
Fax: 01420 592253
enquiries@altoncollege.ac.uk
www.altoncollege.ac.uk

Barton Peveril College
Chestnut Avenue
Eastleigh
Hampshire SO50 5ZA
Tel: 023 8061 7200
www.barton-peveril.ac.uk

Basingstoke College of Technology
Worting Road
Basingstoke
Hampshire RG21 8TN
Tel: 01256 354141
Fax: 01256 306444
information@bcot.ac.uk
www.bcot.ac.uk

Brockenhurst College
Lyndhurst Road
Brockenhurst
Hampshire SO42 7ZE
Tel: 01590 625555
enquiries@brock.ac.uk
www.brock.ac.uk

Cricklade College
Charlton Road
Andover
Hampshire SP10 1EJ
Tel: 01264 360000
Fax: 01264 360010
www.cricklade.ac.uk

Eastleigh College
Chestnut Avenue
Eastleigh
Hampshire SO50 5FS
Tel: 023 8091 1000
goplaces@eastleigh.ac.uk
www.eastleigh.ac.uk

Fareham College
Bishopsfield Road
Fareham
Hampshire PO14 1NH
Tel: 01329 815200
Fax: 01329 822483
info@fareham.ac.uk
www.fareham.ac.uk

Farnborough College of Technology
Boundary Road
Farnborough
Hampshire GU14 6SB
Tel: 01252 407040
info@farn-ct.ac.uk
www.farn-ct.ac.uk

Havant College
New Road
Havant
Hampshire PO9 1QL
Tel: 023 9248 3856
Fax: 023 9247 0621
enquiries@havant.ac.uk
www.havant.ac.uk

Highbury College
Dovercourt Road
Highbury
Portsmouth
Hampshire PO6 2SA
Tel: 023 9238 3131
Fax: 023 9232 5551
info@highbury.ac.uk
www.highbury.ac.uk

Itchen College
Middle Road
Bitterne
Southampton
Hampshire SO19 7TB
Tel: 023 8043 5636
Fax: 023 8042 1911
info@itchen.ac.uk
www.itchen.ac.uk

Peter Symonds College
Owens Road
Winchester
Hampshire SO22 6RX
Tel: 01962 857500
Fax: 01962 857501
www.psc.ac.uk

Portsmouth College
Tangier Road
Portsmouth
Hampshire PO3 6PZ
Tel: 023 9266 7521
Fax: 023 9234 4363
registry@portsmouth-college.ac.uk
www.portsmouth-college.ac.uk

Queen Mary's College
Cliddesden Road
Basingstoke
Hampshire RG21 3HF
Tel: 01256 417500
Fax: 01256 417501
info@qmc.ac.uk
www.qmc.ac.uk

South Downs College
College Road
Waterlooville
Hampshire PO7 8AA
Tel: 023 9279 7979
Fax: 023 9279 7940
college@southdowns.ac.uk
www.southdowns.ac.uk

Southampton City College
St Mary Street
Southampton
Hampshire SO14 1AR
Tel: 023 8048 4848
Fax: 023 8057 7473
www.southampton-city.ac.uk

Southampton Solent University
East Park Terrace
Southampton
Hampshire S014 OYN
Tel: 023 8031 9000
Fax: 023 8033 4161
postmaster@solent.ac.uk
www.solent.ac.uk

Sparsholt College
Westley Lane
Sparsholt
Winchester
SO21 2NF
Tel: 01962 776441
enquiries@sparsholt.ac.uk
www.sparsholt.ac.uk

St Vincent College
Mill Lane
Gosport
Hampshire PO12 4QA
Tel: 023 9258 8311
Fax: 023 9251 1186
info@stvincent.ac.uk
www.stvincent.ac.uk

Taunton's College
Hill Lane
Southampton
Hampshire SO15 5RL
Tel: 023 8051 1811
Fax: 023 8051 1991
admissions@tauntons.ac.uk
www.tauntons.ac.uk

Totton College
Calmore Road
Totton
Southampton
Hampshire SO40 3ZX
Tel: 023 8087 4874
Fax: 023 8087 4879
info@totton.ac.uk
www.totton.ac.uk

Herefordshire

Hereford College of Arts Folly Lane
Hereford
Herefordshire HR1 1LT
Tel: 01432 273359
Fax: 01432 341099
enquiries@hereford-art-col.ac.uk
www.hereford-art-col.ac.uk

Herefordshire College of Technology
Folly Lane
Hereford
Herefordshire HR1 1LS
Tel: 0800 032 1986
enquiries@hct.ac.uk
www.hct.ac.uk

Hertfordshire

Barnet College
Wood Street Centre
Wood Street
Barnet
Hertfordshire EN5 4AZ
Tel: 020 8266 4000
Fax: 020 8441 5236
www.barnet.ac.uk

Hertford Regional College
Broxbourne Centre
Turnford
Broxbourne
Hertfordshire EN10 6AE
Tel: 01992 411411
info@hertreg.ac.uk
www.hertreg.ac.uk

North Hertfordshire College
Stevenage Centre
Monkswood Way
Stevenage
Hertfordshire SG1 1LA
Tel: 01462 424239
enquiries@nhc.ac.uk
www.nhc.ac.uk

Oaklands College
St Albans Smallford Campus
Hatfield Road
St Albans
Hertfordshire AL4 0JA
Tel: 01727 737 080
advice.centre@oaklands.ac.uk
www.oaklands.ac.uk

West Herts College
Hempstead Road
Watford
Hertfordshire WD17 3EZ
Tel: 01923 812000
admissions@westherts.ac.uk
www.westherts.ac.uk

Isle of Wight

Isle of Wight College
Medina Way
Newport
Isle of Wight PO30 5TA
Tel: 01983 526631
Fax: 01983 521707
www.iwcollege.ac.uk

Kent

Bexley College
Tower Road
Belvedere
Kent DA17 6JA
Tel: 01322 422331
Fax: 01322 448403
enquiries@bexley.ac.uk
www.bexley.ac.uk

Bromley College

Rookery Lane Campus
Rookery Lane
Bromley
Kent BR2 8HE
Tel: 020 8295 7000
Fax: 020 8295 7099
info@bromley.ac.uk
www.bromley.ac.uk

Canterbury Christ Church University

Canterbury Campus
North Holmes Road
Canterbury
Kent CT1 1QU
Tel: 01227 767700
Fax: 01227 470442
admissions@cant.ac.uk
www.canterbury.ac.uk

Canterbury College

New Dover Road
Canterbury
Kent CT1 3AJ
Tel: 01227 811111
Fax: 01227 811101
courseenquiries@cant-col.ac.uk
www.cant-col.ac.uk

Dartford Technology College

Heath Lane
Dartford
Kent DA1 2LY
Tel: 01322 224309
Fax: 01322 222445
admin@dtc.kent.sch.uk
www.dtc.kent.sch.uk

Hadlow College

Hadlow
Tonbridge
Kent TN11 0AL
Tel: 01732 850551
enquiries@hadlow.ac.uk
www.hadlow.ac.uk

Hilderstone College

Broadstairs
Kent CT10 2JW
Tel: 01843 869171
Fax: 01843 603877
info@hilderstone.ac.uk
www.hilderstone.ac.uk

Mid-Kent College

Horsted Centre
Maidstone Road
Chatham
Kent ME5 9UQ
Tel: 01634 830633
Fax: 01634 830224
www.midkent.ac.uk

North West Kent College

Dartford Campus
Oakfield Lane
Dartford
Kent DA1 2JT
Tel: 0800 074 1447
Fax: 01322 629468
course.enquiries@nwkcollege.ac.uk
www.nwkcollege.ac.uk

Orpington College

The Walnuts
Orpington
Kent BR6 0TE
Tel: 01689 899700
Fax: 01689 877949
guidance@orpington.ac.uk
www.orpington.ac.uk

Ravensbourne College of Design and Communication

Walden Road
Chislehurst
Kent BR7 5SN
Tel: 020 8289 4900
Fax: 020 8325 8320
info@rave.ac.uk
www.rave.ac.uk

South Kent College

Folkestone Campus
Shorncliffe Road
Folkestone
Kent CT20 2NA
Tel: 01303 858200
www.southkent.ac.uk

Thanet College

Ramsgate Road
Broadstairs
Kent CT10 1PN
Tel: 01843 605040
student_admissions@thanet.ac.uk
www.thanet.ac.uk

West Kent College
Brook Street
Tonbridge
Kent TN9 2PW
Tel: 01732 358101
Fax: 01732 7714415
enquiries@wkc.ac.uk
www.wkc.ac.uk

Lancashire

Accrington and Rossendale College
Sandy Lane Campus
Sandy Lane
Accrington
Lancashire BB5 2AW
Tel: 01254 389933
Fax: 01254 354001
info@accross.ac.uk
www.accross.ac.uk

Adult College
White Cross Education Centre
Quarry Road
Lancaster
Lancashire LA1 3SE
Tel: 01524 60141
Fax: 01524 581137
adcollege.info@ed.lancscc.gov.uk
www.theadultcollege.org

Aquinas College
Nangreave Road
Stockport
Lancashire SK2 6TH
Tel: 0161 483 3237
Fax: 0161 487 4072
enquiries@aquinas.ac.uk
www.aquinas.ac.uk

Blackburn College
Feilden Street
Blackburn
Lancashire BB2 1LH
Tel: 01254 292929
studentservices@blackburn.ac.uk
www.blackburn.ac.uk

Blackpool and The Fylde College
Ashfield Road
Bispham
Blackpool
Lancashire FY2 0HB
Tel: 01253 352352
Fax: 01253 356127
visitors@blackpool.ac.uk
www.blackpool.ac.uk

Bolton Community College
Manchester Road Centre
Manchester Road
Bolton
Lancashire BL2 1ER
Tel: 01204 907000
Fax: 01204 907321
info@bolton-community-college.ac.uk
www.bolton-community-college.ac.uk

University of Bolton
Deane Road
Bolton
Lancashire BL3 5AB
Tel: 01204 900600
Fax: 01204 399074
enquiries@bolton.ac.uk
www.bolton.ac.uk

Burnley College
Shorey Bank
off Ormerod Road
Burnley
Lancashire BB11 2RX
Tel: 01282 711200
Fax: 01282 415063
student.services@burnley.ac.uk
www.burnley.ac.uk

Bury College
Woodbury Centre
Market Street
Bury
Manchester
Lancashire BL9 0BG
Tel: 0161 280 8280
information@burycollege.ac.uk
www.burycollege.ac.uk

Cardinal Newman College
Lark Hill
Preston
Lancashire PR1 4HD
Tel: 01772 460181
Fax: 01772 204671
admissions@cnc.hope.ac.uk
www.cardinalnewman.org.uk

City College Manchester
Abraham Moss Campus
Crescent Road
Crumpsall
Manchester
Lancashire M8 5UF
Tel: 0800 013 0123
www.manchester-city-coll.ac.uk

Cooperative College
Holyoake House
Hanover Street
Manchester
M60 0AS
Tel: 0161 246 2926
Fax: 0161 246 2946
enquiries@co-op.ac.uk
www.co-op.ac.uk

Eccles College
Chatsworth Road
Eccles
Salford
Lancashire M30 9FJ
Tel: 0161 789 5876
Fax: 0161 789 1123
admin@ecclescollege.ac.uk
www.ecclescollege.ac.uk

Hopwood Hall College
St Mary's Gate
Rochdale
Lancashire OL12 6RY
Tel: 01706 345346
Fax: 01706 641426
enquiries@hopwood.ac.uk
www.hopwood.ac.uk

Hugh Baird College
Balliol Road
Bootle
Liverpool
L20 7EW
Tel: 0151 353 4444
Fax: 0151 353 4469
info@hughbaird.ac.uk
www.hughbaird.ac.uk

Lancaster and Morecambe College
Morecambe Road
Lancaster
LA1 2TY
Tel: 01524 66215
Fax: 01524 843078
info@lmc.ac.uk
www.lmc.ac.uk

Liverpool Community College
Bankfield Road
Liverpool
L13 0BQ
Tel: 0151 252 3800
enquiry@liv-coll.ac.uk
www.liv-coll.ac.uk

Loreto College
Chichester Road
Manchester
M15 5PB
Tel: 0161 226 5156
Fax: 0161 227 9174
enquiries@loreto.ac.uk
www.loreto.ac.uk

Manchester College of Arts and Technology
Openshaw Campus
Ashton Old Road
Openshaw
Manchester
M11 2WH
Tel: 0161 953 5995
Fax: 0161 953 3909
enquiries@mancat.ac.uk
www.mancat.ac.uk

Myerscough College
Myerscough Hall
St Michael's Road
Bilsborrow
Preston
Lancashire PR3 0RY
Tel: 01995 642222
Fax: 01995 642333
enquiries@myerscough.ac.uk
www.myerscough.ac.uk

Nelson & Colne College
Scotland Road
Nelson
Lancashire BB9 7YT
Tel: 01282 440 200
Fax: 01282 440 274
info-officer@nelson.ac.uk
www.nelson.ac.uk

North Trafford College of Further Education
Talbot Road
Stretford
Manchester
M32 OXH
Tel: 0161 886 7000
Fax: 0161 872 7921
admissions@ntc.ac.uk
www.northtrafford.ac.uk

The Oldham College
Rochdale Road
Oldham
Lancashire OL9 6AA
Tel: 0161 624 5214
Fax: 0161 785 4234
info@oldham.ac.uk
www.oldham.ac.uk

Ormskirk College
Hants Lane
Ormskirk
Lancashire L39 1PX
Tel: 01695 577140
www.skelmersdale.ac.uk

Pendleton College
Pendleton Centre
Dronfield Road
Salford
Lancashire M6 7FR
Tel: 0161 736 5074
Fax: 0161 737 4103
www.pendcoll.ac.uk

Preston College
Fulwood Campus
St Vincents Road
Preston
Lancashire PR2 8UR
Tel: 01772 225000
Fax: 01772 225002
pc4u@preston.ac.uk
www.preston.ac.uk

Runshaw College
Langdale Road
Leyland
Lancashire PR25 3DQ
Tel: 01772 622677
Fax: 01772 642009
www.runshaw.ac.uk

Salford College
Worsley Campus
Walkden Road
Worsley
Lancashire M28 7QD
Tel: 0161 211 5001
Fax: 0161 211 5020
www.salford-col.ac.uk

Skelmersdale College
Westbank Campus
Yewdale
Skelmersdale
Lancashire WN8 6JA
Tel: 01695 728 744
www.skelmersdale.ac.uk

St Mary's College
Shear Brow
Blackburn
Lancashire BB1 8DX
Tel: 01254 580464
reception@stmarysblackburn.ac.uk
www.stmarysblackburn.ac.uk

Stockport College
Wellington Road South
Stockport
Lancashire SK1 3UQ
Tel: 0161 958 3100
Fax: 0161 480 6636
admissions@stockport.ac.uk
www.stockport.ac.uk

Tameside College
Beaufort Road
Ashton-under-Lyne
Greater Manchester
Lancashire OL6 6NX
Tel: 0161 908 6789
Fax: 0161 908 6612
www.tameside.ac.uk

Wigan and Leigh College
PO Box 53
Parsons Walk
Wigan
Lancashire WN1 1RS
Tel: 01942 761600
Fax: 01942 761603
www.wigan-leigh.ac.uk

Winstanley College
Billinge
Wigan
Lancashire WN5 7XF
Tel: 01695 633244
Fax: 01695 633409
www.winstanley.ac.uk

Xaverian College
Lower Park Road
Manchester
M14 5RB
Tel: 0161 224 1781
Fax: 0161 248 9039
college@xaverian.ac.uk
www.xaverian.ac.uk

Leicestershire

Brooksby Melton College
Brooksby
Melton Mowbray
Leicestershire LE14 2LJ
Tel: 01664 850850
Fax: 01664 855444
course.enquiries@brooksbymelton.ac.uk
www.brooksbymelton.ac.uk

Leicester Adult Education College
2 Wellington Street
Leicester
Leicestershire LE1 6HL
Tel: 0116 233 4343
Fax: 0116 233 4344
admin@laec.ac.uk
www.laec.ac.uk

Leicester College
Painter Street
Leicester
Leicestershire LE1 3WA
Tel: 0116 224 4100
Fax: 0116 253 6553
info@leicestercollege.ac.uk
www.leicestercollege.ac.uk

Loughborough College
Radmoor Road
Loughborough
Leicestershire LE11 3BT
Tel: 0845 166 2950
loucoll@loucoll.ac.uk
www.loucoll.ac.uk

North Warwickshire and Hinckley College
Hinckley College
London Road
Hinckley
Leicestershire LE10 1HQ
Tel: 024 7624 3000
the.college@nwhc.ac.uk
www.nwhc.ac.uk

Regent College
Regent Road
Leicester
Leicestershire LE1 7LW
Tel: 0116 255 4629
Fax: 0116 254 5680
support@regent-college.ac.uk
www.regent-college.ac.uk

South Leicestershire College
Station Road
Wigston
Leicestershire LE18 2DW
Tel: 0116 288 5051
Fax: 0116 288 0823
enquiries@slcollege.ac.uk
www.slcollege.ac.uk

Stephenson College
Thornborough Road
Coalville
Leicestershire LE67 3TN
Tel: 01530 836136
www.stephensoncoll.ac.uk

Lincolnshire

Bishop Grosseteste College
Newport
Lincoln
Lincolnshire LN1 3DY
Tel: 01522 527347
Fax: 01522 530243
info@bgc.ac.uk
www.bishopg.ac.uk

Boston College
Main Campus
Skirbeck Road
Boston
Lincolnshire PE21 6JF
Tel: 01205 365701
Fax: 01205 313252
info@boston.ac.uk
www.boston.ac.uk

Franklin College
Chelmsford Avenue
Grimsby
Lincolnshire DN34 5BY
Tel: 01472 875000
Fax: 01472 875019
college@franklin.ac.uk
www.franklin.ac.uk

Grantham College
Stonebridge Road
Grantham
Lincolnshire NG31 9AP
Tel: 01476 400200
Fax: 01476 400291
enquiry@grantham.ac.uk
www.grantham.ac.uk

Grimsby Institute of Further & Higher Education
Nuns Corner
Grimsby
North East Lincolnshire DN34 5BQ
Tel: 01472 311222
Fax: 01472 879924
infocent@grimsby.ac.uk
www.grimsby.ac.uk

Lincoln College
Monks Road
Lincoln
Lincolnshire LN2 5HQ
Tel: 01522 876000
Fax: 01522 876200
enquiries@lincolncollege.ac.uk
www.lincolncollege.ac.uk

North Lindsey College
Kingsway
Scunthorpe
North Lincolnshire DN17 1AJ
Tel: 01724 281111
Fax: 01724 294020
info@northlindsey.ac.uk
www.northlindsey.ac.uk

Stamford College
Drift Road
Stamford
Lincolnshire PE9 1XA
Tel: 01780 764141
Fax: 01780 763313
enquiries@stamford.ac.uk
www.stamford.ac.uk

London

Albany College
Main Campus
21–24 Queens Road
Hendon
London NW4 2TL
Tel: 020 8202 5965
Fax: 020 8202 8460
info@albany-college.co.uk
www.albany-college.co.uk

Ashbourne College
17 Old Court Place
Kensington
London W8 4PL
Tel: 020 7937 3858
Fax: 020 7937 2207
admin@ashbournecollege.co.uk
www.ashbournecollege.co.uk

Central School of Speech and Drama
Embassy Theatre
Eton Avenue
London NW3 3HY
Tel: 020 7722 8183
enquiries@cssd.ac.uk
www.cssd.ac.uk

City & Islington College
The Marlborough Building
383 Holloway Road
London N7 0RN
Tel: 020 7700 9333
www.candi.ac.uk

City of Westminster College
25 Paddington Green
London W2 1NB
Tel: 020 7723 8826
Fax: 020 7258 2700
www.cwc.ac.uk

College of Central London
73 Great Eastern Street
London EC2A 3HR
Tel: 020 7739 5555
www.central-college.co.uk

College of North East London
High Road
Tottenham
London N15 4RU
Tel: 020 8442 3055
admissions@staff.conel.ac.uk
www.conel.ac.uk

College of North West London
Willesden Centre
Dudden Hill Lane
London NW10 2XD
Tel: 020 8208 5050
courenq@cnwl.ac.uk
www.cnwl.ac.uk

Ealing, Hammersmith & West London College
Gliddon Road
Barons Court
London W14 9BL
Tel: 020 8741 1688
Fax: 020 8563 8247
cic@wlc.ac.uk
www.wlc.ac.uk

Greenwich Community College
95 Plumstead Road
London SE18 7DQ
Tel: 020 8488 4800
Fax: 020 8488 4899
info@gcc.ac.uk
www.gcc.ac.uk

Hackney, The Community College
Shoreditch Campus
Falkirk Street
London N1 6HQ
Tel: 020 7613 9123
enquiries@tcch.ac.uk
www.tcch.ac.uk

Kensington and Chelsea College
Hortensia Road
London SW10 0QS
Tel: 020 7573 3600
Fax: 020 7351 0956
enquiries@kcc.ac.uk
www.kcc.ac.uk

Lambeth College
45 Clapham Common South Side
London SW4 9BL
Tel: 020 7501 5010
courses@lambethcollege.ac.uk
www.lambethcollege.ac.uk

Lewisham College
Lewisham Way
London SE4 1UT
Tel: 0800 834 545
info@lewisham.ac.uk
www.lewisham.ac.uk

Morley College
61 Westminister Bridge Road
London SE1 7HT
Tel: 020 7928 8501
Fax: 020 7928 4074
enquiries@morleycollege.ac.uk
www.morleycollege.ac.uk

Newham College of Further Education
East Ham Campus
High Street South
London E6 6ER
Tel: 020 8257 4000
on-line.enquiries@newham.ac.uk
www.newham.ac.uk

Sir George Monoux College
Chingford Road
Walthamstow
London E17 5AA
Tel: 020 8523 3544
Fax: 020 8498 2443
info@george-monoux.ac.uk
www.george-monoux.ac.uk

South Thames College
Wandsworth High Street
London SW18 2PP
Tel: 020 8918 7777
studentservices@south-thames.ac.uk
www.south-thames.ac.uk

Southgate College
High Street
Southgate
London N14 6BS
Tel: 020 8982 5050
Fax: 020 8982 5051
admiss@southgate.ac.uk
www.southgate.ac.uk

Southwark College
Camberwell Centre
Southampton Way
London SE5 7EW
Tel: 020 7815 1677
Fax: 020 7261 1301
www.southwark.ac.uk

Tower Hamlets College
Poplar Centre
Poplar High Street
London E14 0AF
Tel: 020 7510 7777
Fax: 020 7538 9153
www.tower.ac.uk

Waltham Forest College
Forest Building
Forest Road
Walthamstow
London E17 4JB
Tel: 020 8501 8000
Fax: 020 8501 8001
info@waltham.ac.uk
www.waltham.ac.uk

Westminster Kingsway College
Vincent Square
London SW1P 2PD
Tel: 020 7556 8001
courseinfo@westking.ac.uk
www.westking.ac.uk

Merseyside

Carmel College
Prescot Road
St Helens
Merseyside WA10 3AG
Tel: 01744 452200
Fax: 01744 452222
www.carmel.ac.uk

King George V College
Scarisbrick New Road
Southport
Merseyside PR8 6LR
Tel: 01704 530601
Fax: 01704 548656
enquiries@kgv.ac.uk
www.kgv.ac.uk

Knowsley Community College
Kirkby Campus
Cherryfield Drive
Kirkby
Merseyside L32 8SF
Tel: 0845 155 1055
Fax: 0151 477 5703
info@knowsleycollege.ac.uk
www.knowsleycollege.ac.uk

Southport College
Mornington Road
Southport
Merseyside PR9 0TT
Tel: 01704 500606
Fax: 01704 392794
www.southport-college.ac.uk

St Helens College
Water Street/Town Centre Campus
Water Street
St Helens
Merseyside WA10 1PP
Tel: 01744 733766
Fax: 01744 623400
www.sthelens.ac.uk

Wirral Metropolitan College
Conway Park Campus
Europa Boulevard
Conway Park
Birkenhead
Merseyside CH41 4NT
Tel: 0151 551 7777
Fax: 0151 551 7701
enquiries@wmc.ac.uk
www.wmc.ac.uk

Middlesex

Brooklands College
Church Road
Ashford
Middlesex TW15 2XD
Tel: 01784 248666
Fax: 01784 254132
info@brooklands.ac.uk
www.brooklands.ac.uk

Capel Manor College
Bullsmoor Lane
Enfield
Middlesex EN1 4RQ
Tel: 020 8366 4442
Fax: 01992 717544
enquiries@capel.ac.uk
www.capel.ac.uk

Enfield College
73 Hertford Road
Enfield
Middlesex EN3 5HA
Tel: 020 8443 3434
Fax: 020 8804 7028
courseinformation@enfield.ac.uk
www.enfield.ac.uk

Harrow College
Harrow Weald Campus
Brookshill
Harrow Weald
Middlesex HA3 6RR
Tel: 020 8909 6000
Fax: 020 8909 6050
enquiries@harrow.ac.uk
www.harrow.ac.uk

Richmond upon Thames College
Egerton Road
Twickenham
Middlesex TW2 7SJ
Tel: 020 8607 8000
Fax: 020 8744 9738
courses@rutc.ac.uk
www.richmond-utcoll.ac.uk

Stanmore College
Elm Park
Stanmore
Middlesex HA7 4BQ
Tel: 020 8420 7700
Fax: 020 8420 6502
enquiry@stanmore.ac.uk
www.stanmore.ac.uk

Uxbridge College
Uxbridge Campus
Park Road
Uxbridge
Middlesex UB8 1NQ
Tel: 01895 853333
Fax: 01895 853377
enquiries@uxbridgecollege.ac.uk
www.uxbridge.ac.uk

West Thames College
London Road
Isleworth
Middlesex TW7 4HS
Tel: 020 8326 2020
info@west-thames.ac.uk
www.west-thames.ac.uk

Norfolk

City College Norwich
Ipswich Road
Norwich
Norfolk NR2 2LJ
Tel: 01603 773311
www.ccn.ac.uk

College of West Anglia
Tennyson Avenue
King's Lynn
Norfolk PE30 2QW
Tel: 01553 761144
Fax: 01553 764902
www.col-westanglia.ac.uk

Easton College
Easton
Norwich
Norfolk NR9 5DX
Tel: 01603 731200
Fax: 01603 741438
info@easton-college.ac.uk
www.easton-college.ac.uk

Great Yarmouth College
Southtown
Great Yarmouth
Norfolk NR31 0ED
Tel: 01493 655261
Fax: 01493 653423
info@gyc.ac.uk
www.gyc.ac.uk

Northamptonshire

Moulton College
West Street
Moulton
Northampton
Northamptonshire NN3 7RR
Tel: 01604 491131
Fax: 01604 491127
enquiries@moulton.ac.uk
www.moulton.ac.uk

Northampton College
Booth Lane
Northampton
Northamptonshire NN3 3RF
Tel: 01604 734567
Fax: 01604 734207
enquiries@northamptoncollege.ac.uk
www.northamptoncollege.ac.uk

Tresham Institute
Windmill Avenue
Kettering
Northamptonshire NN15 6ER
Tel: 0845 658 89 90
Fax: 01536 522500
info@tresham.ac.uk
www.tresham.ac.uk

Northern Ireland

Armagh College of Further & Higher Education
Lonsdale Street
Armagh
County Armagh
Northern Ireland BT61 7HN
Tel: 028 3752 2205
Fax: 028 3752 2845
www.armaghcollege.ac.uk

Belfast Metropolitan College
Brunswick Street
Belfast
Northern Ireland BT2 7GX
Tel: 028 9026 5000
Fax: 028 9026 5101
central_admissions@belfastmet.ac.uk
www.belfastmet.ac.uk

Ballymoney and Coleraine Northern Regional College
Union Street
Coleraine
Co Londonderry
Northern Ireland BT52 1QA
Tel: 028 7035 4717
Fax: 028 7035 6377
admissions@causeway.ac.uk
www.causeway.ac.uk

College of Agriculture Food and Rural Enterprise
Greenmount Campus
22 Greenmount Road
Antrim
Co. Antrim
Northern Ireland BT41 4PU
Tel: 028 9442 6601
Fax: 028 9442 6606
enquiries@dardni.gov.uk
www.greenmount.ac.uk

Northern Regional College
400 Shore Road
Newtownabbey
County Antrim
Northern Ireland BT37 9RS
Tel: 028 9085 5000
Fax: 028 9086 2076
info@eaifhe.ac.uk
www.eaifhe.ac.uk

South Eastern Regional College
Market Street
Downpatrick
County Down
Northern Ireland BT30 6ND
Tel: 028 4461 5815
Fax: 028 4461 5817
www.serc.ac.uk

East Tyrone College of Further & Higher Education
Circular Road
Dungannon
County Tyrone
Northern Ireland BT71 6BQ
Tel: 028 8772 2323
Fax: 028 8775 2018
info@etcfhe.ac.uk
www.etcfhe.ac.uk

Limavady College of Further & Higher Education
Main Street
Limavady
County Londonderry
Northern Ireland BT49 OEX
Tel: 028 777 62334
Fax: 028 777 61018
www.limavady.ac.uk

Lisburn Institute
39 Castle Street
Lisburn
County Antrim
Northern Ireland BT27 4SU
Tel: 028 9267 7225
Fax: 028 9267 7291
admissions@liscol.ac.uk
www.liscol.ac.uk

Newry Institute
East Campus
Patrick Street
Newry
County Down
Northern Ireland BT35 8DN
Tel: 028 3025 9696
admissions@nkifhe.ac.uk
www.nkifhe.ac.uk

Northern Regional College
Trostan Avenue
Ballymena
County Antrim
Northern Ireland BT43 7BN
Tel: 028 2565 2871
Fax: 028 2565 9245
www.nrc.ac.uk

**North West Institute of Further &
Higher Education**
Strand Rd
Derry
County Londonderry
Northern Ireland BT48 7BY
Tel: 028 7127 6000
Fax: 028 7126 0520
www.nwifhe.ac.uk

South West College Omagh Campus
2 Mountjoy Road
Omagh
County Tyrone
Northern Ireland BT79 7AH
Tel: 028 8224 5433
Fax: 028 8224 1440
www.omagh.ac.uk

St Mary's College Belfast
191 Falls Road
Belfast
Northern Ireland BT12 6FE
Tel: 028 9032 7678
Fax: 028 9033 3719
www.stmarys-belfast.ac.uk

Stranmillis College
Stranmillis Road
Belfast
Northern Ireland BT9 5DY
Tel: 028 9038 1271
Fax: 028 9066 4423
www.stran.ac.uk

Northumberland

Northumberland College
College Road
Ashington
Northumberland NE63 9RG
Tel: 01670 841200
Fax: 01670 841201
advice.centre@northland.ac.uk
www.northland.ac.uk

Nottinghamshire

Bilborough College
Bilborough Road
Bilborough
Nottingham
Nottinghamshire NG8 4DQ
Tel: 0115 929 9436
Fax: 0115 942 5561
www.bilborough.ac.uk

Broxtowe College
High Road
Chilwell
Nottingham
Nottinghamshire NG9 4AH
Tel: 0115 917 5252
Fax: 0115 917 5200
learn@broxtowe.ac.uk
www.broxtowe.ac.uk

Castle College Nottingham
Maid Marian Way
Nottingham NG1 6AB
Tel: 0845 895 0500
www.castlecollege.ac.uk

New College Nottingham
The Adams Building
Stoney Street
Nottingham
Nottinghamshire NG1 1NG
Tel: 0115 9100 100
enquiries@ncn.ac.uk
www.ncn.ac.uk

Newark College
Friary Road
Newark-On-Trent
Nottinghamshire NG24 1PB
Tel: 01636 680680
Fax: 01636 680681
enquiries@newark.ac.uk
www.newark.ac.uk

North Nottinghamshire College
Carlton Road
Worksop
Nottinghamshire S81 7HP
Tel: 01909 504504
Fax: 01909 504505
contact@nnc.ac.uk
www.nnotts-col.ac.uk

South Nottingham College
Greythorn Drive
West Bridgford
Nottingham
Nottinghamshire NG2 7GA
Tel: 0115 914 6400
Fax: 0115 914 6444
enquiry@snc.ac.uk
www.snc.ac.uk

West Nottinghamshire College
Derby Road
Mansfield
Nottinghamshire NG18 5BH
Tel: 01623 627191
Fax: 01623 623063
www.wnc.ac.uk

Oxfordshire

Abingdon and Witney College
Wootton Road
Abingdon
Oxfordshire OX14 1GG
Tel: 01235 555585
Fax: 01235 553168
enquiry@abingdon-witney.ac.uk
www.abingdon-witney.ac.uk

Henley College
Deanfield Avenue
Henley-on-Thames
Oxfordshire RG9 1UH
Tel: 01491 579988
Fax: 01491 410099
info@henleycol.ac.uk
www.henleycol.ac.uk

North Oxfordshire College and School of Art
Broughton Road
Banbury
Oxfordshire OX16 9QA
Tel: 01295 252221

Oxford & Cherwell Valley College
Oxpens Road
Oxford
Oxfordshire OX1 1SA
Tel: 01865 550550
Fax: 01865 551386
enquiries@oxford.ovc.ac.uk

Ruskin College
Walton Street
Oxford
Oxfordshire OX1 2HE
Tel: 01865 554331
Fax: 01865 554372
enquiries@ruskin.ac.uk
www.ruskin.ac.uk

Scotland

Aberdeen College
Gallowgate Centre
Gallowgate
Aberdeen
Aberdeenshire
Scotland AB25 1BN
Tel: 01224 612000
Fax: 01224 612001
enquiry@abcol.ac.uk
www.abcol.ac.uk

Adam Smith College, Fife
Glenrothes Campus
Stenton Road
Glenrothes
Fife
Scotland KY6 2RA
Tel: 01592 772233
Fax: 01592 568182
enquiries@adamsmith.ac.uk
www.adamsmithcollege.ac.uk

Adam Smith College, Fife
Kirkcaldy Campus
St Brycedale Avenue
Kirkcaldy
Fife
Scotland KY1 1EX
Tel: 01592 268591
Fax: 01592 640225
enquiries@adamsmith.ac.uk
www.adamsmithcollege.ac.uk

Angus College
Keptie Road
Arbroath
Angus
Scotland DD11 3EA
Tel: 01241 432600
Fax: 01241 876169
marketing@angus.ac.uk
www.angus.ac.uk

Anniesland College
19 Hatfield Drive
Glasgow
Lanarkshire
Scotland G12 OYE
Tel: 0141 357 3969
Fax: 0141 357 6557
reception@anniesland.ac.uk
www.anniesland.ac.uk

Ayr College
Dam Park
Ayr
Ayrshire
Scotland KA8 0EU
Tel: 01292 265184
Fax: 01292 263889
information@ayrcoll.ac.uk
www.ayrcoll.ac.uk

Banff & Buchan College
Henderson Road
Fraserburgh
Aberdeenshire
Scotland AB43 9GA
Tel: 01346 586100
Fax: 01346 515370
info@banff-buchan.ac.uk
www.banff-buchan.ac.uk

Barony College
Parkgate
Dumfries
Dumfriesshire
Scotland DG1 3NE
Tel: 01387 860251
Fax: 01387 860395
admin@barony.ac.uk
www.barony.ac.uk

Borders College
Melrose Road
Galashiels
Scotland TD1 2AF
Tel: 08700 505152
Fax: 01896 758179
enquiries@borderscollege.ac.uk
www.borderscollege.ac.uk

Cardonald College
690 Mosspark Drive
Glasgow
Lanarkshire
Scotland G52 3AY
Tel: 0141 272 3333
Fax: 0141 272 3444
enquiries@cardonald.ac.uk
www.cardonald.ac.uk

Central College of Commerce
300 Cathedral Street
Glasgow
Lanarkshire
Scotland G1 2TA
Tel: 0141 552 3941
Fax: 0141 553 2368
information@central-glasgow.ac.uk
www.centralcollege.ac.uk

Clydebank College
College Square
2 Aurora Avenue
Clydebank
Scotland G81 1NX
Tel: 0141 951 7400
Fax: 0141 951 7401
www.clydebank.ac.uk

Coatbridge College
Kildonan Street
Coatbridge
North Lanarkshire
Scotland ML5 3LS
Tel: 01236 422316
Fax: 01236 440266
admissions@coatbridge.ac.uk
www.coatbridge.ac.uk

Cumbernauld College
Tryst Road
Cumbernauld
Lanarkshire
Scotland G67 1HU
Tel: 01236 731811
Fax: 01236 723416
cumbernauld_college@cumbernauld.ac.uk
www.cumbernauld.ac.uk

Dumfries and Galloway College
Herries Avenue
Heathhall
Dumfries
Scotland DG1 3QZ
Tel: 01387 261261
Fax: 01387 250006
info@dumgal.ac.uk
www.dumgal.ac.uk

Dundee College
Kingsway Campus
Old Glamis Road
Dundee
Scotland DD3 8LE
Tel: 01382 834834
Fax: 01382 858117
enquiry@dundeecoll.ac.uk
www.dundeecoll.ac.uk

Elmwood College
Carslogie Road
Cupar
Fife
Scotland KY15 4JB
Tel: 01334 658800
Fax: 01334 6558888
www.elmwood.ac.uk

Forth Valley College
Clackmannan Campus
Branshill Road
Alloa
Clackmannanshire
Scotland FK10 3BT
Tel: 01259 215121
Fax: 01259 222789
info@forthvalley.ac.uk
www.forthvalley.ac.uk

Forth Valley College
Falkirk Campus
Grangemouth Road
Falkirk
Stirlingshire
Scotland FK2 9AD
Tel: 01324 403000
Fax: 01324 403222
info@forthvalley.ac.uk
www.forthvalley.ac.uk

Forth Valley College
Stirling Campus
Kerse Road
Stirling
Stirlingshire
Scotland FK7 7QA
Tel: 01786 406000
Fax: 01786 406070
info@forthvalley.ac.uk
www.forthvalley.ac.uk

Glasgow Metropolitan College
North Hanover Street Campus
60 North Hanover Street
Glasgow
Lanarkshire
Scotland G1 2BP
Tel: 0141 566 6222
Fax: 0141 566 6226
enquiries@glasgowmet.ac.uk
www.glasgowmet.ac.uk

Glasgow Metropolitan College
60 North Hanover Street
Glasgow
Scotland G1 2BP
Tel: 0141 566 6222
Fax: 0141 566 6226
enquiries@glasgowmet.ac.uk
www.glasgowmet.ac.uk

Glasgow College of Nautical Studies
21 Thistle Street
Glasgow
Lanarkshire
Scotland G5 9XB
Tel: 0141 565 2500
Fax: 0141 565 2599
enquiries@gcns.ac.uk
www.glasgow-nautical.ac.uk

Inverness College
Longman Campus
3 Longman Road
Longman South
Inverness
Scotland IV1 1SA
Tel: 01463 273000
Fax: 01463 711977
info@inverness.uhi.ac.uk
www.inverness.uhi.ac.uk

James Watt College of Further & Higher Enducation
Finnart Street
Greenock
Scotland PA16 8HF
Tel: 01475 724433
Fax: 01475 888079
enquiries@jameswatt.ac.uk
www.jameswatt.ac.uk

Jewel and Esk Valley College
24 Milton Road East
Edinburgh
Scotland EH15 2PP
Tel: 0131 660 1010
Fax: 0131 657 2276
info@jevc.ac.uk
www.jevc.ac.uk

John Wheatley College
2 Haghill Road
Glasgow
Scotland G31 3SR
Tel: 0141 588 1500
Fax: 0141 763 2384
advice@jwheatley.ac.uk
www.jwheatley.ac.uk

Kilmarnock College
Holehouse Road
Kilmarnock
Ayrshire
Scotland KA3 7AT
Tel: 01563 523501
Fax: 01563 538182
enquiries@kilmarnock.ac.uk
www.kilmarnock.ac.uk

Langside College
50 Prospecthill Road
Glasgow
Scotland G42 9LB
Tel: 0141 636 3600
Fax: 0141 632 5252
enquireuk@langside.ac.uk
www.langside.ac.uk

Lauder College
Halbeath
Dunfermline
Fife
Scotland KY11 8DY
Tel: 01383 845000
Fax: 01383 845001
customerservices@lauder.ac.uk
www.lauder.ac.uk

Lews Castle College
Stornoway
Isle of Lewis
Scotland HS2 0XR
Tel: 01851 770000
Fax: 01851 770001
aofficele@lews.uhi.ac.uk
www.lews.uhi.ac.uk

Moray College
Moray Street
Elgin
Morayshire
Scotland IV30 1JJ
Tel: 01343 576000
Fax: 01343 576001
www.moray.ac.uk

Motherwell College
Dalzell Drive
Motherwell
Scotland ML1 2DD
Tel: 01698 232425
Fax: 01698 232527
information@motherwell.co.uk
www.motherwell.ac.uk

Newbattle Abbey College
Newbattle Road
Newbattle
Dalkeith
Midlothian
Scotland EH22 3LL
Tel: 0131 663 1921
Fax: 0131 654 0598
office@newbattleabbeycollege.ac.uk
www.newbattleabbeycollege.co.uk

North Glasgow College
110 Flemington St
Glasgow
Scotland G21 4BX
Tel: 0141 558 9001
Tel: 0141 588 9905
www.north-gla.ac.uk

North Highland College
Ormlie Road
Thurso
Caithness
Scotland KW14 7EE
Tel: 01847 889000
Fax: 01847 889001
northhighlandcollege@thurso.uhi.ac.uk
www.nhcscotland.com

Oatridge Agricultural College
Ecclesmachen
Broxburn
West Lothian
Scotland EH52 6NH
Tel: 01506 864800
Fax: 01506 853373
info@oatridge.ac.uk
www.oatridge.ac.uk

Orkney College
East Road
Kirkwall
Orkney
Scotland KW15 1LX
Tel: 01856 569000
Fax: 01856 569001
orkney.college@orkney.uhi.ac.uk
www.orkney.uhi.ac.uk

Perth College
Crieff Road
Perth
Perthshire
Scotland PH1 2NX
Tel: 01738 877000
Fax: 01738 877001
pc.enquiries@perth.uhi.ac.uk
www.perth.ac.uk

Queen Margaret University College
Corstorphine Campus
Clerwood Terrace
Edinburgh
Scotland EH12 8TS
Tel: 0131 317 3247
Fax: 0131 317 3248
admissions@qmuc.ac.uk
www.qmced.ac.uk

Reid Kerr College
Renfrew Road
Paisley
Renfrewshire
Scotland PA3 4DR
Tel: 0800 052 7343
sservices@reidkerr.ac.uk
www.reidkerr.ac.uk

Sabhal Mòr Ostaig
Sleat
Isle of Skye
Scotland IV44 8RQ
Tel: 01471 888000
Fax: 01471 888001
sm.oifis@groupwise.uhi.ac.uk
www.smo.uhi.ac.uk/beurla

Scottish Agricultural College
King's Buildings
West Mains Road
Edinburgh
Scotland EH9 3JG
Tel: 0131 535 4000
information@sac.co.uk
www.sac.ac.uk

Shetland College of Further Education
Gremista
Lerwick
Shetland
Scotland ZE1 0PX
Tel: 01595 771000
Fax: 01595 771001
www.shetland.uhi.ac.uk

South Lanarkshire College
Hamilton Road
Cambuslang
Scotland G72 7NY
Tel: 0141 641 6600
Fax: 0141 641 4296
admissions@slc.ac.uk
www.south-lanarkshire-college.ac.uk

Stevenson College
Bankhead Avenue
Edinburgh
Scotland EH11 4DE
Tel: 0131 535 4700
Fax: 0131 535 4708
info@stevenson.ac.uk
www.stevenson.ac.uk

Stow College
43 Shamrock Street
Glasgow
Lanarkshire
Scotland G4 9LD
Tel: 0141 332 1786
enquiries@stow.ac.uk
www.stow.ac.uk

Telford College
Crewe Toll
Edinburgh
Scotland EH4 2NZ
Tel: 0131 332 2491
Fax: 0131 343 1218
mail@ed-coll.ac.uk
www.ed-coll.ac.uk

West Lothian College
Almondvale Crescent
Livingston
West Lothian
Scotland EH54 7EP
Tel: 01506 418181
Fax: 01506 409980
enquiries@west-lothian.ac.uk
www.west-lothian.ac.uk

Shropshire

Harper Adams University College
Newport
Shropshire TF10 8NB
Tel: 01952 820280
Fax: 01952 814783
www.harper-adams.ac.uk

Ludlow College
Castle Square
Ludlow
Shropshire SY8 1GD
Tel: 01584 872846
Fax: 01584 876012
info@ludlow-college.ac.uk
www.ludlow-college.ac.uk

New College Telford
King Street
Wellington
Telford
Shropshire TF1 1NY
Tel: 01952 641892
www.newcollegetelford.ac.uk

Shrewsbury College of Arts and Technology
London Road
Shrewsbury
Shropshire SY2 6PR
Tel: 01743 342342
Fax: 01743 342343
prospects@shrewsbury.ac.uk
www.shrewsbury.ac.uk

Telford College of Arts & Technology
Haybridge Road
Wellington
Telford
Shropshire TF1 2NP
Tel: 01952 642200
Fax: 01952 642263
studserv@tcat.ac.uk
www.tcat.ac.uk

Walford and North Shropshire College
Shrewsbury Road
Oswestry
Shropshire SY11 4QB
Tel: 01691 688000
Fax: 01691 688001
enquiries@wnsc.ac.uk
www.wnsc.ac.uk

Somerset

Bath Spa University
Newton Park Campus
Newton St Loe
Bath
Somerset BA2 9BN
Tel: 01225 875875
Fax: 01225 875444
enquiries@bathspa.ac.uk
www.bathspa.ac.uk

Bridgwater College
Bath Road
Bridgwater
Somerset TA6 4PZ
Tel: 01278 455464
Fax: 01278 444363
information@bridgwater.ac.uk
www.bridgwater.ac.uk

City of Bath College
Avon Street
Bath
Somerset BA1 1UP
Tel: 01225 312191
Fax: 01225 444213
enquiries@citybathcoll.ac.uk
www.citybathcoll.ac.uk

Norton Radstock College
South Hill Park
Radstock
Bath
Somerset BA3 3RW
Tel: 01761 433161
Fax: 01761 436173
courses@nortcoll.ac.uk
www.nortcoll.ac.uk

Richard Huish College
South Road
Taunton
Somerset TA1 3DZ
Tel: 01823 320800
Fax: 01823 320801
enquiries@richuish.ac.uk
www.richuish.ac.uk

Somerset College of Arts and Technology
Wellington Road
Taunton
Somerset TA1 5AX
Tel: 01823 366366
enquiries@somerset.ac.uk
www.somerset.ac.uk

Strode College
Church Road
Street
Somerset BA16 OAB
Tel: 01458 844400
Fax: 01458 844411
courseinfo@strode-college.ac.uk
www.strode-college.ac.uk

Weston College
Knightstone Road
Weston-super-Mare
North Somerset BS23 2AL
Tel: 01934 411 411
Fax: 01934 411 410
www.weston.ac.uk

Yeovil College
Mudford Road
Yeovil
Somerset BA21 4DR
Tel: 01935 423921
info@yeovil.ac.uk
www.yeovil-college.ac.uk

Staffordshire

Burton College
Lichfield Street
Burton on Trent
Staffordshire DE14 3RL
Tel: 01283 494400
Fax: 01283 494800
www.burton-college.ac.uk

Cannock Chase Technical College
The Green
Cannock
Staffordshire WS11 1UE
Tel: 01543 462200
Fax: 01543 574223
enquiries@cannock.ac.uk
www.cannock.ac.uk

Leek College
Stockwell St
Leek
Staffordshire ST13 6DP
Tel: 01538 398866
Fax: 01538 399506
admissions@leek.ac.uk
www.leek.ac.uk

Newcastle-under-Lyme College
Liverpool Road
Newcastle-under-Lyme
Staffordshire ST5 2DF
Tel: 01782 715111
Fax: 01782 717396
enquiries@nulc.ac.uk
www.nulc.ac.uk

Rodbaston College
Rodbaston
Penkridge
Staffordshire ST19 5PH
Tel: 01785 712209
Fax: 01785 715701
rodenquiries@rodbaston.ac.uk
www.rodbaston.ac.uk

Stafford College
Earl Street
Stafford
Staffordshire ST16 2QR
Tel: 01785 223 800
Fax: 01785 259 953
enquiries@staffordcoll.ac.uk
www.staffordcoll.ac.uk

Stoke on Trent College
Cauldron Campus
Stoke Road
Shelton
Stoke on Trent
Staffordshire ST4 2DG
Tel: 01782 208208
info@stokecoll.ac.uk
www.stokecoll.ac.uk

Tamworth and Lichfield Colleges
Croft Street
Upper Gungate
Tamworth
Staffordshire B79 8AE
Tel: 01827 310202
Fax: 01827 59437
enquiries@tamworth.ac.uk
www.tlc.ac.uk

Suffolk

Lowestoft College
St Peters Street
Lowestoft
Suffolk NR32 2NB
Tel: 01502 583521
Fax: 01502 500031
info@lowestoft.ac.uk
www.lowestoft.ac.uk

Otley College
Charity Lane
Otley
Ipswich
Suffolk IP6 9EY
Tel: 01473 785543
info@otleycollege.ac.uk
www.otleycollege.ac.uk

Suffolk College
Ipswich
Suffolk IP4 1HY
Tel: 01473 255885
Fax: 01473 230054
info@suffolk.ac.uk
www.suffolk.ac.uk

West Suffolk College
Out Risbygate
Bury St Edmunds
Suffolk IP33 3RL
Tel: 01284 701301
info@westsuffolk.ac.uk
ww2.westsuffolk.ac.uk

Surrey

Brooklands College
Heath Road
Weybridge
Surrey KT13 8TT
Tel: 01932 797700
Fax: 01932 797800
info@brooklands.ac.uk
www.brooklands.ac.uk

Carshalton College
Nightingale Road
Carshalton
Surrey SM5 2EJ
Tel: 020 8544 4444
Fax: 020 8544 4440
cs@carshalton.ac.uk
www.carshalton.ac.uk

Coulsdon College
Placehouse Lane
Old Coulsdon
Surrey CR5 1YA
Tel: 01737 551176
Fax: 01737 551282
info@coulsdon.ac.uk
www.coulsdon.ac.uk

Croydon College
College Road
Croydon
Surrey CR0 1DX
Tel: 020 8686 5700
info@croydon.ac.uk
www.croydon.ac.uk

East Surrey College
Gatton Point
Claremont Road
Redhill
Surrey RH1 2JX
Tel: 01737 772611
Fax: 01737 768641
studentservices@esc.ac.uk
www.esc.ac.uk

Esher College
Weston Green Road
Thames Ditton
Surrey KT7 0JB
Tel: 020 8398 0291
Fax: 020 8339 0207
eshercollege@esher.ac.uk
www.esher.ac.uk

Farnham College
Morley Road
Farnham
Surrey GU9 8LU
Tel: 01252 716988
Fax: 01252 723969
enquiries@farnham.ac.uk
www.farnham.ac.uk

Godalming College
Tuesley Lane
Godalming
Surrey GU7 1RS
Tel: 01483 423526
Fax: 01483 417079
college@godalming.ac.uk
www.godalming.ac.uk

Guildford College
Stoke Park Campus
Stoke Road
Guildford
Surrey GU1 1EZ
Tel: 01483 448585
Fax: 01483 448600
info@guildford.ac.uk
www.guildford.ac.uk

Hillcroft College
South Bank
Surbiton
Surrey KT6 6DF
Tel: 020 8399 2688
Fax: 020 8390 9171
enquiry@hillcroft.ac.uk
www.hillcroft.ac.uk

John Ruskin College
Selsdon Park Road
South Croydon
Surrey CR2 8JJ
Tel: 020 8651 1131
Fax: 020 8651 4011
info@johnruskin.ac.uk
www.johnruskin.ac.uk

Kingston College
Kingston Hall Road
Kingston upon Thames
Surrey KT1 2AQ
Tel: 020 8546 2151
info@kingston-college.ac.uk
www.kingston-college.ac.uk

Guildford College
Merrist Wood Campus
Worplesdon
Guildford
Surrey GU3 3PE
Tel: 01483 884000
info@guildford.ac.uk
www.merristwood.ac.uk

Merton College
Morden Park
London Road
Morden
Surrey SM4 5QX
Tel: 020 8408 6400
Fax: 020 8408 6666
info@merton.ac.uk
www.merton.ac.uk

North East Surrey College of Technology
Reigate Road
Ewell
Epsom
Surrey KT17 3DS
Tel: 020 8394 1731
info@nescot.ac.uk
www.nescot.ac.uk

Reigate College
Castlefield Road
Reigate
Surrey RH2 0SD
Tel: 01737 221118
Fax: 01737 222657
enquiries@reigate.ac.uk
www.reigate.ac.uk

Richmond Adult and Community College
Parkshot
Richmond
Surrey TW9 2RE
Tel: 020 8891 5907
Fax: 020 8332 6560
info@racc.ac.uk
www.racc.ac.uk

Strode's College
High Street
Egham
Surrey TW20 9DR
Tel: 01784 437506
Fax: 01784 471794
info@strodes.ac.uk
www.strodes.ac.uk

Woking College
Rydens Way
Woking
Surrey GU22 9DL
Tel: 01483 761036
Fax: 01483 728144
wokingcoll@woking.ac.uk
www.woking.ac.uk

Tyne and Wear

City of Sunderland College
Bede Centre
Durham Road
Sunderland
Tyne and Wear SR3 4AH
Tel: 0191 511 6060
Fax: 0191 511 6380
www.citysun.ac.uk

Newcastle College
Rye Hill Campus
Scotswood Road
Newcastle upon Tyne
Tyne and Wear NE4 5BR
Tel: 0191 200 4000
Fax: 0191 200 4517
enquiries@ncl-coll.ac.uk
www.ncl.coll.ac.uk

South Tyneside College
St. George's Avenue
South Shields
Tyne and Wear NE34 6ET
Tel: 0191 427 3500
Fax: 0191 427 3535
info@stc.ac.uk
www.stc.ac.uk

Tyne Metropolitan College
Embleton Avenue
Wallsend
Tyne and Wear NE28 9NJ
Tel: 0191 229 5000
Fax: 0191 229 5301
enquiries@tynemet.ac.uk
www.tynemet.ac.uk

Wales

Aberdare College
Cwmdare Road
Aberdare
Rhondda Cynon Taff
Wales CF44 8BR
Tel: 01685 887511
Fax: 01865 876635
www.aberdare.ac.uk

Barry College
Colcot Road
Barry
Wales CF62 8YJ
Tel: 01446 725000
Fax: 01446 732667
enquiries@barry.ac.uk
www.barry.ac.uk

Bridgend College
Cowbridge Road
Bridgend
Mid Glamorgan
Wales CF31 3DF
Tel: 01656 302302
Fax: 01656 663912
enquiries@bridgend.ac.uk
www.bridgend.ac.uk

Coleg Ceredigion
Park Place
Cardigan
Ceredigion
Wales SA43 1AB
Tel: 01239 612032
www.ceredigion.ac.uk

Coleg Glan Hafren
Trowbridge Road
Rumney
Cardiff
Wales CF3 1XZ
Tel: 0845 045 0845
Fax: 029 20 250339
enquiries@glan-hafren.ac.uk
www.glan-hafren.ac.uk

Coleg Gwent
The Rhadyr
Usk
Wales NP15 1XJ
Tel: 01495 333333
Fax: 01495 333526
info@coleggwent.ac.uk
www.coleggwent.ac.uk

Coleg Harlech
Harlech
Gwynedd
Wales LL46 2PU
Tel: 01766 781900
Fax: 01766 780169
info@harlech.ac.uk
www.harlech.ac.uk

Coleg Llandrillo
Llandudno Road
Rhos-on-Sea
Colwyn Bay
North Wales LL28 4HZ
Tel: 01492 546666
Fax: 01492 543052
www.llandrillo.ac.uk

Coleg Llysfasi
Pentrecelyn
Ruthin
Denbighshire
Clwyd
Wales LL15 2LB
Tel: 01978 790263
Fax: 01978 790468
admin@llysfasi.ac.uk
www.llysfasi.ac.uk

Coleg Meirion-Dwyfor
Ffordd Ty'n y Coed
Dolgellau
Gwynedd
Wales LL40 2SW
Tel: 01341 422827
Fax: 01341 422393
coleg@meiriondwyfor.ac.uk
www.meirion-dwyfor.ac.uk

Coleg Menai
Ffriddoedd Road
Bangor
Gwynedd
North Wales LL57 2TP
Tel: 01248 370125
Fax: 01248 370052
www.menai.ac.uk

Coleg Powys
Brecon Campus
Penlan
Brecon
Powys
Wales LD3 9SR
Tel: 0845 4086400
Fax: 01874 622165
www.coleg-powys.ac.uk

Coleg Powys
Llandrindod Campus
Spa Road
Llandrindod Wells
Powys
Wales LD1 5ES
Tel: 0845 4086300
Fax: 01597 825122
www.coleg-powys.ac.uk

Coleg Powys
Newtown Campus
Llanidloes Road
Newtown
Powys
Wales SY16 4HU
Tel: 0845 4086200
Fax: 01686 622246
www.coleg-powys.ac.uk

Deeside College
Kelsterton Road
Connah's Quay
Deeside
Flintshire
Wales CH5 4BR
Tel: 01244 831531
Fax: 01244 814305
www.deeside.ac.uk

Gorseinon College
Belgrave Road
Gorseinon
Swansea
Wales SA4 6RD
Tel: 01792 890700
Fax: 01792 898729
admin@gorseinon.ac.uk
www.gorseinon.ac.uk

Merthyr Tydfil College
Ynysfach
Merthyr Tydfil
Wales CF48 1AR
Tel: 01685 726000
college@merthyr.ac.uk
www.merthyr.ac.uk

Neath Port Talbot College
Dwr-y-Felin Road
Neath
West Glamorgan
Wales SA10 7RF
Tel: 01639 648000
Fax: 01639 648009
enquiries@nptc.ac.uk
www.nptc.ac.uk

Pembrokeshire College
Haverfordwest
Pembrokeshire
Wales SA61 1ZZ
Tel: 01437 753000
Fax: 01437 753001
admissions@pembrokeshire.ac.uk
www.pembrokeshire.ac.uk

Pontypridd College
Ynys Terrace
Rhydyfelin
Pontypridd
Rhondda Cynon Taff
Wales CF37 5RN
Tel: 01443 662800
Fax: 01443 663028
www.pontypridd.ac.uk

Swansea College
Tycoch Road
Tycoch
Swansea
West Glamorgan
Wales SA2 9EB
Tel: 01792 284000
Fax: 01792 284074
enquiries@swancoll.ac.uk
www.swancoll.ac.uk

Welsh College of Horticulture
Northop
Mold
Flintshire
Wales CH7 6AA
Tel: 01352 841000
Fax: 01352 841031
info@wcoh.ac.uk
www.wcoh.ac.uk

Ystrad Mynach College
Twyn Road
Ystrad Mynach
Hengoed
Wales CF82 7XR
Tel: 01443 816888
Fax: 01443 816973
enquiries@ystrad-mynach.ac.uk
www.ystrad-mynach.ac.uk

Warwickshire

North Warwickshire and Hinckley College
Main Site
Hinckley Road
Nuneaton
Warwickshire CV11 6BH
Tel: 024 7624 3000
the.college@nwhc.ac.uk
www.nwhc.ac.uk

Stratford-upon-Avon College
The Willows North
Alcester Road
Stratford-Upon-Avon
Warwickshire CV37 9QR
Tel: 01789 266 245
Fax: 01789 267 524
college@stratford.ac.uk
www.stratford.ac.uk

Warwickshire College
Leamington Centre
Warwick New Road
Leamington Spa
Warwickshire CV32 5JE
Tel: 01926 318000
Fax: 01926 318111
www.warkscol.ac.uk

Warwickshire College
Rugby Centre
Lower Hillmorton Road
Rugby
Warwickshire CV21 3QS
Tel: 01788 338800/0800 834 254
Fax: 01788 338575
www.warkscol.ac.uk

West Midlands

Birmingham College of Food, Tourism and Creative Studies
Summer Row
Birmingham
West Midlands B3 1JB
Tel: 0121 604 1000
Fax: 0121 608 7100
marketing@bcftcs.ac.uk
www.bcftcs.ac.uk

Birmingham Community College

8 Colmore Row
Birmingham
West Midlands B3 2QX
Tel: 0121 694 6461
Fax: 0121 694 6463
www.bcomcol.ac.uk

Birmingham Institute of Art and Design (BIAD)

Grosta Green
Corporation Street
Birmingham
West Midlands B4 7DX
Tel: 0121 331 5800/01
Fax: 0121 331 7814
enquiries@students.uce.ac.uk
www.biad.uce.ac.uk

Bournville College of Further Education

Bristol Road South
Northfield
Birmingham
West Midlands B31 2AJ
Tel: 0121 483 1000
Fax: 0121 411 2231
info@bournville.ac.uk
www.bournville.ac.uk

City College Birmingham

Garretts Green Lane
Garretts Green
Birmingham
West Midlands B33 0TS
Tel: 0121 743 4471
Fax: 0121 743 9050
enquiries@citycol.ac.uk
www.citycol.ac.uk

Coventry City College

Butts Centre
Butts
Coventry
West Midlands CV1 3GD
Tel: 024 7679 1000
Fax: 024 7679 1670
info@staff.covcollege.ac.uk
www.covcollege.ac.uk

Dudley College of Technology

The Broadway
Dudley
West Midlands DY1 4AS
Tel: 01384 363000
Fax: 01384 363311
studentservices@dudleycol.ac.uk
www.dudleycol.ac.uk

Fircroft College of Adult Education

1018 Bristol Road
Selly Oak
Birmingham
West Midlands B29 6LH
Tel: 0121 472 0116
Fax: 0121 471 1503
www.fircroft.ac.uk

Halesowen College

Whittingham Road
Halesowen
West Midlands B63 3NA
Tel: 0121 602 7777
Fax: 0121 585 0369
info@halesowen.ac.uk
www.halesowen.ac.uk

Henley College Coventry

Henley Road
Bell Green
Coventry
West Midlands CV2 1ED
Tel: 024 7662 6300
Fax: 024 7661 1837
www.henley-cov.ac.uk

Hereward College

Bramston Crescent
Tile Hill Lane
Coventry
West Midlands CV4 9SW
Tel: 024 7646 1231
enquiries@hereward.ac.uk
www.hereward.ac.uk

Matthew Boulton College of Further & Higher Education

Jennens Road
Birmingham
West Midlands B4 7PS
Tel: 0121 446 4545
Fax: 0121 503 8590
ask@mbc.ac.uk
www.matthew-boulton.ac.uk

Queen Alexandra College
Court Oak Road
Harborne
Birmingham
West Midlands B17 9TG
Tel: 0121 428 5050
Fax: 0121 428 5048
enquiries@qac.ac.uk
www.qac.ac.uk

Sandwell College
Oldbury Campus
Pound Road
Oldbury
West Midlands B68 8NA
Tel: 0121 556 6000
Fax: 0121 253 6836
enquiries@sandwell.ac.uk
www.sandwell.ac.uk

Solihull College
Blossomfield Campus
Blossomfield Road
Solihull
West Midlands B91 1SB
Tel: 0121 678 7001
Fax: 0121 678 7200
enquiries@solihull.ac.uk
www.solihull.ac.uk

South Birmingham College
Hall Green Centre
Cole Bank Road
Birmingham
West Midlands B28 8ES
Tel: 0121 694 5000
info@sbc.ac.uk
www.sbirmc.ac.uk

Stourbridge College
Hagley Road
Stourbridge
West Midlands DY8 1QU
Tel: 01384 344344
Fax: 01384 344345
info@stourbridge.ac.uk
www.stourbridge.ac.uk

Sutton Coldfield College
Sutton Campus
34 Lichfield Road
Sutton Coldfield
West Midlands B74 2NW
Tel: 0121 355 5671
Fax: 0121 362 1192
infoc@sutcol.ac.uk
www.sutcol.ac.uk

Walsall College of Arts & Technology
St Paul's Street Campus
Walsall
West Midlands WS1 1XN
Tel: 01922 657000
Fax: 01922 657083
info@walcat.ac.uk
www.walcat.ac.uk

City of Wolverhampton College
Paget Road
Wolverhampton
West Midlands WV6 0DU
Tel: 01902 836000
Fax: 01902 423070
mail@wolvcoll.ac.uk
www.wolverhamptoncollege.ac.uk

West Sussex

Central Sussex College
College Road
Crawley
West Sussex RH10 1NR
Tel: 0845 1550043
Fax: 01293 442399
www.centralsussex.ac.uk

Chichester College
Westgate Fields
Chichester
West Sussex PO19 1SB
Tel: 01243 786321
Fax: 01243 539481
info@chichester.ac.uk
www.chichester.ac.uk

Northbrook College, Sussex
West Durrington Campus
Littlehampton Road
Worthing
West Sussex BN12 6NU
Tel: 01903 606060
Fax: 01903 606073
www.northbrook.ac.uk

The College of Richard Collyer
Hurst Road
Horsham
West Sussex RH12 2EJ
Tel: 01403 210822
admin@collyers.ac.uk
www.collyers.ac.uk

West Dean College
West Dean
Chichester
West Sussex PO18 0QZ
Tel: 01243 811301
enquiries@westdean.org.uk
www.westdean.org.uk

Wiltshire

New College
New College Drive
Swindon
Wiltshire SN3 1AH
Tel: 01793 611470
Fax: 01793 436437
admissions@newcollege.ac.uk
www.newcollege.co.uk

Salisbury College
Southampton Road
Salisbury
Wiltshire SP1 2LW
Tel: 01722 344344
Fax: 01722 344345
enquiries@salisbury.ac.uk
www.salisbury.ac.uk

Swindon College
North Star Avenue
Swindon
Wiltshire SN2 1DY
Tel: 01793 491591
admissions@swindon-college.ac.uk
www.swindon-college.ac.uk

Wiltshire College
Cocklebury Road
Chippenham
Wiltshire SN15 3QD
Tel: 01249 464644
Fax: 01249 465326
info@iltscoll.ac.uk
www.wiltscoll.ac.uk

Worcestershire

Evesham College
Davies Road
Evesham
Worcestershire WR11 1LP
Tel: 01386 712600
Fax: 01386 712640
information@evesham.ac.uk
www.evesham.ac.uk

Kidderminster College
Market Street
Kidderminster
Worcestershire DY10 1LX
Tel: 01562 820811
Fax: 01562 512006
studentservices@kidderminster.ac.uk
www.kidderminster.ac.uk

New College
Bromsgrove Campus
Blackwood Road
Bromsgrove
Worcestershire B60 1PQ
Tel: 01527 570020
Fax: 01527 572900
www.ne-worcs.ac.uk

Pershore Group of Colleges
Avonbank
Pershore
Worcestershire WR10 3JP
Tel: 01386 552443
Fax: 01386 556528
pershore@pershore.ac.uk
www.pershore.ac.uk

Worcester College of Technology
Deansway
Worcester
Worcestershire WR1 2JF
Tel: 01905 725555
Fax: 01905 28906
college@wortech.ac.uk
www.wortech.ac.uk

Yorkshire

Askham Bryan College
Askham Bryan
York
Yorkshire YO23 3FR
Tel: 01904 772211
www.askham-bryan.ac.uk

Barnsley College
PO Box 266
Church Street
Barnsley
South Yorkshire S70 2YW
Tel: 01226 216216
Fax: 01226 216553
programme.enquiries@barnsley.ac.uk
www.barnsley.ac.uk

Bishop Burton College
York Road
Bishop Burton
Beverley
Yorkshire HU17 8QG
Tel: 01964 553000
Fax: 01964 553101
www.bishopburton.ac.uk

Bradford College
Great Horton Road
Bradford
West Yorkshire BD7 1AY
Tel: 01274 433004
Fax: 01274 741060
admissions@bilk.ac.uk
www.bradfordcollege.ac.uk

Calderdale College
Francis Street
Halifax
Yorkshire HX1 3UZ
Tel: 01422 357357
www.calderdale.ac.uk

Castle College
Granville Road
Sheffield
Yorkshire S2 2RL
Tel: 0114 260 2600
Fax: 0114 260 2101
http://my.sheffcol.ac.uk

Cleveland College of Art and Design
Green Lane
Linthorpe
Middlesbrough
Yorkshire TS5 7RJ
Tel: 01642 288000
Fax: 01642 288828
www.ccad.ac.uk

Craven College
High Street
Skipton
North Yorkshire BD23 1JY
Tel: 01756 791411
Fax: 01756 794872
enquiries@craven-college.ac.uk
www.craven-college.ac.uk

Dearne Valley College
Manvers Centre
Manvers Park
Wath-upon-Dearne
Rotherham
Yorkshire S63 7EW
Tel: 01709 513333
Fax: 01709 513110
learn@dearne-coll.ac.uk
www.dearne-coll.ac.uk

Dewsbury College
Halifax Road
Dewsbury
Yorkshire WF13 2AS
Tel: 01924 436221
Fax: 01924 457047
info@dewsbury.ac.uk
www.dewsbury.ac.uk

Doncaster College
Waterdale
Doncaster
Yorkshire DN1 3EX
Tel: 0800 358 7575
Fax: 01302 553559
infocentre@don.ac.uk
www.don.ac.uk

East Riding College
Longcroft Hall
Gallows Lane
Beverley
Yorkshire HU17 7DT
Tel: 0845 1200037
Fax: 01482 866784
info@eastridingcollege.ac.uk
www.eastridingcollege.ac.uk

Greenhead College
Greenhead Road
Huddersfield
West Yorkshire HD1 4ES
Tel: 01484 422032
Fax: 01484 518025
college@greenhead.ac.uk
www.greenhead.ac.uk

Huddersfield New College
New Hey Road
Huddersfield
Yorkshire HD3 4GL
Tel: 01484 652341
Fax: 01484 649923
info@huddnewcoll.ac.uk
www.huddnewcoll.ac.uk

Huddersfield Technical College
New North Road
Huddersfield
Yorkshire HD1 5NN
Tel: 01484 536521
Fax: 01484 511885
info@huddcoll.ac.uk
www.huddcoll.ac.uk

Hull College
Park Street Centre
Park Street
Hull
Yorkshire HU2 8RR
Tel: 01482 329988
Fax: 01482 589989
info@hullcollege.ac.uk
www.hull-college.ac.uk

Joseph Priestley College
Peel Street
Morley
Leeds
Yorkshire LS27 8QE
Tel: 0113 307 6111
helpline@joseph-priestley.ac.uk
www.joseph-priestley.ac.uk

Keighley College
Cavendish Street
Keighley
North Yorkshire BD21 3DF
Tel: 01535 618600
Fax: 01535 618556
info@keighley.ac.uk
www.keighley.ac.uk

Leeds College of Art and Design
Blenheim Walk
Leeds
West Yorkshire LS2 9AQ
Tel: 0113 202 8000
Fax: 0113 202 8001
info@leeds-art.ac.uk
www.leeds-art.ac.uk

Leeds College of Building
North Street
Leeds
West Yorkshire LS2 7QT
Tel: 0113 222 6000
Fax: 0113 222 6001
info@lcb.ac.uk
www.lcb.ac.uk

Leeds Thomas Danby
Roundhay Road
Leeds
West Yorkshire LS7 3BG
Tel: 0113 249 4912
Fax: 0113 240 1967
info@thomasdanby.ac.uk
www.leedsthomasdanby.ac.uk

Middlesbrough College
Roman Road
Linthorpe
Middlesbrough
Yorkshire TS5 5JP
Tel: 01642 333333
courseinfo@mbro.ac.uk
www.mbro.ac.uk

New College Pontefract
Park Lane
Pontefract
Yorkshire WF8 4QR
Tel: 01977 702139
Fax: 01977 600708
reception@newcollpont.ac.uk
www.newcollpont.ac.uk

Norton College
Dyche Lane
Sheffield
Yorkshire S8 8BR
Tel: 0114 260 3603
Fax: 0114 260 3655
marketing@sheffcol.ac.uk
http://my.sheffcol.ac.uk

Park Lane College
Park Lane
Leeds
Yorkshire LS3 1AA
Tel: 0845 045 7275
Fax: 0113 216 2020
course.enquiry@parklanecoll.ac.uk
www.parklanecoll.ac.uk

Parson Cross College
Remington Road
Sheffield
Yorkshire S5 9PB
Tel: 0114 260 3603
Fax: 0114 260 3655
http://my.sheffcol.ac.uk

Peaks Centre
Waterthorpe Greenway
Sheffield
Yorkshire S20 8LY
Tel: 0114 260 3603
Fax: 0114 260 3655
http://my.sheffcol.ac.uk

Rotherham College of Arts and Technology
Rother Valley Campus
Doe Quarry Lane
Dinnington
Yorkshire S25 2NF
Tel: 08080 722777
www.rotherham.ac.uk

Rotherham College of Arts and Technology
Town Centre Campus
Eastwood Lane
Rotherham
Yorkshire S65 1EG
Tel: 08080 722777
www.rotherham.ac.uk

Selby College
Abbott's Road
Selby
North Yorkshire YO8 8AT
Tel: 01757 211000
Fax: 01757 213137
info@selby.ac.uk
www.selby.ac.uk

Sheffield College
PO Box 345
Sheffield
Yorkshire S2 2YY
Tel: 0114 260 3603
Fax: 0114 260 3655
http://my.sheffcol.ac.uk

Shipley College
Exhibition Road
Saltaire
West Yorkshire BD18 3JW
Tel: 01274 327222
Fax: 01274 327201
enquiries@shipley.ac.uk
www.shipley.ac.uk

Thomas Rotherham College
Moorgate Road
Rotherham
Yorkshire S60 2BE
Tel: 01709 300600
Fax: 01709 300601
enquiries@thomroth.ac.uk
www.thomroth.ac.uk

Trinity and All Saints College
Brownberrie Lane
Horsforth
Leeds
Yorkshire LS18 5HD
Tel: 0113 283 7100
Fax: 0113 283 7200
enquiries@leedstrinity.ac.uk
www.tasc.ac.uk

Wakefield College
Whitewood Campus
Four Lane Ends
Castleford
West Yorkshire WF10 5NF
Tel: 01924 789 789
Fax: 01924 789 340
info@wakcoll.ac.uk
www.wakcoll.ac.uk

Wilberforce College
Saltshouse Road
Hull
Yorkshire HU8 9HD
Tel: 01482 711688
enquiry@wilberforce.ac.uk
www.wilberforce.ac.uk
York College
Tadcaster Road
York
Yorkshire YO24 1UA
Tel: 01904 770400
Fax: 01904 770499
www.yorkcollege.ac.uk

York St John University
Lord Mayor's Walk
York
YO31 7EX
Tel: 01904 624624
Fax: 01904 612512
admissions@yorksj.ac.uk
www.yorksj.ac.uk

Yorkshire Coast College
Lady Edith's Drive Campus
Lady Edith's Drive
Scarborough
Yorkshire YO12 5RN
Tel: 0800 731 7410
enquiries@ycoastco.ac.uk
www.yorkshirecoastcollege.ac.uk

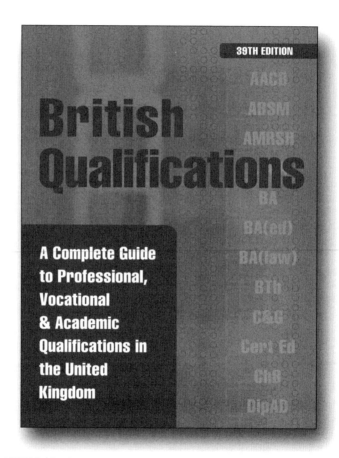

ALSO AVAILABLE FROM KOGAN PAG